Exploring Empathy

At the Interface/Probing the Boundaries

VOLUME 92

The titles published in this series are listed at *brill.com/aipb*

Exploring Empathy

Its Propagations, Perimeters and Potentialities

Edited by

Rebeccah J. Nelems
L.J. Theo

BRILL

RODOPI

LEIDEN | BOSTON

GUELPH HUMBER LIBRARY
205 Humber College Blvd
Toronto, ON   M9W 5L7

Cover illustration: Title: *Backstory.* Copyright Fiona Larkin, 2013.

Names: Nelems, Rebeccah J., editor. | Theo, L.J., editor.
Title: Exploring empathy : its propagations, perimeters and potentialities /
   edited by Rebeccah J. Nelems, L.J. Theo.
Description: Leiden ; Boston : Brill, [2018] | Series: At the
   interface/probing the boundaries, ISSN 1570-7113 ; 92 | Includes
   bibliographical references and index.
Identifiers: LCCN 2017046257 (print) | LCCN 2017047517 (ebook) | ISBN
   9789004360846 (E-book) | ISBN 9789004350748 (pbk. : acid-free paper)
Subjects: LCSH: Empathy.
Classification: LCC BF575.E55 (ebook) | LCC BF575.E55 E86 2018 (print) | DDC
   152.4/1--dc23
LC record available at https://lccn.loc.gov/2017046257

Typeface for the Latin, Greek, and Cyrillic scripts: "Brill". See and download: brill.com/brill-typeface.

ISSN 1570-7113
ISBN 978-90-04-35074-8 (paperback)
ISBN 978-90-04-36084-6 (e-book)

Table of Contents

Introduction: Exploring Empathy

Rebeccah J. Nelems* and L.J. Theo

In November 2014, the 1ˢᵗ Global Conference on Empathy was held in Prague, the Czech Republic, organised by the international network for research and publishing, Inter-Disciplinary.Net. Conference participants from around the world represented a wide range of professional and disciplinary backgrounds, and their interest in empathy arose in relation to diverse areas of human life. At the close of the conference, however, the lively debate and discussions initiated there seemed like they were only just beginning, and the idea for this dialogic volume was born.

Research on the origin, use, value and development of empathy is on the rise across regions and professions, as the term is increasingly invoked and referenced in sectors ranging from ethics to education. However, while there is apparent consensus across the political, regional and disciplinary spectrum on the unquestionable 'good' that results from practices of empathy, the supposed stable nature of empathy and the social constructions derived from it have not been sufficiently examined. During the conference, debates emerged around the popular, 'common sense' conception of empathy as the 'capacity to stand in another's shoes', and participants considered what might be at stake in this definition itself. Discussion around its cognitive and/or affective aspects abounded. Challenges to common assumptions that empathy is always a noble pursuit that necessarily benefits the 'empathisee' opened up onto critical explorations of the production of power with respect to how and when empathy is harnessed or promoted, by whom, and to what end. Assumptions about how empathy is fostered or promoted were explored and challenged by participants in a diversity of contexts, from the realms of education, psychology, and health care, to the media, videogame culture, and new technologies.

Empathy, it seems, is not so simple.

This volume's dialogic structure came about through the contributors' interest in engaging with one another's work amidst differences in viewpoint, disciplines and contexts – so as to contribute to furthering the debate about the value, role, potentiality and limits of empathy in the 21ˢᵗ century. The result of months of engagement, this volume reflects this dialogue amidst diversity. Contributors, who represent five different world regions, were encouraged to present their distinct ideas, writing styles, and epistemological approaches to the topic of empathy – whilst considering what the implications of one another's approaches were to their own. In this way, the dialogical volume models the very type of interactive, inter-disciplinary and inter-sectoral debate its authors believe needs to happen if we are to deepen our understanding of empathy and its offerings.

Within this diversity, two cross-cutting themes emerge.

First, there is a shared sense across authors that empathy is not always as it seems – whether defining it, or trying to foster it. The volume examines notions of

---

* In memory of my dad, Bill Nelems (1939–2017), whose way of being and relating on this planet has profoundly inspired my work on the topic of empathy.

the propagations, perimeters, and potentialities of empathy as a concept beyond the common consensus assumptions about its inherent 'goodness', and its apparent distinction from 'antipathy' and 'sympathy'. In this way, many of the contributors aim to destabilise and de-familiarise empathy as a concept such that it can be critically explored from a fresh perspective.

For this reason, Section I – the book's starting point – consists of two chapters that challenge perhaps the three most commonly held assumptions about empathy. In his chapter, 'Empathy as Orientation Rather than Feeling: Why Empathy Is Ethically Complex,' Steve Larocco challenges the notion that empathy is a 'feeling', arguing instead it is an orientation towards an 'other' that is devoid of ethical content. He further takes on, what Gavin Fairbairn (in Section II) calls, the 'cosy view' that empathy is inherently good. In her chapter, 'What Is This Thing Called Empathy?', Rebeccah J. Nelems explores what is at stake in the commonly held definition of empathy as (no more and no less than) 'the capacity to stand in another's shoes'. Nelems proposes that this common definition reflects a passive conception of empathy that reproduces an individualist worldview and divests empathy of its transformative and interdependent potentiality.

This brings us to the second cross-cutting theme in this volume: While theoretically engaged, all of the contributors are all also fundamentally interested in the everyday implications of such propagations with respect to lived experience. In other words, the volume engages in theoretical debates infused by considerations of the applied and the concrete – driven by an appreciation that what is at stake in a conversation about empathy are questions of ethics, care, relationality, altruism, social action, well-being and social change. At its core, authors share a commitment and engaged concern that a discussion about empathy – whether it is deemed good or not – is ultimately about how we relate to, treat and are treated by others (human and otherwise) and the world around us.

Contributors to section II engage in this dialectics of theory and praxis by drawing on their own personal and professional experiences to consider the cognitive and affective workings of empathy. This section's authors delve into the role of empathy, and its facilitation (or lack thereof), in domains as diverse as the psyche, the policy world, and in the context of institutions such as education, healthcare and the nation.

In 'Empathy, Complex Thinking and Their Interconnections,' Camilla Pagani presents the findings and analysis of a research study on youth's relationship with cultural diversity. She considers three ideas: the generation of empathy from the perspective of critical thinking, the complexity of the empathetic process and how youth experience it in the context of multicultural classrooms and communities in Italy. Gavin Fairbairn's chapter 'Reflecting on Empathy' dialogically relates to all of the chapters in this section, touching on discussions about empathy and education, predominant views of empathy and autism, and empathy and disability. Fairbairn also explores the role of intuition in empathy, and integrates discussions from Section I into various applied contexts, destabilising commonly or widely accepted 'cosy' views of empathy as good. Veronica Wain considers how policy contexts and policymakers in Australia rely on and in turn (re-)generate constructions of alterity in the context of the intellectually impaired. Her chapter, 'Empathy with the Enemy: Can the Intellectually Gifted Experience Empathy with the Intellectually Impaired,' is inspired by her lived and academic navigations of the policy and service delivery world, as mother to a young woman with an intellectual impairment. Through exploring the story of E and other adolescents with whom she works, Nurit Sahar reflects in her chapter 'Cognitive Milestones on Mutual Paths towards Empathy: A Four-Step Model' on the extent to which the ability to empathise and to act upon empathy can be learned and developed in therapy, in the face of cognitive and emotional deficits.

Contributors to Section III take a turn towards examining the generation (or lack thereof) of empathy through the use of different mediums for different ends in the media, popular culture and the arts. Implicit in this section is a consideration of the motivating and performative conditions of empathy, as well as its outcomes.

In his chapter, 'Empathic New(s) Orientations in Narratives about Sexuality,' LJ (Nic) Theo reflects on the location of empathy within the media, through a discussion of narrative constructions of sexual orientations in Sub-Saharan African news. He considers how the written word, and in particular political identity representations in news media, might reflect on notions of empathetic engagement, and how such representations might reflect non-normative sexualities in counter-productive ways. In 'Art or Science? Formulating Empathy in *Breaking Bad*,' Abby Bentham reflects on what might be considered as the 'dark side' of empathetic engagement, considering how characters such as Walter White in the television show 'Breaking Bad' might revise consensus notions of empathy as being inherently about positive socio-political engagement. In his chapter, '"Gays Are the New Jews": Homophobic Representations in African Media versus Twitterverse Empathy', Charles King reflects on empathy-generating and empathy-inhibiting journalistic practices in online social media in light of homophobic representations which abound in African mainstream news. He argues that non-traditional media such as Twitter offer a new platform upon which users can make ethical decisions to retaliate against state-sanctioned homophobia and hatred. Finally, Fiona Larkin's chapter 'Seeing the Loop: Examining Empathy through Art Practice' considers the complex mechanisms by which empathy might be generated, in light of its expanded definitions. She considers the relationship between the written word and the visual in empathy generation, particularly through art practice, in her consideration of phenomenological constructions of empathic generation.

As an exploration, this volume intends to provoke and ask more questions than it intends to answer or resolve. Greater debate and exploration about empathy, such as the authors in this book engage in, is required, if we are to wrestle with empathy in all its complexity. By expanding upon some of the inter-disciplinary and distinctive perspectives presented at the conference, and generating further thinking about what is at stake in discussions and practices of empathy, the volume aims to contribute to debate about empathy and its potentialities and limitations in different domains of society. As such, it aims to encourage a move beyond the bounds of the expected, and to serve as a contribution to homes as varied as a sociology or psychology lecturer's bookshelf; a psychologist's or medical doctor's consulting rooms; a journalist's desk; the library of a television commissioning editor; the offices of a literary agent, or a fine arts institution.

Key to the uniqueness of the volume is its implicit questioning of certain elements about empathy that remain largely uninterrogated: that it is a stable and easily-understood notion; that it is always and necessarily a positive thing; that it is applicable only in the 'soft sciences'; that it is only relevant to developmental agendas; that it is necessarily an exclusively psycho-dynamic idea; that it is a belief, rather than, perhaps, a process or performance.

With the beginnings of such a deeper interrogation, perhaps the doors can be opened to ever more complex ways of understanding empathy, and thereby ever more effective ways of invoking it for the benefit of individuals, communities, societies and existence itself.

Part I

Exploring Empathy's 'Goods' and Limits

Empathy as Orientation Rather than Feeling: Why Empathy Is Ethically Complex

Steve Larocco

Abstract

The relation between empathy and ethics is complex and, at times, fairly ambiguous. Empathy is often sentimentalised as synonymous to 'care,' but this chapter argues that empathy is not a particular feeling or type of feeling in itself. Rather, empathy is an orientation to the other, one that attunes to some aspect of the other's feelings or emotions or thoughts (or some combination of all three), yet which may not engage with the other's otherness at all. Empathy may simply construe the other as 'like me,' and therefore not engage with the specificity and alterity of what the other is fully feeling. Empathy may only orient to what in the other seems or feels familiar. To put the point succinctly: feeling-with is not the same as feeling-for. How one responds to the feelings produced by the empathic orientation depend on other dispositions, behavioural habits and inclinations, as well as the cognitive frames and self-narratives in which one is embedded. Empathy, for ethical behaviour, is a crucial intersubjective focaliser, but by itself as an orientation it may not direct the better angels of our nature to direct action.

Key Words: Empathy, compassion, ethics, affect, emotion, care, feeling-for, orientation, dysregulation.

*****

1. What Is Empathy?

There has been a fresh spurt of interest, both scholarly and otherwise, in the phenomena pulled together by the term 'empathy.' The primatologist Frans de Waal, in a recent book on the subject, dubbed ours 'the age of empathy.'[1] This interest has been fashioned in part by the tragedies and empathic failures of our times, in part by the ongoing migrations of diverse populations globally who bring cultural difference and attendant, distinct emotional palettes with them to their new places of residence, in part by global media, which press divergent populations into virtual contact without the necessity of movement or migration, in part by the still burgeoning cultural force of psychotherapy in first-world nations, and in part by the growing interest in the emotions, the rise of neuroscience, and the discovery of mirror neurons. Additionally, this interest may also be an effect of what Natan Sznaider calls the emergence of the 'compassionate temperament' in modernity, an interest in the distant suffering of others.[2] Because empathy and compassion are often conflated, which I will argue is an intellectual mistake, it is often treated as obvious that a rise in compassion would also entail an extension or increase of empathy, and this accentuates interest. In a world in which there seems to be an

© KONINKLIJKE BRILL NV, LEIDEN, 2018 | DOI 10.1163/9789004360846_002

excess of suffering, the idea that fully understanding and fostering empathy might lead to much more kind, interpersonal behaviour is alluring. Such interest in its current manifestations responds to the two major domains in which empathy seems to operate: as a form of intersubjective apprehension, an ability to understand (and/or interpret) minds other than our own—their aims, their motives, their framing of the world, their form of life; and the ability to feel what others feel, not simply reactively, as in emotional contagion, but projectively, by an openness to feeling beyond oneself. In this latter domain, empathy is conceived as a form of emotional attunement.

Concurrently, as empathy has become melded in common thinking and in the public sphere with compassion, there has also been a sentimentalisation of empathy, a sense that empathy is inherently positive and lies at the core of community, morality, and care for the other. This is what Gavin Fairbairn refers to, with insightful analytic concern, as the 'cosy' view of empathy.[3] There is some truth in this version of empathy. Empathy towards the other can lead to concern and care. However, empathy is not limited to such feelings or impulses; rather, it is a much more complex phenomenon, functioning in diverse ways in interpersonal and group relations. There are several reasons for this: first, empathy itself is not any particular emotion or feeling; it is not a *content*. Rather, it is an orienting or perhaps even focalising of attention, feeling and cognition toward and through the other. This may include emotional attunement to the other, a sharing of at least some of the other's feelings, but it need not. Rather, it is structured 'between' people, having no specific content of its own. Whom it imitates and what feelings it mimes are situationally and subjectively specific, and may not have much to do with care for the other. Typically, empathy is construed as feeling the other's *distress* or *suffering*, though there is no necessary reason to limit it to that. Second, empathy is not simply emotional, but invariably a combination of emotion and cognition (structured by prior familial experiences and culturally specific learning, often in the form of conditioning, yet also, at times, highly imaginative). Third, empathy is selective, culling out, often non-consciously, specific others and specific feelings of those others. Typically, a person doesn't empathise with all of the other's feelings or with the other's full world-orientation, but only with what one finds to be the salient aspects of that person's feelings, emotions or perspective (with that salience being defined by intensely subjective as well as other-oriented processes).

The selective aspect of empathy is crucial to emphasise, for even if empathy and care might be aligned, one critical problem for the sentimentalisation of empathy is that in normal social life a person clearly doesn't empathise with *all* others. One chooses, according to both conscious and often, more frequently, non-conscious promptings and biases, precisely whom one will engage with empathically and whom (often the many) one will ignore. This selectivity is actually a bit complex, as one may, at times, fail to empathise with people whom one feels one should, whilst empathising in certain ways with people one might consider as not being deserving of empathy, within one's ethical purview. The issue here is that one may have inclinations to empathise with certain feelings and emotions and not others, so those who display those emotions (friend or, at the time, foe) may garner empathic attention, while a family member displaying feelings one is not inclined to empathise with may garner no empathic orientation. As one can see, empathy is allocated according to subjective biases. This is true even if one isn't making a *choice*, as much of the underpinnings of empathic orientation happen out of conscious awareness. In this sense, empathy is a phenomenon of attention and focus, of what one attends to, voluntarily or involuntarily.

A final issue is that empathy can produce feelings that are potentially destructive (one can empathise with resentment, aggression, outrage, contempt, disgust, etc., or one can focus only on the feelings in oneself that empathy generates—empathy can be a staging for narcissistic assimilation of the other's emotions). This is a major problem if one considers empathy only to be a form of compassion. But if it is true, as I believe it is, that one can orient and attune to the other's aggressive or negative emotions, then empathy needs to be considered not simply as a disposition to care, but as a multivalent (bimodal) structure of interpersonal orientation. Empathy *is* at the core of life together, but it functions in complex ways: oscillating between facilitating interpersonal bonds by the sharing of feelings and minds, but also providing much of the cognitive/affective infrastructure for the manipulation of others according to their recognised dispositional vulnerabilities, as in the grooming of a child for sexual abuse, or for the kinds of contagious groupthink that lead to the aggressive sanctioning of those within a collective as well as the shared hostility towards those outside. In the American South of the 1930s, for example, empathy for the husband who thought an African-American man had looked at his white wife erotically could lead to lynching. There are surviving postcards of lynchings in which there is an excess of exuberant, shared feelings among the lynchers and the mobs that supported them, but none for the person lynched. Empathy does not only involve an orientation that induces pro-social behaviour. Empathy does open us, in sometimes accurate and in sometimes distorted ways, to the feeling-life and world-orientation of others. How we as individuals and as societies use that possibility remains ethically complex and, at times, troubling. It is an intersubjective terrain of both possibility and disappointment.

2. Differing Conceptions of Empathy

Part of the problem I am pointing to in how empathy functions results simply because of differing conceptions of precisely what empathy is. Daniel Batson, for example, sketches out eight different possibilities for how the term 'empathy' is used.[4] One of the problems in dealing with empathy, according to Batson, is that the term is so conceptually muddy that different people talking about empathy are often talking about different phenomena. Additionally, as Amy Coplan and Peter Goldie outline in their introduction to their 2011 Oxford anthology on empathy, researchers on empathy often diverge on whether and to what extent empathy involves what might be called higher and lower level processes.[5] According to Coplan and Goldie, what are designated as lower level processes are those that are more automatic, more immediately affective or emotional, and entail less involved cognitive processing. What is at stake in this distinction between higher and lower forms is the extent to which empathy not only involves the simulation or replication of the emotional and/or cognitive states of others, but also whether such an orientation or matching will 'lead one to respond with sensitivity and care to the suffering of another.'[6] The move from emotional (and cognitive) matching to caring behaviour is neither simple nor straightforward, with what is termed lower order empathy typically regarded as less likely to induce an altruistic or pro-social response (as if that were the only or predominant aim of empathy as it actually functions in human life). What Coplan and Goldie implicitly recognise is the problem with empathy as simply shared feeling; if empathy is only that (it's 'lower' form), it may not do much to motivate compassion or care.

To illustrate why 'lower forms' of empathy may not induce prosocial behaviour in any straightforward way, take, for example, the phenomenon of emotional contagion,[7] an often non-conscious and non-intentional form of emotional transfer or synchronisation, which perhaps serves as the base level for lower level empathy and even for empathy as a whole. In emotional contagion, we feel what others feel, in part because at the level of emotions and affect, self and other often have permeable or even porous boundaries.[8] When one is around someone who is anxious or distressed, for example, one often becomes anxious or distressed as well. This phenomenon is particularly salient in crowds, where panic or trance-like ecstasy may 'leap' from person to person. In such contexts, one feels what the other feels, often non-consciously, without necessarily focusing any attention on the other. In emotional contagion, there may be little or no interest in taking the other's perspective or in feeling the world from the other's viewpoint. What occurs instead is simply emotional or affective resonance, a movement of one's own emotional life in synchronous response to the emotional life of an other or others. I may feel the other's joy, or panic, or awe, but I may have no interest or concern in the other herself. When watching a fireworks show, my own emotions may intensify due to the joyous awe of those around me, even if I have neither care nor concern for what they are actually feeling. In emotional contagion, there is emotional attunement, in a sense, without explicit attention to or focalisation on the other. Nonetheless, if empathy is simply shared feeling or emotion, then such experiences should be construed as empathic, though collective panic and emotional entrainment at a rock concert or rave seem odd as instances of empathy.

Some thinkers would argue that emotional contagion isn't a form of empathy, as it involves no necessary other-orientation or hint of perspective taking. One simply feels what others feel, seemingly automatically and often with no reference to the other, as I outlined above. At stake here is the role of the focalisation of attention in what we construe as empathy. If I am at a sporting event, my emotions will tend to match those of other spectators, somewhat independently of what happens on the field, and also relatively independently of whether I attend to the emotion of those around me. I may focus almost entirely on the action itself, yet my emotions may mirror those of other spectators beyond my awareness. My jubilation over a team victory is typically dramatically enhanced if others around me are also jubilant, even if I don't notice them. I may believe that it is simply the success of my team that is producing my feeling, even though my elation would almost certainly be substantially curtailed were I alone. Similarly, if I am in a crowd that panics, I will be very likely to panic too, even if I don't know what is inducing the panic. I *feel* with the other, even if the other's orientation to the world remains opaque to me. I share the dominant feeling, but not the other's singular existence. What is crucial in emotional contagion is that there is emotional transfer but no necessary, connected orientation. There is emotional attunement, as it were, without focused attention on the other as other. In emotional contagion, I assume other's feelings often without knowing I am doing so, as if the emotional difference between self and other had, to some degree, vanished. The neurological work on mirror neurons points to the human capability of such kinds of response to others.[9]

What this discussion of emotional contagion shows is that orientation to the other, based on focalised attention, seems as necessary to what we consider to be empathy as attunement to the other's feelings, for attunement without attention doesn't seem to be empathic. The explanation for this response to what I might call 'subjectless' emotional resonance is not difficult to imagine: it is focalised attention to the other (not necessarily *for* the other, unfortunately) that is at the heart of what we consider empathy to be. One must attend to the other to empathise with the other, and this attention to the other is a necessary, if only implicit, component of almost all conventional forms of empathy, whether in a higher or lower form. Of course, what must follow from such attention for empathy to occur is some form of attunement, but whether such attunement is about emotion and feeling, or about the other's perspective, or both, remains to some degree open-ended. Empathy can entail a focus on and attunement to (or with) the other's emotions, state of mind, perspective or overall form of life.

Different persons may have differing capacities for each kind of empathic response. Some people readily feel what others feel, but don't have an easy time taking the other's perspective or thinking their way into the other's form of life, while others may take the other's perspective cognitively or intellectually while not attuning effectively to what the other is actually feeling. The people I have known in each category have differed fairly substantially in response to the other's suffering or distress, as those who feel what the other feels often have a much more immediate, visceral response. This leads them either immediately to strive to relieve the other's suffering, or to turn away or tune the other out. In either case, because the emotional intensity is often high and disturbing or dysregulating, these people often feel a need to *act*, though that pressure doesn't necessarily mean that either compassion or care will follow. Those in the other category, who imagine the other's perspective but don't feel the other's emotions intensely, have an easier time staying oriented to the other's suffering, but may have less of a motive to act. They may recognise the other's suffering, but not necessarily be disturbed by it. Since the other's difficulty doesn't have an intense, dysregulating emotional effect, it is not a problem that necessarily needs to be solved. Those people who have an ample capacity for both emotional attunement and imaginative perspective-taking may do best in reflectively acting in accord with the particulars of the other's need.

3. The Other's Suffering May Be Aversive

One problem with empathic orientation, as my account of those who intensely feel the emotions of others has raised, is that such attention and attunement may be and often is aversive, especially when the other is suffering intensely or in pain, the very situation in which compassion might be conventionally most salient. Even if we have tendencies to synchronise our emotional states with those of others (through mirror neurons, through our propensity to imitate, through the dispositions generated by the residual sway of the dynamic, modulated emotional attunement between infant and mother in healthy early development), such synchronisation may cause us to feel badly (it may powerfully disrupt our ability to regulate the intensity and tone of our affective arousal), and as a consequence shift our attention/orientation away from the other. As Batson points out, in a situation in which an other is distressed, emotional contagion, mirroring or 'higher forms' of empathy may simply make one also feel distressed.[10] Paradoxically, as Batson argues, this may actually inhibit the desire to relieve the other's unease, as it can lead one to focus on and try to relieve one's own distress rather than attending to that of the other. In such a situation, empathic orientation may not lead to compassion but rather to its failure, as the other's suffering feels unbearable to the empathiser. The often aggressive response to persons in distress, particularly when that distress cannot be easily alleviated, is one result of emotional transmission. Caretakers with infants who won't stop crying, for example, may well shift from empathy and care to rage to make an infant's crying stop. The very permeability or porousness of our emotional boundaries to the feelings of others makes us constantly susceptible to emotional dysregulation due to the other's distress or suffering, and this can lead to an aggressive effort to try to force the other to self-regulate or to the empathiser's reactive distanciation or dissociation (entailing either cultivated indifference to the other's feelings and plight, or physical separation). Our propensity to mirror the emotions of others can and often does induce *defensive* responses that foster care of the self rather than care of the other.

At issue is the constant need for all people to regulate and modulate their emotional and affective states and flows in relation to both environmental and internal pressures and stimuli. Because individuals, as social beings, are constitutionally open at least in some ways to the feelings, affects and emotions of the other, a significant aspect of our intersubjective lives is the management of our own emotional self-regulation in response to the emotional environment in which we are immersed. Allan Schore argues, from a neurological perspective, that there is always right brain to right brain unconscious resonance and sharing going on between individuals in proximity due to non-verbal signalling of various kinds.[11] This means that one does not regulate one's emotional life in an isolated or solitary way, but rather that one, paradoxically, self-regulates one's states of arousal, moods and emotional tones in and through others. In some ways, we are *always* sharing others' affective lives, and this can be either positive (we look to friends, for example, to help pick up our mood or to mirror our joy) or disruptive (consider how feelings of joy dissipate when not met by a mirroring response in the other). This intersubjectivity in feeling is especially salient in situations of the other's distress (the conventional situation of empathic orientation), because the more one shares the other's feelings, the more one risks dysregulating one's own emotional state, which is typically aversive. The more one orients to the other, the more one opens oneself to emotions and affective intensities that are not one's own, and that may be difficult to manage or modulate. The other's feelings, particularly those of distress, suffering and pain, are often disruptive, and may invoke defensive responses to preserve self-regulation, and this may block compassion, care and concern.

4. 'Real Empathy'

Here, in relation to the problems of emotional and affective intersubjectivity, we return to a definitional problem: is simply feeling distress at an other's distress really empathy or just a form of emotional contagion? Because it entails an orientation to the other, even if that leads to de-orientation to the other or the deflection of attention, I would argue that it is a form of empathy. Coplan, however, argues that it is not, for it doesn't require perspective-taking, which to her is a necessary attribute of higher form (i.e. 'real') empathy.[12] She would relegate emotional contagion or mirroring the distress of an other to a lesser or crude form of affective matching, as it is 'a direct, automatic, unmediated process,'[13] rather than one that involves some aspect of imaginative perspective-taking. At stake is the effort to distinguish differing possibilities of emotional transmission, with those that involve a subject who is imaginatively open to the other but appropriately bounded being the highest, as only this form provides 'experiential understanding.'[14] As much as this definition is alluring, it tends to want to exclude the ethical ambiguity of empathy as an orientation. Because one orients towards the other, because one *pays attention* to the other, even towards the other as other and not as a version of oneself, does not mean that one is altruistically or compassionately concerned with the other's suffering or distress or that one will act towards that other pro-socially. One strategy in the current military when thinking about an opponent *who one wishes to kill* is to empathise *selectively* with that other (which means, to use Coplan's rubric, to be able to simulate or at least match the other's affect, to imagine the other's perspective *as* the other experiences it, and to maintain self-other differentiation). In this circumstance emotional matching may be thin, but as Batson and Coplan herself point out in the case of emotional contagion, feeling what the other feels may have no ethical or care dimension to it at all. Because one is oriented to the other doesn't mean that one cares about or for the other. While imaginative perspective-taking may be crucial to an other-oriented ethics, to take such a perspective doesn't necessarily entail either feelings or acts of care. Empathic orientation can simply be used instrumentally, to facilitate manipulation or control of the other. In this sense, empathy and compassion are clearly different (even if related) phenomena, and should not be conflated.

5. Empathy and Its Problems

There is a three-fold problem with empathy as an orientation. The first problem is that as an orientation empathy has no necessary content, and consequently, in isolation, it is not necessarily pro-social. In this I am to some degree following de Waal's distinction between empathy and sympathy, in which he defines empathy as 'the process by which we gather information about someone else,'[15] making it an orientation and a mode of apprehension. In contrast, he defines sympathy as an inclination that 'reflects concern about the other and a desire to improve the other's situation.'[16] While some writers may treat what de Waal terms sympathy as a form of empathy, his distinction between the two gets at the difference between empathy as a mode of orienting to, feeling with and experiencing the other and the related but separate issue of how one *feels towards* and *treats* that other.

Empathy as an emotional, cognitive and often imaginative opening of oneself to the other remains ethically limited without supplementation. I might call attention here to the phenomenon of what I might paradoxically call 'narcissistic empathy,' an orientation towards and attunement to the world of the other in order to bring that world and the person who defines it within the domain of one's own form of life. Rebeccah Nelems cites the work of Megan Boler in calling this, in its less solipsistic forms, 'passive empathy,' by which she means empathy that peruses the other from a stance of self-focused affective control.[17] Such empathy neither destabilises nor mobilises the affective life of the self. Rather, the other's emotions, feelings, life-experience, even life-history are passively consumed and metabolised, as if they exist to feed the self's appetite for manageable emotional arousal. In a society of the spectacle, one feels good about oneself because one cares, not because one actually wrestles with the real alterity of the other's experience, and especially not because one *acts*. Passive empathy, as Nelems argues in the context of school programs, can be an empty exercise in self-affirmation: I feel bad about the other's tragedy; therefore, I am good. But as Nelems argues, if empathy is to be a significant component in ethical motivation, it must be motivating and transformative. This means shared feeling and perspective must be supplemented by an attention to, orientation towards, and compassion for the otherness of the other. Transformative empathy attends to the alterity of the other; it is curious, exploratory, open and concerned, dealing with difference not as a marker of absolute separation but as a spur to vulnerable, potentially destabilising engagement. Passive empathy shows little of this, and narcissistic empathy exhibits none.

Empathy, as lived, always entails a dialectical relation between narcissistic and/or passive empathy and its more altruistic, other-inclined, transformative forms. Most people, depending on situational context and their own dispositions, have tendencies towards one or the other empathic mode, but almost invariably have the capacity for both. And this division in both the form and functioning of empathy serves as a salient reminder: *feeling-with is not the same as feeling-for*. I would add, however, the caveat that empathy's absence, even the absence of passive empathy, *is* anti-social, as not having some capacity for an interested orientation to the other will have necessarily adverse effects for life in community, which is how all humans, to a greater or lesser extent, live. If I can't (or won't) feel the other's feelings or motivations in some way, if my response to the other is autistic or insistently defensive, the other's behaviour will simply appear to me as incomprehensible, irrational and therefore, most likely, as aberrant. Moral aggression is a typical response when one defensively refuses the risk of the other's suffering, vulnerability and need, and often is a socially licensed response to what one perceives as the other's incomprehensibly aberrant behaviour or emotional states.

The second problem with empathy as an orientation is that empathy is, as I mentioned previously, selective. This selectivity has two dimensions: first, one doesn't empathise with all people. We are selective in whose emotional lives and minds are of concern to us. In situations of social hierarchy, for example, there are conventions (or, perhaps, more powerfully, ideologically driven rules) about whom one can or ought to empathise with. As feminists have pointed out, men in sexist societies have often had a very poor record of empathising with the lives of women. Part of the reason for this is the failure of other-oriented perspective taking, the most significant aspect of empathy in Coplan's model. But part of it also involves a non-conscious defensive response to potential emotional contagion, in which what one does is block access to the other's emotions in order to avoid the possibility of dysregulation of one's own. Emotional contagion can be a form of vulnerability, because emotional regulation is often hard. Consequently, there is a bias against certain kinds of affective matching—when the other's affects are dystonic or negative or would create ethical dissonance. Culturally cultivated dispositions shape and support such biases. This phenomenon produces empathic non- or even dis-orientation.

A related but second selectivity concerns empathy's orientation towards only some and not all aspects of the feelings and world-perspective of the people with whom one empathises. I may empathise with my partner's distress about her family, for example, but not her distress about my behaviour. There are clearly ego-related inhibitions in terms of empathic orientation, such as exist in narcissistic empathy, and we may be much less inclined to empathise with the feelings of the other whom we perceive as emotionally dystonic or hostile to our selves. Additionally, the other's feelings may be complex, and empathy may only be able to orient itself towards the dominant portion of the palette of the other's feelings. Someone who is angry may also feel shame or humiliation or sadness or even remorse, but the anger may block those feelings from empathic availability. Consequently, one may only empathise with the other's dominant feeling state, and not with the complexity of affect that underpins it. Such a limitation may distort the apprehension of the other as other that one may wish to derive from empathy.

The third problem is that empathy, as orientation, is not itself a form of motivation. It is not an affect, not a means, by itself, of mobilisation. It can generate emotions as it attunes to and matches them, but how one responds to those emotions depends on the complex set of inclinations and dispositions which that person has developed in relation to his or her emotional repertoire and life history. This affects whether one resists empathy, experiences it passively, or feels it transformatively. If I am (or have been) disposed to care, then the distress of the other can lead to prosocial behaviour, but only *if* I don't feel overwhelmed by the distress I experience by emotional contagion and by perspective taking, identification and by other-inflected imagining. If I am already prone to emotional dysregulation, even if I am disposed to care *and* engage with the other empathically, I may not be able or willing to help, and whatever care I feel I may strive to damp or curb (and start defensive processes to isolate myself from the other's distress). If I am not disposed to care, either characterologically or situationally, I may feel the other's distress, but only as an irritant; if I have trouble with emotional regulation and am prone to cathartic outbursts, empathy may lead to defensive violence, *even if I imagine the other's perspective*, either from my own vantage point or from the other's. How one responds to the other is more the result of unconscious, entrenched dispositions than empathic orientation *per se*.[18] There is nothing inherent in the empathic orientation itself that mandates how the emotions and thoughts conjured in me by opening myself to the other will actually play out.

6. Conclusion

Consequently, and in contrast to much that has been written, the relation between empathy and ethics is complex and at least at times fairly ambiguous. While a lack of empathy clearly has adverse ethical consequences as it accentuates the other's difference, the presence of empathy doesn't necessarily establish a relation of care or pro-social behaviour towards a given other and may not engage the other's alterity at all. That depends on other factors, especially the relations between the empathiser's emotional repertoire and conditioned dispositions and other learned forms of social orientation and behaviour. One doesn't care automatically because one empathises, at least not in a way that means alleviating the other's distress or suffering. As we know from the behaviour of toddlers, the distress of others may simply lead to empathic distress. You cry because you're sad; I cry because you're crying. Whether such distress is adequately shared, leads to other-oriented perspective taking, or, more significantly, to an emotional orientation of care and behavioural action, to *transformative* empathy, remains uncertain. Empathy well may be a necessary component aspect of the better angels of our nature. But by itself it is not enough to ensure that those angels don't emulate the feelings, behaviour and ethical failings of their darker doubles.

Notes

[1] Frans de Waal, *The Age of Empathy* (London: Souvenir Press, 2010).
[2] Natan Sznaider, *The Compassionate Temperament: Compassion and Cruelty in the Modern World* (Lanham, Maryland: Rowen and Littlefield, 2001), 1-5.
[3] Gavin Fairbairn, 'Reflecting on Empathy', in this volume.
[4] C. Daniel Batson, 'These Things Called Empathy: Eight Distinct but Related Phenomena,' *The Social Neuroscience of Empathy,* ed. Jean Decety and William Ickes (Cambridge, MA: MIT University Press, 2011), 8.
[5] Amy Coplan and Peter Goldie, 'Introduction' to *Empathy: Philosophical and Psychological Perspectives*, ed. Amy Coplan and Peter Goldie (New York: Oxford University Press, 2011), xxxii-xxxiii.
[6] Batson, 'These Things Called Empathy,' 3, 9-10.
[7] Elaine Hatfield, J. T. Cacciopo and Richard Rapson, *Emotional Contagion* (New York: Cambridge University Press, 1993).
[8] Theresa Brennan, *The Transmission of Affect* (Ithaca, New York: Cornell University Press, 2004).
[9] Marco Iacoboni, *Mirroring People: The Science of Empathy and How We Connect with Others* (New York: Picador, 2009); Iacoboni, 'Within Each Other: Neural Mechanisms for Empathy in the Primate Brain,' *Empathy: Philosophical and Psychological Perspectives*, ed. Amy Coplan and Peter Goldie (New York: Oxford University Press, 2011); and Christian Keysers, *The Empathic Brain: How the Discovery of Mirror Neurons Changes Our Understanding of Human Nature*

(Social Brain Press, 2011). The work on mirror neurons may too quickly conflate mirroring neuron responses and empathy. Mirror neurons do suggest an *automatic* responsiveness to both the behaviour and feeling of others.
[10] Batson, 'These Things Called Empathy,' 10.
[11] Allan Schore, 'Foreword' to *The Neuropsychology of the Unconscious: Integrating Brain and Mind in Psychotherapy*, by Efrat Ginot (New York: Norton, 2015), xiii. See also Allan Schore, *Affect Regulation and the Origin of the Self: the Neurobiology of Emotional Development* (New York: Norton, 1994).
[12] Amy Coplan, 'Understanding Empathy: Its Features and Effects,' *Empathy: Philosophical and Psychological Perspectives*, ed. Amy Coplan and Peter Goldie (New York: Oxford University Press, 2011), 9.
[13] Coplan, 'Understanding Empathy,' 8-9.
[14] Ibid., 17.
[15] de Waal, *The Age of Empathy*, 88.
[16] Ibid.
[17] Rebeccah J. Nelems, 'What Is This Thing Called Empathy?', in this volume.
[18] Efrat Ginot, *The Neuropsychology of the Unconscious: Integrating Brain and Mind in Psychotherapy* (New York: Norton, 2015), 1-55. She attributes this phenomenon to the laying down of unconscious self-systems in early intersubjective life.

Bibliography

Batson, C. Daniel. 'These Things Called Empathy: Eight Distinct but Related Phenomonena.' *The Social Neuroscience of Empathy*, edited by Jean Decety and William Ickes, 3-15. Cambridge, Massachusetts: MIT University Press, 2011.

Brennan, Theresa. *The Transmission of Affect*. Ithaca, New York: Cornell University Press, 2004.

Coplan, Amy. 'Understanding Empathy: Its Features and Effects,' *Empathy: Philosophical and Psychological Perspectives*, edited by Amy Coplan and Peter Goldie, 3-18. New York: Oxford University Press, 2011.

Coplan, Amy and Peter Goldie. 'Introduction' to *Empathy: Philosophical and Psychological Perspectives*, edited by Amy Coplan and Peter Goldie, ix-xlvii. New York: Oxford University Press, 2011.

de Waal, Frans. *The Age of Empathy: Nature's Lessons for a Kinder Society*. London: Souvenir Press, 2009.

Ginot, Efrat. *The Neuropsychology of the Unconscious: Integrating Brain and Mind in Psychotherapy*. New York: Norton, 2015.

Hatfield, Elaine, J. T. Cacciopo and Richard Rapson. *Emotional Contagion*. New York: Cambridge University Press, 1993.

Iacoboni, Marco. *Mirroring People: The Science of Empathy and How We Connect with Others*. New York: Picador, 2009.

Iacoboni, Marco. 'Within Each Other: Neural Mechanisms for Empathy in the Primate Brain.' *Empathy: Philosophical and Psychological Perspectives*, edited by Amy Coplan and Peter Goldie, 45-57. New York: Oxford University Press, 2011.

Keysers, Christian. *The Empathic Brain: How the Discovery of Mirror Neurons Changes Our Understanding of Human Nature*. Social Brain Press, 2011.

Schore, Allan. *Affect Dysregulation and the Disorders of the Self*. New York: Norton, 2004.

Schore, Allan. 'Foreword' to *The Neuropsychology of the Unconscious: Integrating Brain and Mind in Psychotherapy*, by Efrat Ginot, xi-xxx. New York: Norton, 2015.

Sznaider, Natan. *The Compassionate Temperament: Compassion and Cruelty in the Modern World*. Lanham, Maryland: Rowen and Littlefield, 2001.

Steve Larocco teaches theory and literature at Southern Connecticut State University in the USA. He has published work on shame, personality, ideology, forgiveness, forms of imitation, seduction and tragedy. He is currently working on a book on forgiveness.

What Is This Thing Called Empathy?

Rebeccah J. Nelems

Abstract

While psychologists have been talking about it for decades, empathy as a topic of popular interest has emerged relatively recently. This chapter examines the emergence of empathy as a social 'good' in the past decade, particularly in North America. Drawing on phenomenological and sociological theory, empathy is approached not as a singular, knowable phenomenon, but as a multi-dimensional, ethical and social construct that means different things to different people across time and place. By critically exploring common conceptions about empathy, this chapter examines what the growing interest in empathy at this moment in time might tell us about North American worldviews, beliefs and values. The chapter then considers how these worldviews and beliefs act as 'canopies of meaning' that may frame how people both experience and understand empathy. It is argued that the popular conception of empathy as 'the capacity to stand in another's shoes' – whether conceived of in affective or cognitive terms – constitutes a 'passive' and individualist orientation towards the Other that divests empathy of its transformative potential. Conceived of and experienced within a worldview of interdependence and relationality, other possible orientations towards the Other appear, which open up the potential for empathy to not only transform the Self, but also to be a driver of social change. Building on Larocco's conception of empathy as an orientation, the author proposes a diagram, which maps out how distinctive orientations towards the 'Other' relate to and diverge from one another.

Key Words: Empathy, phenomenology, individualism, sociology, passive empathy, transformative empathy, interdependence, worldview, experiential hegemony.

*****

1. Context

Popular interest in empathy has emerged relatively recently in Western history. As a reference point, nearly three time more academic articles referenced the term 'empathy' in 2016 alone (41,000) than those published cumulatively between 1900 and 1970 (14,900).[1] While academic interest in empathy has been steadily gaining in the past two decades, mainstream interest in the topic has explosively grown in the past 2-5 years. For example, the number of 'empathy' google search results in the first five months of 2015 alone (5,860,000) were 3 times the number of posts in 2013, 15 times more than those that appeared in 2010, and 65 times more than those that appeared in 2005.[2]

The growing focus on empathy has emerged along two prominent storylines. The first of these is that empathy is a fundamentally important human capacity that represents an invaluable 'good' for society. This narrative is bolstered and cultivated by a growing number of research studies across disciplines, offering evidence that empathy is positively correlated with numerous other socially desired capacities and traits, such as conflict resolution,[3] critical thinking,[4] and leadership.[5] A certain urgency has been lent to this storyline by popular theorist Jeremy Rifkin, who argues that empathy is the most critical capacity humans have to address the unprecedented challenges that lie ahead, such as climate change, migration and population growth.[6] However, while Rifkin believes that as a species we are becoming more empathetic, he argues that humanity is now in a race for time as to whether or not it will develop its empathic capacity in time to reverse the collision course it is on.

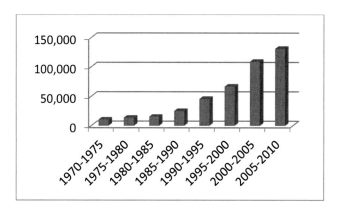

Graph 1: Number of academic articles that reference 'empathy', by half-decade

The second storyline about empathy in North America is that we suffer from an 'empathy deficit'. Since this phrase was coined by US President Barack Obama in 2006, a range of studies measuring empathy decreases have been conducted in the US. This narrative has consistently focused on youth as being empathy deficient, with one study citing that 75% of 20-year olds today are less empathetic than their cohort 30 years ago – the sharpest decline having occurred in the past ten years.[7] In Canada, research has focused more on high levels of bullying and violence, used as proxy indicators for a lack of empathy, with similarly discouraging findings. For instance, Canada holds the sixth highest ranking in the world for bullying of boys,[8] and nearly one-third of high school students in the province of Ontario report having been victims of bullying in the past year.[9]

Given the intersection of these narratives, it is not surprising that investments in both the US and Canada are increasingly being made in empathy education, premised on the now commonly held belief that empathy can be taught or learned.[10] Movements with an explicit focus to foster empathy are also appearing at the local, national and international levels, such as Ashoka, whose Empathy Initiative aims 'to create a world committed to ensuring that every child masters empathy.'[11]

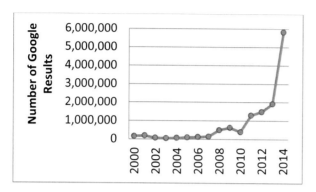

Graph 2: Number of Google Search Results for 'Empathy', by year[12]

But why is an interest in empathy emerging at this particular juncture in North America's history? While the scientific discovery of mirror neurons in macaques in the early 1990s may be credited with some of the interest in the topic, as Larocco observes,[13] it is arguably the case that without additional factors in play, such data would not have resonated with the popular imagination to the extent that it has. After all, many scientific discoveries fail to capture the popular imagination – even those with significant implications for our existence.

It seems more than coincidental that the surge of interest in empathy coincides with the digitalisation and globalisation of the world. The digitalised world is unquestionably transforming the ways humans interact with both existing and new connections, enabling us to encounter a potentially diverse range of humans and their distinctive 'emotional palettes',[14] as well as other species or forms of existence with whom we may never have crossed paths with before. Whether through an awareness of climate change or a YouTube video gone viral, one cannot escape an awareness of our interconnectedness. If empathy is a fundamentally interactive and intersubjective experience between people and/or beings, an ongoing question to be explored as we move forward, is what happens to empathy when relationships are digitalised and globalised?

The emergence of empathy as a prominent social good also emerges in a North American culture steeped in individualist ways of thinking and being in the world, wherein acting out of self-interest is viewed as an entirely rational (if not financially prudent) way to act.[15] It is striking that such interest in empathy – a phenomenon infused with the potential of being the most interdependent and relational of experiences – emerges in this context. Could the relatively sudden interest in empathy be but one expression of how a rationality founded upon the unit of the individual falls short, in a world where the interconnectedness of life is undeniable? However, does being embedded in an individualist worldview have any implications for how one might experience or think about empathy? Does an individualist worldview and way of being in the world shape, frame or limit the potential for empathy? In order to consider this, it will be critical to explore how empathy is being defined and understood within these contexts. However, before doing that, it is important to first clarify my approach to empathy, not as a fixed, knowable phenomenon out there, but as a multi-dimensional social and ethical construct.

2. Empathy as a Multi-Dimensional Construct

What are the parameters of empathy? For the purposes of this chapter, phenomenological and interpretive sociological theory is used to establish a non-positivist approach to this question. Such an approach diverges from a positivist approach, by maintaining that empathy is not something 'out there' to be discovered and understood in its singularity as a phenomenon in the natural world might be. The question is not thus one of what empathy *truly* is, as the decades-old debate in psychology over whether empathy is primarily affective (emotional) or cognitive assumed. Rather, as a phenomenon that can and does mean different things to different people and societies at different points in time, empathy is viewed as a multi-dimensional, ethical and social construct.

While inherited from those who came before, social constructs are co-created with others around us – intersubjectively – and evolve over time, like language.[16] They are constructs, not because there is no reality or 'facts' out there as postmodernists might claim, but because it is not possible to ever fully 'know' or represent that reality.[17] There is always a distance or gap. In other words, reality is socially constructed in so far as knowledge of this reality is necessarily socially constructed. Magritte's painting of the pipe, 'The Treachery of Images', which features an image of a pipe and then the line 'Ceci n'est pas une pipe' ('This is not a pipe') demonstrates this point in one simple visual: words, images and concepts are only ever representations of a reality that, necessarily, can never be that reality itself. While a pipe enjoys a physical existence, the concept and word 'pipe' do not. The concept is created and maintained collectively within a society, and assigned a meaning so that we may understand one another and communicate about the pipe. Assigning a conceptual category to a phenomenon is a way of ordering the world around us such that two extremely different-looking pipes are equally recognised as pipes.

As with any word or concept, however, social constructs are not random or free floating, but appear within a broader system of language and understanding. For phenomenologists, these systems cohere into worldviews, which act as 'canopies of meaning' within which people organise and make sense of the world around them and everything they encounter.[18] These worldviews act as historical frames, that both enable and limit our understanding and experience of the world. Phenomena that do not make sense within our worldview either appear to us as 'non-sense' or simply remain unseen.[19] On the other hand, conceptions of phenomena that are given a place within the system or canopy of meaning are naturalised as 'common sense' norms of just 'how things are', and reified as representative of objective reality. To borrow a term from indigenous legal scholar Aaron Mills, they become 'settled answers';[20] not open for debate or negotiation, they become assumed 'truths' that we take as for granted as the air we breathe. Due to their reification as 'common sense' truths, the fact of their social constructedness remains hidden. Not seeing the social constructedness of the world is referred to by phenomenologists as maintaining a 'natural attitude' or orientation towards the world.[21]

Through his concept of 'experiential hegemony', Vahabzadeh argues that these canopies of meaning place parameters not only around one's understanding of a given phenomenon but also on their encountered experience of it.[22] If we are to accept this possibility, this suggests that our understanding and very experience of a phenomenon such as empathy is framed – both in terms of being enabled and limited – by the worldview/s within which we are embedded.

To say that our worldview *frames* our understanding and experience, however, is not to suggest it *determines* it. Of course, we do not need theory to tell us this. We need only history. Social movements such as the anti-slavery, women's suffragette and civil rights movements are clear examples that worldviews and their accompanying systems of meaning can be changed and transgressed. However, how does one see beyond the frames of a given worldview in order to begin to imagine – let alone create – an alternative?

The notion of our experience and understanding being framed by a worldview or system of meaning does not suggest we cannot change and challenge it – or that we are without agency, structurally determined by the worldviews within which we are born or to which we subscribe – as ideology theorists such as Althusser inevitably (and I believe, inadvertently) imply.[23] The work of Foucault (Althusser's student) and many discourse theorists he inspired was precisely to theoretically explore how existing systems of meaning can be challenged.[24] Vahabzadeh theorizes that the 'natural attitude' can be transgressed when one experiences something that stands outside of the given canopy of meaning[25] e.g., the individual who experiences being transgendered within a worldview that does not imagine (or indeed accept) this as a possibility. It is through such 'surplus' experience that an individual 'steps back' and the social constructedness of the reified world is rendered visible. From this vantage point, it is possible to 'withdraw consent',[26] to refuse reification, and to unsettle or disrupt a settled construct. Vahabzadeh adds that other conditions that make this possible include when the horizon a worldview produces 'turns bleak' or 'fails to emanate possibilities'.[27] For Berger and Luckmann, tears in the canopy or system of meaning appear when the system fails to offer sufficient explanation or meaning for emerging phenomena – such as when certain members of society fail to conform to established norms, when alternative norms are encountered such as in another society, or when a duelling 'coterie of experts' emerges, casting commonly held assumptions or beliefs into stark relief.[28] A contemporary example of this would be economists vs. environmentalists on climate change.

Unsettling naturalised constructs and norms is thus a key way through which dominant worldviews and systems of meaning can not only be transgressed, but also by which they are first rendered visible. Through 'stepping back' from one's 'natural attitude' into a 'phenomenological attitude' towards the world,[29] one can thus 'liberate…herself from the blinding light of proximity'[30] – from the norms and settled answers that underpin a given worldview – and begin to imagine other potential worldviews. Similarly, Marcuse believes such a stance is made possible through a willed estrangement from, or refusal to identify with, the worldview within which one is immersed.[31] Stuart Hall analogously suggests that we must 'address ourselves "violently" towards the present as it is, if we are serious about transforming it.'[32]

The significance of the above for the purposes of this chapter is fourfold. First, if empathy is an ethical and social construct that is intersubjectively created, a critical review of taken-for-granted conceptions of empathy offer us glimpses of the worldview in which these make sense. For this reason, 'settled' conceptions of empathy reveal as much about our society's epistemic frames and worldviews as they do about this phenomenon called empathy. The central questions in understanding empathy then become what do popular conceptions of empathy in the West tell us about Western values and worldviews, and how do these worldviews in turn frame one's potential understanding and experience of empathy?

It follows that when conceptions of empathy are left un-interrogated as 'settled answers', one's understanding and indeed one's potential experience of empathy will likely be framed by the worldview to which one subscribes. This fundamentally changes the question of whether empathy can be taught or not by reframing it as a question of how distinctive worldviews frame, limit and/or enable different potential experiences and conceptions of empathy.

Third, if one does not accept the 'given' definitions of empathy as the only possible definitions – a stance this author encourages readers to take – then how should one begin to imagine other potential conceptions of empathy? Through 'stepping back' to consider the epistemic perimeters that worldviews place on experiences or conceptions of empathy, what new potentialities for empathy emerge? What do these potentialities offer to a society that some argue suffers from an 'empathy deficit'?

Finally if empathy is a multi-dimensional ethical and social construct that can and does mean different things to different people, it can reference distinctive or even incompatible worldviews and their accompanying moral frameworks. As such, it is not possible to conceive of empathy as a range of ideas that neatly fall along a shared spectrum or under a shared umbrella. Empathy understood as a constellation[33] of concepts and experiences offers a broader, more pluralistic metaphor.

3. A Critical Exploration of Popular Conceptions of Empathy

What is most striking about the way empathy is referenced and understood in mainstream North America is how taken for granted it is as a concept. It is referenced as if it were a single, common sense concept, which (of course) we all know. Such a simple conception, however, is based on various assumptions about empathy. First, as Fairbairn and Larocco observe, empathy is assumed to be inherently good, and thus, by extension can only lead to good things.[34] Fairbairn and Larocco make significant contributions on this front – presenting strong evidence of cases in which empathy can or is used in ways that could not be deemed particularly 'good'. However, this 'cosy' view of empathy persists,[35] effectively inoculating the concept from interrogation, despite the fact that there is enough research and debate to suggest it is neither simple, nor settled as a concept.

Advocates of the 'cosy view' back up their case with the growing array of research referenced in Section 1, which argues that empathy is positively correlated to numerous other socially desired human traits such as leadership, conflict resolution, and critical thinking. It is crucial to note, however, that 'empathy' itself is seldom defined in these studies. In the happy consensus about the unquestionable good of empathy,[36] it seems empathy as a concept has itself gone unquestioned. It is a 'settled answer'[37] – in this case, an unquestionable good – that is not up for debate.

The lack of broader interrogation has led to a notable imprecision and vagueness surrounding the concept. Such nebulousness has arguably been a key factor enabling the continual conflation of empathy with other concepts, such as sympathy and compassion, as Fairbairn and Larocco respectively observe.[38] The haziness around empathy is particularly manifest in North America's education sector,[39] where this feel-good vagueness has manifest in a view of empathy as a silver bullet that will address any number of societal ills from climate change to social responsibility to bullying and violence.[40] Its do-no-harm and inherently moral status has meant that in the culture of audit that is North American education, empathy education programs have largely flown under (or over, if we think in moral terms) the radar and have not been systematically or comparatively evaluated.[41]

However, while such happy imprecision persists everywhere around the concept, a singular, fixed definition of empathy has simultaneously emerged. Empathy is declared to be (no more or less than) 'the capacity to take another's perspective by standing in their shoes'. Just as the inherent goodness of empathy is taken for granted, so too has this definition acquired a 'common sense' status. This definition is backed by a surprising number of experts, with the online Wikipedia chiming in, in agreement – where this definition is posited as fact alongside the many other Wikipedia-approved 'settled answers', whether pertaining to national boundaries, historical events, cultural traditions or individual biographies.

While this definition is frequently touted about, what it offers and what it fails to offer have not been carefully examined. However, the definition of empathy as (no more and no less than) 'the capacity to stand in another's shoes' enacts an reproduces an individualist worldview in so far as it keeps the Self at the centre of both the concept and experience. At its core, this definition frames empathy as a capacity, trait or skill that belongs to an *individual*. While this explains society's obsessive interest in the biological line of questioning of whether empathy is innate to individuals or not, it dispossesses alternate conceptions of empathy that might not conceive of empathy as a personal trait or skill. These conceptions might, for example, imagine empathy to be something that cannot be possessed by an individual, but rather, as a fundamentally relational or collective experience that is created and shared with an Other in a context of interdependence and mutuality.

By inviting one to subscribe to the view that to be empathetic is to try and feel, imagine or rationally entertain what it is like to *be* the Other, this definition assumes it is possible to know what it is like to be an Other. However, it is not possible to engage in any such acts without necessarily projecting one's own perceptions, experiences, knowledge, beliefs, hopes, expectations, assumptions and fears onto the Other. Despite this, one's own shoes – and the worldview within which these shoes are embedded – never come into question or are even acknowledged. As such, this empathy not only does not require one to step back from their 'natural attitude', it relies upon one invoking it. One's own worldview, accepted beliefs and common sense understanding of the world is both start and end point.

What happens to the Other in this encounter? Tapping into the imagination is argued by many to be one of the most powerful routes to empathy.[42] However, conceiving of empathy as the act of one individual imagining they are in an Other's situation suggests not only that empathy is a capacity that is individually possessed and enacted, but that the Other is not actually required to stick around for the experience. It is an act of imagined occupation whereby I consume and colonise the other's experience. In the act of projecting my Self onto an Other, just as a video game player does onto an avatar, the presence of a real live Other is no longer a requirement. Indeed, how would an Other remain, with someone standing in their shoes?

The notion that the Other need not remain for the experience (they just need to leave their shoes behind) implies that empathy is (no more or less than) a feeling *for*, as opposed to a feeling *with*. Feeling *for* has historically been distinguished from feeling *with*, the former harkening back to Aristotle's notion of pity where concern for the Other is based on fear for the Self.[43] Any resultant feelings or thoughts that emerge thus reflect more about the empathiser than they do the empathisee. In this context, it becomes easy to understand why empathy is so frequently conflated with sympathy. This conception is quite distinct from early psychological conceptions of empathy discussed by Nurit Sahar in her chapter, whereby empathy was not understood as an act of 'identifying' or 'becoming' the other. Rather, she argues that the state of empathy 'allows the individual to be aware of the other's feelings and emotions, while simultaneously still being aware of their own feelings and emotions.'[44]

The contemporary individualist conception of empathy has significant repercussions for the empathy one might potentially experience. If perspective-taking or 'feeling for' relies on one's own worldview as a frame of reference, how might one encounter or experience a 'very distant other',[45] whose potentially radically different experience or worldview are not easily comprehensible within one's own frame of experience? Does this simply imply that we can only empathise with those who are at least to some extent comprehensible to us? Veronica Wain wrestles with precisely this challenge, on the question of how someone who does not have an intellectual disability could possibly empathise with someone who does.[46] Further, by extension, does this rule out the possibility of experiencing empathy for other species? Moreover, such individualist empathy relies on one's choice or willingness to 'stand in another's shoes'. Will the self-declared self-made Wall Street investment banker care to imagine or feel what it might be like to be the homeless person just outside? This not only places parameters around 'the ability to empathise with the very distant other' but also a disavowal of one's own potential participation in the Other's experience – as Boler writes, the ability 'to recognise oneself as implicated in the social forces that create the climate of obstacles the other must confront.'[47]

Operationalised in North American society, this mainstream understanding of empathy has also assumed a deeply moral tone: framed as a capacity, standing in an Other's shoes is not only declared possible, it is assumed to be the *good* and *ethical* thing to do. In the very moment of this empathy, however, the Other has been occupied, dispossessed of their own shoes – quite possibly without having ever invited the occupant – and subsequently silenced from conveying what it is they would want. As Boler asks, does the Other even want empathy or might they instead want something altogether different, such as justice?[48] Identifying the colonial affront of such a notion, this view also betrays its consumer or marketing accents: one betters oneself by acquiring this capacity and consuming an Other's experience.[49] Empathy here, has become akin to tourism, a controlled act of exposing oneself to another's alterity with minimal risk to the Self. It becomes an act of stepping onto a fairground ride (of one's choosing) with the safe knowledge that one can walk away unscathed at any time. The empathiser's ability to control the experience and enjoy closure and/or exoneration from the experience itself are key features of this empathy.[50]

Those who subscribe to a view of empathy as a continuum might argue that all of the above is a semantic argument, and that perspective-taking or feeling *for* another could easily be but the starting point down a path towards a 'deeper' empathy, or what Nowak calls 'empathic action'.[51] What this argument would miss, however, is that all empathy is not equal. Different conceptions of empathy reference distinct and sometimes oppositional worldviews and value systems. The predominant view of empathy as 'standing in another's shoes' is underpinned by an individualist worldview that precludes a worldview of interdependence. What is lacking from this individualist conception of empathy is an orientation towards the Other that reflects a worldview of interdependence as central to existence, which requires both the Self and Other to remain for the experience.

Within such a frame, the Other plays a critical role in the experience of empathy, and standing in their shoes is seen as neither possible nor moral. In this latter formulation, closure and exoneration are not something one can bestow upon oneself. Such empathy entails a vulnerability – both that one may not be invited to be or feel with the Other, and that one might be forever changed through the experience. Such an empathy might transform the 'empathiser' more than the 'empathisee', turning on its head the notion that being empathetic to an other is a noble and charitable thing to do.

Educator Meagan Boler's distinction between 'passive' and 'transformative' empathy is particularly helpful here. Boler refers to identification-based, perspective-taking empathy as passive, because it results in no change in the Self or in orientation towards the Other, other than a temporary, fleeting experience. For Boler, 'passive empathy' enables a sense of closure as the experience is directed by and controlled by the empathiser in terms of with whom one empathises, when and why. In contrast, she conceives of 'transformative empathy' as entailing an act of self-reflection and a willingness to part with one's worldview or frame of understanding, in order to try and encounter the Other. Acknowledging that the Other does not understand or make sense of their experience within the same frames of reference as the Self demands a degree of openness that puts one's own worldview in a position of risk and instability. Transformative empathy is thus distinct from passive empathy to the extent that the Other must remain intact (and in their own shoes), while the Self opens themselves up to potential change. In this way, 'transformative empathy' entails 'self-reflective participation' in which one becomes aware of, and willing to challenge, one's own frame of reference, including beliefs and assumptions. Table 1, below, summarises Boler's distinction between 'passive' and 'transformative' empathy.

Table 1: Boler's Passive vs. Transformative Empathy

Passive Empathy	Transformative Empathy
• Identification-based: imagining and/or feeling what it is like to be in another's shoes • Based on fear for oneself (*that could happen to me*) and imagining similar points of vulnerability between self and other • Empathiser projects own experiences and ideas onto the Other • Stays within the Self's comfort zone: they choose what experiences to consume and establish themselves as judge/evaluator of Other's experience • Does not require self-reflection • Produces no action towards justice • Enables a sense of closure	• Recognition and respect that the Other's experience (and shoes) can never be fully felt or known • Focus on listening to and hearing the other in their own terms and frame of reference • Requires 'self-reflective participation' of becoming aware of one's own assumptions and beliefs • Entails risk and unfamiliarity • Opens up the possibility of empathising with the very distant other • Invites action and the ability 'to recognise oneself as implicated in the social forces' that contribute to the Other's experience • Refuses closure

Envisioned as such, transformative empathy actually describes the act of phenomenologically 'stepping back' from one's natural attitude – the moment in which the worldview or 'canopy of meaning' within which one exists and by which one makes sense of the world is rendered visible, so that one might encounter the Other in their alterity, rather than merely encountering a projected Self. This would suggest that in order to step towards an Other, one must first be willing to 'step back' from themselves. It is a gesture towards engaging the unknown alterity of the Other, rather than an act of projection onto the Other of one's own worldview, experiences, expectations, hopes and fears, as one might project oneself onto an avatar in a video game. It suggests a distinctive potential for empathy as an experience of being 'led by the foreign', as Stein proposed.[52]

In contrast to passive empathy, where one believes it is possible to stand in an Other's shoes and *know* their experience, in transformative empathy, the Self strives to understand the Other by only knowing they can never fully know the Other's experience. It is a fundamentally relational experience in which the Other always retains a degree of impenetrability; in which the gap of which Fiona Larkin speaks[53] is recognised, respected and retained. This orientation towards the Other is thus marked not by an intended end goal of intelligibility or occupation of the Other, but by an acceptance of the Other's ultimate unintelligibility. This acknowledgement that any understanding of the Other is only ever partial and never fully representative runs parallel to the notion that the concept or word can never fully represent or reflect the reality it is meant to capture. In the same way that phenomenologists call for a stepping back or estrangement from predominant rationalities in order to challenge them, transformative empathy refuses 'cosy', feel-good identification and requires that an element of estrangement remain a part of the relational experience. Transformative empathy conceived of in these ways thus directly undermines the belief that one ever could – or should – try to stand in an Other's shoes.

This conceptualisation of empathy touches on related concepts elaborated across this volume in different ways. Exploring empathy through the visual arts, Fiona Larkin argues: 'it is impossible to engage empathetically with the image without being first aware of the separation between self and other.'[54] To stand in 'another's shoes' would be to erase this gap in a single move. In her chapter, Nurit Sahar returns to Kohut's understanding of empathy, stating that empathy 'allows the individual to be aware of the other's feelings and emotions, while simultaneously still being aware of their own feelings and emotions.'[55] It is not an act of 'identifying' with or 'becoming' the other. LJ (Nic) Theo addresses the inherent problematics with representation when a journalist, however compassionate their intentions might be, speaks for the Other as other.[56] Such a 'speaking for' is conducted as if they could stand in the Other's shoes. Charles King argues that the Twitterverse holds promise for empathetic engagement precisely because using Twitter, the subject who has been objectified as 'Other' in the mainstream media, can remain and speak for themselves.[57] Wain argues that the path to empathy with an Other, who to some extent will always be unknowable, is one of 'undoing and unknowing of all that I thought I knew'.[58] Finally, Gavin Fairbairn speaks about the leap of intuition entailed in empathy, which can never entail a secure 'knowing', one of the bases upon which he critiques Simon Baron-Cohen's definition of empathy.[59]

Building on Boler's claim that the experience of passive empathy actually obstructs the possibility of experiencing transformative empathy, I propose that an individualist conception of empathy, gone unquestioned, may impede one from experiencing empathy as a fundamentally relational and interdependent phenomenon. In this way, the popular and singular definition of empathy as 'the ability to stand in another's shoes' is not just the mark of a naïve, happy consensus; rather, it directly reproduces individualistic ways of thinking and being that risk draining empathy of its more transformative and radical potentialities. Popular conceptions of empathy in North America thus individualise the experience and dispossess it of its more intersubjective and transformative potential.

However, if it is possible to challenge and change worldviews through questioning the 'settled answers' and concepts upon which a worldview is founded, exploring alternate potentialities for empathy that stand in surplus to a conception of it as an individual 'capacity to stand in another's shoes' may be a pathway through which an individualist worldview itself might be disrupted. This suggests that empathy might just carry the transformative potentiality it has been suspected of having – though not because it will produce good citizens that do good things (as Larocco effectively argues, empathy itself has no content, ethical or otherwise.[60]) The true potency of empathy lies not in the perceived social 'good' that comes from *knowing* what it is like to be another (passive empathy), but in its potential to transform worldviews through an openness to the *un*known and a willingness to unlearn what has been naturalised (transformative empathy). This invites us to consider an experience of empathy that is not an individual act of identifying, consuming or colonising the Other. Rather, it invites an experience of empathy as a phenomenological 'stepping back' from one's worldview through a fundamentally relational and interdependent experience of encountering an Other in their alterity. It is only through the phenomenological act of critically 'stepping back' from an individualist worldview that a different type of empathy becomes a potentiality.

4. Towards a Multi-Dimensional Understanding of Empathy

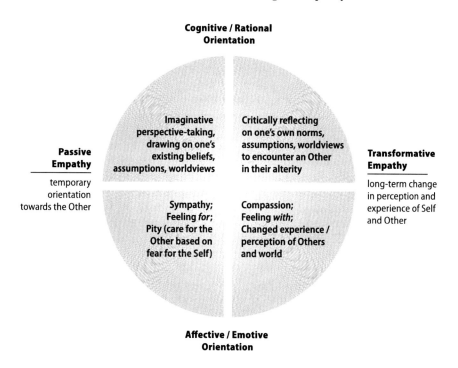

Diagram 1: A Constellation of Orientations towards the 'Other'

I have argued that empathy is neither a single concept representing some external truth, nor a continuum of related ideas, but a constellation that includes distinct orientations towards the Other, which reflect divergent worldviews. How do we start to conceptualise this constellation, and where do these orientations stand in relation to one another? Diagram 1 offers a starting point for mapping out this constellation, building on Larocco's conception of empathy as an orientation towards an Other.[61]

Reflected in the diagram, empathy understood as 'standing in another's shoes' – whether through imaginative perspective taking or feeling *for* – is considered passive in orientation, and thus situated on the left hand side of the diagram. As these orientations entail a projection of the Self onto the Other, no change in the Self is observed, and the experience is temporary. Thus, any change in state experienced when standing in another's shoes is only temporary in nature; no transformation ensues from the experience – whether internal to the Self or in the external actions of the Self.

The orientations towards the Other listed on the right-hand side are distinct from the left precisely on this point: the extent to which the Self is open to change through their orientation towards an Other. Both critically reflecting on one's worldview, and feeling *with* another, may entail long-term shifts in the Self, which may or may not lead to any concrete, external acts of change, but which may transform one's perception or experience of the world – arguably a prerequisite of any sustained change in external acts. Transformative orientations towards the Other reflect a non-individualist, interdependent worldview.

It is important to acknowledge that this diagram selects and thereby prioritises two poles (cognitive-affective; passive-transformative), which frame the conceptions put forward – both in terms of enabling and limiting them. Other frames would invariably reveal different aspects of the constellation. However, it is critical to note that this diagram is not intended to be exhaustive or definitive, but serves as one frame through which one can think through distinctive orientations towards the Other and how they relate to one another within a broader constellation – all of which could never be contained in a single diagram. Also, emotional contagion is left off the diagram, concurring with Larocco's argument that it does not represent an orientation towards an Other.[62]

The diagram's use of these poles is not intended to reproduce binaries, but acknowledge the way in which these categories of analysis have and continue to frame conceptions. It is acknowledged that the cognitive-affective binary reproduces an age-old Cartesian dualism of mind and body, which denies the inevitable interconnectedness of mind and body, of lived experience and thought. As a phenomenologist, I explicitly reject such dualism, and assert that it would not be possible to render one's worldview visible (top right quadrant in Graph 3) without simultaneously having a transformed experience of Others and the world (bottom right quadrant in Graph 3).

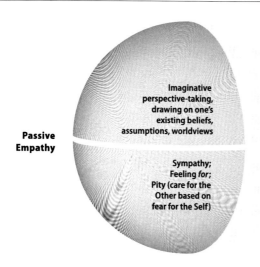

Diagram 2: View of Constellation within an Individualist Worldview

However, I do argue that a passive orientation towards an Other that emerges within an individualist, passive orientation towards the Other divests one of a transformative orientation or experience, in which I suggest the radical potentiality and social potency of empathy lies. Conceived of as a constellation, we as human actors are always embedded in a worldview, which situates us in a particular location within this constellation. Where we are positioned within the diagram shapes our vantage point, delineating what is both proximal to us – those concepts that are normalised and obvious in their visibility – and those that remain distant or obscured, eclipsed from our line of sight, precisely by that which is proximal to us.

5. Concluding Remarks

What is really at stake here? Why does it matter how we understand or define empathy? I offer three answers to these questions.

First, if, as I have argued, not all conceptions of empathy are equal – nor even compatible – then it is not enough to foster or teach 'empathy'. It is essential to clarify just what is meant by empathy in terms of both what is thought to be missing or needed, and how it might best be fostered. The growing popularity of the argument that empathy is the most important human capacity to addressing the unprecedented challenges that lie ahead of us (such as climate change, depletion of natural resources, growing economic inequalities, and population growth[63]) makes it easy to understand why empathy has been such a settled concept in North America. If it is so unquestionably good and important for society, we had better get on with it! However, it is precisely the vagueness that underlies this common sense concept that renders it meaningless and creates an impasse for those interested in fostering it. A vague conception of empathy is insufficient for identifying how to foster it. Diagram 1 offers the starting point for a typology of empathy, intended to support those wanting to promote empathy to clarify what it is they mean by empathy, so that they might identify the most relevant pedagogical approaches.

Second, the popular consensus that empathy (in all its vagueness) is an unquestionable social good that should be promoted, funded and fostered suggests that contemporary formulations of empathy 'make sense' within prevailing ways of thinking. In this context, any un-interrogated acceptance of 'settled answers' about what empathy is in contemporary North America will merely reproduce the same ways of thinking and being that have produced an empathy deficit in the first place. Might the casting of empathy as 'the capacity to stand in another's shoes' not represent the crowning glory of an individualist worldview, whereby this phenomenon, reframed as an individual trait and capacity, is divested of its intersubjective, relational, interdependent, experiential and transformative potential?

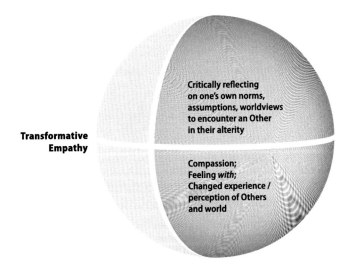

Transformative Empathy

Critically reflecting on one's own norms, assumptions, worldviews to encounter an Other in their alterity

Compassion; Feeling *with*; Changed experience / perception of Others and world

Diagram 3: View of Constellation from an Interdependent Worldview

Third, as Heidegger and others have observed, taken-for-granted, fixed concepts have a way of arresting meaning and stifling other potential interpretations.[64] In other words, unquestioned fixed concepts conceal and restrict more than they reveal and enable, and are a key way through which social norms and values are re-/produced. Vahabzadeh argues that this stifles not only other understandings of a phenomenon, but other potential experiences of it.[65] The singular conception of empathy as 'the capacity to stand in another's shoes' not only impedes other conceptions of empathy that reference different worldviews, but may dispossess those who remain settled within an individualist worldview of a potentially transformative experience of empathy.

A more radical conception of empathy as an interdependent encounter, experienced and enacted in relationship with an Other, does not limit empathy to being an individual asset or feather in one's cap, but opens up the possibility that empathy is a process or experience of being led by 'the foreign'.[66] Such a conception suggests that in order to encounter an Other in their alterity, one must step back from one's naturalised worldviews by questioning one's 'settled answers'. Mahatma Gandhi said, 'As human beings, our greatness lies not so much in being able to remake the world…as in being able to remake ourselves.'[67] Perhaps empathy does have the transformative potential it is suspected of having – but not because it is a good thing that makes us good people. Perhaps empathy's transformative potential is in the way this relational experience can change the way we see, experience and understand the world, and by doing this, we change the world itself.

Notes

[1] Google Search Results, viewed on 17 June 2017, http://www.google.com.

[2] Ibid.

[3] Leslie S. Greenberg, et al., 'Empathy', *Psychotherapy* 38.4 (2001): 380-384.

[4] Kathleen Holtz Deal, 'The Relationship between Critical Thinking and Interpersonal Skills: Guidelines for Clinical Supervision', *The Clinical Supervisor* 22.2 (2004): 3-19.

[5] E. Isaac Mostovicz, Nada K. Kakabadse and Andrew P. Kakabadse, 'A Dynamic Theory of Leadership Development', *Leadership & Organization Development Journal* 30.6 (2009): 563-576.

[6] Jeremy Rifkin, *The Empathic Civilization: The Race to Global Consciousness in a World in Crisis* (New York: Penguin Group, 2009).

[7] Sara H. Konrath, Edward H. O'Brien, and Courtney Hsing, 'Changes in Dispositional Empathy in American College Students over Time: A Meta-Analysis,' *Personality and Social Psychology Review* 15.2 (2011): 180-198.

[8] Wendy M. Craig, Lyndall Schumann, M. E. Edge, and C. Teske, 'Are Bullying and Victimization on the Rise in Canada?' Department of Psychology, Queen's University (paper presented at the Ontario: Canadian Public Health Association Conference, 2012).

[9] Angela Paglia-Boak, et al., *Ontario Student Drug Use and Health Survey (OSDUHS): Mental Health and Well-Being Report 1991-2011* (Toronto: Centre for Addiction and Mental Health, 2012).

[10] Mark H. Davis, 'Empathy', *Handbook on the Sociology of Emotions*, eds. Jan E. Stets and Jonathan H. Turner (Riverside, CA: Springer Press, 2006), 443-466.

[11] Ashoka Empathy Initiative, viewed on 20 October 2013, http://empathy.ashoka.org/.

[12] Google Search Results, viewed on 14 June 2015, http://www.google.com.

[13] Stephen Larocco, 'Empathy as Orientation Rather than Feeling: Why Empathy Is Ethically Complex,' in this volume.

[14] Ibid.

[15] While not elaborated here, this argument draws on Herbert Marcuse's conception of technocratic rationality in *One-Dimensional Man* (Boston: Beacon Press, 1964) as a means of engaging in the distinctive rationalities that accompany any historical worldview.

[16] Peter L. Berger and Thomas Luckmann, *Social Construction of Reality: A Treatise in the Sociology of Knowledge* (New York: Anchor Books, 1966).

[17] Ibid.

[18] Ibid.

[19] Ibid.

[20] Aaron Mills, 'Constitutional Stories,' *The Cairo Review of Global Affairs*, 6 April 2015, accessed 15 June 2015, http://www.aucegypt.edu/GAPP/CairoReview/Pages/articleDetails.aspx?aid=797.

[21] Alfred Schutz, *On Phenomenology and Social Relations: Selected Writings* (Chicago: University of Chicago Press, 1973).

[22] Peyman Vahabzadeh, *Articulated Experiences: Toward a Radical Phenomenology of Contemporary Social Movements* (Albany: State University of New York Press, 2003), 97.

[23] Louis Althusser, 'Ideology and Ideological State Apparatuses', *Lenin and Philosophy and Other Essays*. Trans. Ben Brewster (London: NLB, 1969): 121-173.

[24] Michel Foucault, 'The Subject and Power', *Critical Inquiry* 8 (1982): 777-795.

[25] Vahabzadeh, *Articulated Experiences*.

[26] Ibid., 98.

[27] Ibid., 97.

[28] Berger and Luckmann, *Social Construction of Reality*.

[29] Schutz, *On Phenomenology and Social Relations*.

[30] Vahabzadeh, *Articulated Experiences*, 101.

[31] Marcuse, *One-Dimensional Man*, 67.

[32] Stuart Hall, 'The Great Moving Right Show', *Marxism Today*, January 1979, 14.

[33] Susan Verducci, 'A Conceptual History of Empathy and a Question it Raises for Moral Education', *Educational Theory* 50.1 (2000): 63-80.

[34] Larocco, 'Empathy as Orientation'; Gavin Fairbairn, 'Reflecting on Empathy', in this volume.

[35] Fairbairn, 'Reflecting on Empathy'.

[36] Meagan Boler, *Feeling Power* (London: Routledge, 1999), 156.

[37] Mills, 'Constitutional Stories'.

[38] Larocco, 'Empathy as Orientation'; Fairbairn, 'Reflecting on Empathy.

[39] Jeffrey S. Dill, 'Durkheim and Dewey and the Challenge of Contemporary Moral Education', *Journal of Moral Education* 36.2 (2007): 221-237; Verducci, 'A Conceptual History of Empathy'.

[40] Megan Boler, 'The Risks of Empathy: Interrogating Multiculturalism's Gaze', *Cultural Studies* 11.2 (1997): 253-273.

[41] Davis, 'Empathy'.

[42] Louise Rosenblatt, *Literature as Exploration* (New York: Noble and Noble, 1938).

[43] Boler, 'The Risks of Empathy.'

[44] Nurit Sahar, 'Cognitive Milestones on Mutual Paths towards Empathy: A Four-Step Model,' in this volume.

[45] Meagan Boler, *Feeling Power* (London: Routledge, 1999), 159.

[46] Veronica Wain, 'Empathy with the Enemy: Can the Intellectually Gifted Experience Empathy with the Intellectually Impaired?,' in this volume.

[47] Ibid., 159.

[48] Ibid., 157.

[49] Ibid., 159.

[50] Ibid.

[51] Katie Collins, 'Extending Empathy Is Key to Human Survival, Says Academic', *Wired*, 20 May 2014, viewed on 14 June 2015, http://www.wired.co.uk/news/archive/2014-05/20/the-empathy-revolution-anita-nowak.

[52] Edith Stein, *On the Problem of Empathy* (Washington DC: ICS Publications, 1989).

[53] Fiona Larkin, 'Seeing the Loop: Examining Empathy through Art Practice,' in this volume.

[54] Ibid.

[55] Sahar, 'Cognitive Milestones on Mutual Paths to Empathy.'

[56] LJ (Nic) Theo, 'Empathic New(s) Orientations in Narratives about Sexuality,' in this volume.

[57] Charles King, '"Gays Are the new Jews": Homophobic Representations in African Media versus *Twitterverse* Empathy,' in this volume.

[58] Wain, 'Empathy with the Enemy.'

[59] Fairbairn, 'Reflecting on Empathy.'
[60] Stephen Larocco, 'Empathy as Orientation.'
[61] Ibid.
[62] Ibid.
[63] Collins, 'Extending Empathy Is Key to Human Survival'; Jeremy Rifkin, *The Empathic Civilization.*
[64] Martin Heidegger, *Being and Time.* Trans. John MacQuarrie and Edward Robinson (New York: Harper & Row, Publishers, Inc., 1962).
[65] Vahabzadeh, *Articulated Experiences.*
[66] Stein, *On the Problem of Empathy.*
[67] Mahatma Gandhi, quoted in Michael K. McCuddy, 'Fundamental Moral Orientations: Implications for Values-Based Leadership', *The Journal of Values-Based Leadership* 1.1 (2008): 1-13.

Bibliography

Althusser, L. 'Ideology and Ideological State Apparatuses'. *Lenin and Philosophy and Other Essays.* Translated by Ben Brewster. London: NLB, 1969.

Berger, Peter L. and Thomas Luckmann. *Social Construction of Reality: A Treatise in the Sociology of Knowledge.* New York: Anchor Books, 2003.

Boler, Megan. 'The Risks of Empathy: Interrogating Multiculturalism's Gaze'. *Cultural Studies* 11.2 (1997): 253-273.

Boler, Megan. *Feeling Power.* London: Routledge, 1999.

Collins, Katie. 'Extending Empathy Is Key to Human Survival, Says Academic'. *Wired.* 20 May 2014. Viewed on 14 June 2015. http://www.wired.co.uk/news/archive/2014-05/20/the-empathy-revolution-anita-nowak.

Craig, W. M., L. Schumann, M. E. Edge, and C. Teske. 'Are Bullying and Victimization on the Rise in Canada?' Paper presented at the Ontario: Canadian Public Health Association Conference, 2012.

Davis, Mark H. 'Empathy'. *Handbook on the Sociology of Emotions,* edited by Jan E. Stets and Jonathan H. Turner, 443-466. Riverside, CA: Springer Press, 2006.

Deal, K. H. 'The Relationship between Critical Thinking and Interpersonal Skills: Guidelines for Clinical Supervision'. *The Clinical Supervisor* 22.2 (2004): 3-19.

Dill, Jeffrey S. 'Durkheim and Dewey and the Challenge of Contemporary Moral Education'. *Journal of Moral Education* 36.2 (2007): 221-237.

Foucault, Michel. 'The Subject and Power'. *Critical Inquiry* 8 (1982): 777-795.

Greenberg, L. S., J. C. Watson, R. Elliott and A. C. Bohart. 'Empathy'. *Psychotherapy* 38.4 (2001): 380-384.

Hall, Stuart. 'The Great Moving Right Show'. *Marxism Today*, January 1979, 14-20.

H. Haste, and A. Hogan. 'Beyond Conventional Civic Participation, Beyond the Moral-Political Divide: Young People and Contemporary Debates about Citizenship'. *Journal of Moral Education* 35.4 (2006): 473-493.

Heidegger, Martin. *Being and Time*. Translated by John MacQuarrie and Edward Robinson. New York: Harper & Row, 1962.

Holt, S. and J. Marques. 'Empathy in Leadership: Appropriate or Misplaced?' *Journal of Business Ethics* 105.1 (2012): 95-105.

Kennedy, D. 'Philosophy for Children and the Reconstruction of Philosophy'. *Metaphilosophy* 30.4 (1999): 338-359.

Konrath, S. H., E. H. O'Brien, and C. Hsing. 'Changes in Dispositional Empathy in American College Students over Time: A Meta-Analysis'. *Personality and Social Psychology Review* 15.2 (2011): 180-198.

Marcuse, Herbert. *One-Dimensional Man.* Boston: Beacon Press, 1964.

Mills, Aaron. 'Constitutional Stories'. *The Cairo Review of Global Affairs*. 6 April 2015. Accessed 15 June 2015. http://www.aucegypt.edu/GAPP/CairoReview/Pages/articleDetails.aspx?aid=797.

Mostovicz, E. I., N. K. Kakabadse, and A. P. Kakabadse. 'A Dynamic Theory of Leadership Development'. *Leadership & Organization Development Journal* 30.6 (2009): 563-576.

Paglia-Boak, A., E. M. Adlaf, H. A. Hamilton, J. H. Beitchman, D. Wolfe and R. E. Mann. *Ontario Student Drug Use and Health Survey (OSDUHS): Mental Health and Well-Being Report 1991-2011.* Toronto: Centre for Addiction and Mental Health, 2012.

Rifkin, Jeremy. *The Empathic Civilization: The Race to Global Consciousness in a World in Crisis.* New York: Penguin Group, 2009.

Rosenblatt, Louise. *Literature as Exploration.* New York: Noble and Noble, 1938.

Schutz, Alfred. *On Phenomenology and Social Relations: Selected Writings.* Chicago: University of Chicago Press, 1973.

Stedman, N. L. P., and A. C. Andenoro. 'Identification of Relationships between Emotional Intelligence Skill & Critical Thinking Disposition in Undergraduate Leadership Students'. *Journal of Leadership Education* 6.1 (2007): 192-220.

Stein, Edith. *On the Problem of Empathy.* Washington D.C.: ICS Publications, 1989.

Vahabzadeh, Peyman. *Articulated Experiences: Toward A Radical Phenomenology of Contemporary Social Movements.* Albany, NY: State University of New York Press, 2003.

Verducci, Susan. 'A Conceptual History of Empathy and a Question It Raises for Moral Education'. *Educational Theory* 50.1 (2000): 63-80.

Weir, E. 'Preventing Violence in Youth'. *Canadian Medical Association Journal* 172.10 (2005): 1291-1292.

Rebeccah J. Nelems is conducting her PhD on empathy and youth at the University of Victoria, Canada. She is a 2015 Trudeau Scholar, and the grateful recipient of the Social Sciences and Humanities Research Council doctoral fellowship, and a Canadian Federation of University Women award.

Part II

Exploring the Affective and Cognitive Workings
of Empathy

Empathy, Complex Thinking and Their Interconnections

Camilla Pagani

Abstract

The chapter aims to examine the interconnections between empathy and complex thinking. Part of the considerations presented here draw on a research study on youths' relationship with cultural diversity through the analysis of anonymous open-ended essays written by secondary school pupils. The different components of empathy, and the emotional component in particular, are examined. Also the constituent aspects of complex thinking are presented and analysed. The risks of a 'mutilated' thought, characterised by a lack or a scarcity of complexity, are mentioned. The importance of fostering youths' complex thinking and empathic abilities is emphasised and the role of the arts, especially of literature, in shedding more light on the complexity of human mind, including its empathic abilities, is also underlined. The definition of empathy is examined and suggestions for enriching the debate on the nature of empathy are proposed.

Key Words: Empathy, complex thinking, emotions, cultural diversity, open-ended essays, education, youth, literature.

*****

1. Empathy and Complex Thinking: Some Definitions

Like other kinds of artistic expressions, since its beginnings literature has contributed enormously to bolstering humans' efforts to comprehend themselves, their relationships, and reality in general. In particular, literature has shed much light on the complexity of human 'identity,' as well as on the experiences of empathy and of compassion.[1] One example is to be drawn from Milan Kundera's most renowned book:

> … to have compassion (co-feeling) means not only to live with the other's misfortune but also to feel with him any emotion – joy, anxiety, pain. This kind of compassion … therefore signifies the maximal capacity of affective imagination, the art of emotional telepathy. In the hierarchy of sentiments, then, it is supreme.[2]

Though in these lines Kundera only refers to the emotional sphere of human interactions and mentions 'compassion' and not 'empathy,' it is clear that: a) compassion and empathy share some basic components (e.g., the capacity, at least to some degree, to feel an emotion with *the other*, as indicated in the above quotation); and b) like compassion, empathy also implies the use and the development of complex cognitive and emotional abilities (e.g., affective imagination, which Kundera considers to be the most sublime of sentiments). It is a fact that one of the most refined expressions of the complexity of the human mind is the empathic experience.

Indeed, empathy involves a broad range of complex emotional and cognitive states and abilities. Other elements characterising the nature of empathy strongly contribute to underpinning the complexity of the empathic experience. For example, in the empathic process: a) cognitive empathy and empathic emotions continuously and in various ways interact;[3] b) the empathiser experiences a sort of identification with *the other* and at the same time maintains her/his identity, and, hence, the self-other differentiation.[4] Beyond reasonable doubt, these are two fundamental characteristics of the empathic experience.

Given the 'complexity' of the issue which is the object of this chapter – complex thinking and empathy and their interconnections – I will first provide some definitions of the main psychological constructs to which I will refer in this context. More precisely, I will try to define the basic meanings I attach to these constructs.

By complex thinking I mean a group of cognitive and emotional processes through which individuals try to understand themselves, the others, and all the aspects of reality in which they are interested.[5] Some of the most meaningful cognitive and emotional processes involved in complex thinking are: awareness of the complexity of one's emotions and thoughts, multiple perspective-taking, creativity, constant and uninterrupted openness to new dimensions and realities, the acceptance of uncertainty, of incompleteness and of contradiction, the incessant involvement in a constructive relationship with diversity, and the co-occurrence of the sense of unity and multiplicity in a continuous and strenuous attempt towards integration.[6] By integration I mean the awareness of the necessity of different perspectives and at the same time the awareness of the necessity of an effort towards a sort of reconciliation and unification of these perspectives.

Most of the various meanings (e.g., perspective-taking, integration, and coherence) attached to these constructs will be discussed in the course of the chapter itself. By empathy I mean a situation-specific affective and cognitive state in which a person understands (or tries to understand), feels (or partly feels) and is moved by his/her understanding of the other's inner experience.[7] In conclusion, when research studies indicate that in the empathic experience cognitive empathy and empathic emotions interact *in various ways*, it means that in this interaction the amount and the role of these two components can vary according to the characteristics of the situation. I will especially deal with the emotional constituent of the empathic experience and will focus on the different levels of complexity that may be present in the emotional constituent itself.

Later on in this chapter I will address the issue regarding Fairbairn and Larocco's caveats about an often too simplistic use and interpretation of the concept of empathy and I will connect this short discussion with a reference to the notion of 'transformative empathy' as it is presented in Nelems' chapter.[8] Suffice it here to specify that in this chapter I will generally use the term 'empathy' with a positive connotation. I will develop this point later on.

I will examine the interconnections between empathy and complex thinking in the context of my research studies on youths' relationship with diversity, and, in particular, cultural diversity. I will put forth my considerations through the analysis of some extracts from anonymous open-ended essays written by Italian secondary school pupils, where they expressed their attitudes towards multiculturalism in present Italian society. These texts should help us more concretely to understand the link between empathic attitude and complex thinking. As a matter of fact, an assumption of my research work is that all the cognitive and emotional processes that characterise complex thinking are also unavoidably reflected in the various forms of linguistic communication, including written texts.

2. Emotional Complexity and Its Main Constituents

As I said above, I will especially deal with the emotional constituent of the empathic experience and with the different levels of complexity that may be present in the emotional constituent itself. I will briefly touch on the relationship between affective and cognitive empathy. And then I will analyse the interconnections between emotional complexity and complex thinking. As mentioned above, some extracts from participants' essays will help us in this task.

By emotional complexity I mean both the quantity of emotions that belong to a person's conceptual system and the individual and intra-individual variations in the experience and in the conceptualisation, of a specific emotion.[9] More precisely, emotional complexity could also be defined as having emotional experiences that are 'broad in range and well differentiated'.[10] Lindquist and Barrett especially identified two aspects of emotional complexity, namely dialecticism and granularity. Dialecticism refers to the experience of positive and negative emotional states (e.g., pleasantness and unpleasantness) 'in a coincidental or temporarily related fashion'.[11] Consequently, in our case, we can evaluate the degree of dialecticism from pupils' concurrent or almost concurrent experiences of positive and negative emotions as are portrayed in their essays. However, I would further develop Lindquist and Barrett's theorizations and argue that dialecticism should also imply individuals', at least partial, awareness of their contradictory emotions.

Emotion granularity refers to the precision and accuracy with which individuals describe their emotional experiences.[12] Individuals differ in this ability as some are more able to describe than others. Some people are more capable of clearly distinguishing different emotional experiences and of using precise and accurate emotion adjectives when they describe them. Others, on the other hand, represent their emotions in more general and broader terms. Even when they use adjectives to describe emotion (e.g., sad, unhappy, angry, etc.) they are not deeply aware of the variety and complexity of the meanings attached to each of these terms. Thus, the representations of their emotional experiences are more vague, confused, less precise and less defined. What is more, those who are good at emotional granularity can probably also be aware that their own experiences of specific emotions can vary over the course of time.

3. Methods

The research study I am referring to here represents a first stage of a wider research work on the relation between youths' complex thinking and empathy. At the same time it also represents a further development of a previous study I conducted with my research collaborators on youths' attitudes towards multiculturalism.[13] The formula (context and methodology) we had used seemed to be satisfactory, so in the present study a part of it was kept, namely the context (school), the use of anonymous open-ended essays, the preference for the use of qualitative data and, in particular, the distinction between explicit and implicit meaning of the texts. It is clear that I share Wójcik's view regarding the importance of analysing youths' attitudes toward outgroups and of developing effective anti-prejudice educational interventions.[14]

In this study we aimed to analyse the relationship between complex thinking and empathic attitude especially through the analysis of the implicit meaning of the texts.[15] This includes a consideration not only of their factual content, but also, and above all, of their implicit meaning.[16] We are all aware that for numerous reasons in human communication what is said, written or shown may diverge from what is really and deeply felt and thought.

The implicit meaning of a text, which is the *real* meaning, is the outcome of many components (including its factual content), some of which are more related to the formal characteristics of the text itself,[17] while others are more related to the characteristics of its content. For our purposes, we identified some of these characteristics and we evaluated the level of their presence in the texts. In particular, we examined *coherence, honesty, concreteness,*[18] *multiple perspective-taking,* and *creativity.*

By *coherence* we mean the extent to which the concepts and the experiences presented in a text, even if they are diverse, are sufficiently integrated. *Honesty,* which is different from *politeness,* refers to participants' disposition and motivation to express their views and feelings openly and truly.[19] *Concreteness* indicates if and to what extent participants support their argumentations by referring to precise direct or indirect experiences, thus possibly revealing a deeper involvement in the issue on their part. *Multiple perspective-taking* is related to the awareness of the complexity of the issue at stake and of the absolute necessity of considering other perspectives beyond one's own. Finally, *creativity* characterises a novel and original content, as well as a style that combines linguistic correctness and originality. For example, the use of appropriated, personally constructed metaphors that convey new and clearly elaborated meanings can be regarded as an indication of creativity.

Through these instruments it is easier to identify the participants' real feelings and thoughts which are explicitly and implicitly expressed in their essays. In the same way as, in an eye to eye oral communication, we are aware of the importance of nonverbal behaviour in understanding others' real feelings and attitudes,[20] so it is necessary to understand the importance of those signs in a written text that can help us understand its implicit meaning. In other words, when we try to understand the implicit meaning of a text, what we are doing is nothing but trying to empathically fathom the true attitudes and feelings of the author of the text. Indeed, we tried to move forward, for example beyond the level of participants' most evident culturally induced motivations and ideas, including their stereotypes or their possible conformity to social desirability norms, and to reach that 'inner core' where the role of culture is less strong and where more essential and profound motivations and thoughts prevail. We believe that this type of text analysis helped us to attain a deeper insight into youths' real feelings and thoughts.

In this study we collected and analysed 79 open-ended essays anonymously written in 4 classes by 79 secondary school pupils (41 F and 38 M) aged 14-18. Regarding this specific method, I agree with Barrett's point of view, according to which 'self-reports, despite their obvious limitations…do appear to contain valid information about fundamental aspects of experience'[21] and that the best way to understand a person's experience is to ask them.

All the pupils in the participating classes took part in the research. Their participation was presented as part of the normal activities of the classes and as an integral part of their curriculum. Thus, only school administration approval was required (a common research practice in Italian schools). In each class the author and a research assistant illustrated the principal activities of their Research Institute and the aim of the study. Teachers were asked not to be present in order to avoid any kind of interference with the research work.

The following are the exact words (contained in a brief note we gave to each pupil) we used when we asked our participants to write about their views and experiences in a society that has unequivocally become multicultural:

> For a long time now Italy has been inhabited not only by Italians but also by people coming from other countries. We are interested in what you think about this topic. Tell us about your experiences and the experiences of others, also referring to what happens both at school and in society in general.

Pupils were given an hour and a half to complete their assignment. They were asked to indicate only their gender and were not requested to specify whether they are an immigrant or an Italian. It is worth mentioning here that in the last few years the number of immigrant pupils enrolled in Italian schools has considerably increased, with 9% in the 2013/2014 school year.[22] The pupils' age could be inferred from the grades they were attending, as their essays were collected separately from each class.

Every effort was made to create a trustful and collaborative atmosphere. We assured participants that their essays would not be graded and they would not be judged for what and how they wrote, but that they should rather try to express their views and feelings freely. We also assured them that their teachers would not have access to what they wrote. Finally, we told them that if they wanted to, they would be informed about the results of the research and that we could organise a meeting with them for further discussion. We met each class some time afterwards and addressed with participants those points that seemed to be most relevant for them.

The analysis of these texts was largely based on principles of textual analysis, discourse analysis, ethnographic analysis, and content analysis. The pupils' essays were repeatedly read by the author and a research assistant, who independently conducted a qualitative analysis of data and, afterwards, compared the results of their analyses. As I said above, the essays were mainly analysed in terms of the categories of *coherence, honesty, concreteness, multiple perspective-taking,* and *creativity,* whose presence was assessed using a five-point Likert scale, and especially focusing on the implicit meaning of the texts themselves.

4. Analysis of Some Extracts

In order to better understand the relationship between complex thinking and empathy, we will start by examining some extracts from an essay written by a 16-year-old-boy. The following are the first lines of it:[23]

> Well, unfortunately this is a very difficult topic. I would start by
> saying that I think that accepting all these people in a country
> like Italy is unfair. This is because by accepting so many people
> in our country, we are losing our identity as Italians.[24]

In the first sentence of his essay the boy uses a style characterised by a certain degree of originality and, thus, *creativity,* as he directly and apparently sincerely, seems to be addressing the researchers themselves. This kind of originality could resemble the quality of 'inequivalence' described by Tsoukas and Hatch[25] in their consideration of complexity in social organisations, with specific reference to George Soros, as the ability to generate 'more inequivalent descriptions of a situation'.[26] The two authors relate this ability to complexity. However, though the pupil's sentence might be defined, in a way, as 'novel' and 'unexpected' – attributes that approximately correspond to 'inequivalent' – its meaning is not really clear. In particular, it is not completely clear whether the pupil is specifically referring to the difficulty related to the issue per se – multiculturalism – or to the difficulty of the assignment, or to both. Thus, even in this first line where he seems to be more open and *honest*, this pupil has not been able to express his point of view unambiguously.

Besides, another element that does not support the idea of originality connected with this text is the fact that from the second sentence the idea of multiculturalism is almost automatically associated with the problems of immigration and that immigration is perceived as an 'invasion,' in the wake of the opinions expressed by a large part of the media and by a part of the Establishment. So, only the negative effects implied in such a situation are suggested. No other perspective – for example, the possibility of a positive coexistence of culturally diverse people – is considered, neither in this first paragraph nor in the rest of the essay.

From the second sentence of the paragraph ('I would start by saying that I think that accepting all these people in a country like Italy is unfair') we are introduced more profoundly into the pupil's emotional experience as regards multiculturalism. Given that he identifies multiculturalism with immigration and immigration with an invasion, it necessarily follows that the principal emotion that the boy experiences is fear. Fear is the result of a perception of threat. At the beginning of the essay the threat is 'numerical' ('all these people' and 'so many people'). Here, we come across a well-known and strong prejudice, namely the idea that shortly or even in the present time in Italy there will be or there are more immigrants than Italians. We named this kind of fear *'unjustified,'* as it is not grounded on real, concrete and verifiable circumstances.[27]

In the third sentence, the boy better specifies his fear: it is the fear of losing his identity, as a consequence of the purported 'invasion' of 'hordes' of immigrants. In our previous study we had identified *'fear of losing their identity,'* together with *'fear of losing their own safety and welfare'* and *'fear of losing other people's affection'* as youths' three most significant fears related to their relationship with multiculturalism.[28]

From many respects, some attitudes of a number of our pupils could be defined as "racist" and, thus, be very close to those expressed by Ezekiel's participants in his ethnographic fieldwork with neo-Nazi and Klan leaders and followers. In the analysis of his research study, Ezekiel frequently underlines the fact that in the interviewing he felt that these youths were 'fearful at the core'[29] and that at 'an unspoken but deep level' they seemed to feel 'extremely vulnerable'.[30]

'Fear of losing one's identity' is a strong emotional state which is usually triggered by a powerful, often negative event, like for example a catastrophe, which produces a distinct demarcation between the time before and the time after it. Obviously, this boy's fear is also fuelled by a simplistic, distorted, and unrefined conceptualisation of 'identity.' Certainly, a discussion in class on the concept of identity would improve pupils' levels of complex thinking and of empathic attitudes towards 'diverse' individuals. This way, the idea of identity would not coincide with the idea of a presumed 'race' or ethnic group. As also Ezekiel points out, the idea of 'race' as a real entity, as a 'biological category with absolute boundaries, each race having a different essence – just as a rock is a rock and a tree is a tree, a White is a White and a Black is a Black',[31] characterises neo-Nazi and Klan youths' view of reality. I will not consider here the fact that the concept of race should have no relevance whatsoever since as social scientists we are aware (but pupils may not be aware) that the biological bases of race have been widely confuted and that the concept of race is a social construction.[32] For example, in a discussion in class, students might question the traditional criteria people often use when defining identity and might embark on an effort to provide a new definition of 'human being.' Later in this chapter, we will see how this issue is smartly addressed by another participant, a girl of 14.

The boy's simplistic and partly distorted conceptualisation of identity and, more importantly, his insufficient awareness of the various components of his experience of fear, fuel feelings of anger and resentment against immigrants to the extent that his mental representation of them changes. This change can be easily tracked in the paragraph below:

> Then the most important question is: what do all these immigrants want? Do they want a job? Do they want money? Do they want to live in peace? Or rather, they want our jobs? They want our money? And steal our peace earned throughout centuries of wars and of our ancestors' efforts?[33]

While at the very beginning of his essay immigrants were implicitly considered to be apparently honest people who leave their countries because they are needy and look for better economic and social conditions, later on immigrants are implicitly presented as malicious individuals, whose main purpose is to steal Italians' jobs, money, and presumed tranquillity. Cognitive distortions and a scarce awareness of his cognitive and emotional experiences nullify the boy's empathic abilities.

Morin defines the result of this process as a mutilation of thought and underpins the role of complex thinking in countervailing this destructive process. It is important to quote his words as they are particularly poignant, terse, and direct:

> Complexity is situated at a point of departure for a richer, less mutilating action. I strongly believe that the less a thought is mutilating, the less it will mutilate human beings. We must remember the ravages that simplifying visions have caused, not only in the intellectual world, but in life. Much of the suffering of millions of beings results from the effects of fragmented and one-dimensional thought.[34]

A similar position is held by Ezekiel when he describes the world of neo-Nazi and Klan leaders and followers as 'impoverished of half the range of human feeling and thought – like the army, like prison',[35] characterised as it is by *'spiritual poverty'*.[36] Though in this chapter my considerations basically focus on the relationship between complex thinking and empathic attitudes, which places my analysis on a different and more general level as compared to those studies that investigate the relationship between formal education and ethnic prejudice, it is interesting to point out that these studies generally indicate a negative correlation between a level of formal education and prejudice against ethnic minorities.[37] On his part, Ezekiel similarly describes the neo-Nazi and Klan youths as 'poorly educated',[38] given that they had usually left school early.

Now I will quote a different essay, written by a 14-year-old Italian boy, who, from some respects, regards himself as a stranger and probably also as a diverse individual. No rage or fear characterise this pupil's attitudes towards multiculturalism at the time he writes his essay. Instead, interest and curiosity concerning himself and immigrants (the culturally diverse people) can be vividly felt. He provides a brief but tight, brilliant and, above all, dialectic description of the transformation of his attitudes in the course of time towards multiculturalism. His views are marked by emotional complexity and emotional granularity. He also puts forth his 'complex' definition of 'stranger' and, accordingly, a 'complex' concept of identity. The boy is now living in Rome:

> As I came from a little town, I was scared and intrigued by a multi-ethnic city. I was scared by the rumours on immigrants and intrigued by the many cultures I was coming across. As I started living here I found out that the rumours were all wrong, instead the opposite was true ....

> As I was born in a big city and then moved to a little town, the people there saw me as a stranger but then, as I came here people coming from other states became the strangers, I can say that the definition of stranger depends on the perspective from which someone sees the situation so I cannot express a real opinion on this subject.[39]

The boy seems to be aware of the transformations that have occurred in his views and attitudes regarding multiculturalism which he seems to have autonomously developed. His style is direct, original, and personal. He is analysing himself and the changes that have taken place in his perspectives. The term 'rumours' remind us of stereotypes and prejudices, but he was able to discard them in the end through a direct contact with multiculturalism itself. This reality is examined in its complexity. The representation of a multicultural society is not characterised by a simplistic and Manichaean language, which tends to represent multiculturalism in a dichotomous way (e.g., good/bad, honest/criminal, referring either to immigrants or to Italians).[40] He is aware of and accepts uncertainty and the concrete possibility of new perspectives and of new developments in social contexts and in people's attitudes towards them. It is clear how complex thinking and a mature and constructive relationship with cultural diversity are deeply interconnected. We are very far from neo-Nazi and Klan youths' view of reality, whereby the implicit definition of identity implies the existence of fixed and rigid borders ('each race having a different essence – just as a rock is a rock and a tree is a tree, a White is a White and a Black is a Black'[41]) and the consequent rejection of all those territories stretching beyond the borders.

Another participant, a girl of 14, in her essay introduces the theme of the definition of 'human being,' a term that *per se* implies the idea that borders between countries and cultures can in a way lose any kind of relevance. First, the girl criticises all those people that judge others on the basis of exterior criteria, like, for example, their origins, social status, and physical features. She maintains that these people are lacking in something, namely knowledge and the capacity to think autonomously:

> I think that people who judge others on the ground of their origin, or worse, of the economic situation of their country, well, I think these people are not free to think with their own head, I think they don't know a single thing, History, Psychology, Science; people who limit themselves to skin colour, to eyes or hair colour ....[42]

In the lines immediately following, the girl seems to suggest that these limitations in the capacity of thinking inevitably result in limitations in cognitive and emotional empathy:

> ... people who just look at this and are not able to OBSERVE the other's self, people who are not able to think that deeply, in the most inner and profound place in the other's heart there is a soul
> ....

Hence, the girl indirectly suggests a link between complex thinking and empathy. But she even goes further on by suggesting that this soul:

> ... is far away from any possibility of being judged simply because nobody can compare something if no criterion to refer to is available, and what is this criterion? Simply it does not exist. It will never exist.

In these two lines the girl makes three important statements: a) presently a model, a prototypical idea of 'human being' does not exist; b) without this model or prototypical idea no judgment is possible on how much someone exhibits the characteristics of a human being; and c) this model or prototypical idea will never exist. The girl thereby accepts the complexity of the problem of the definition of human being and the uncertainty related to the possibility that this definition does not and will never exist.

However, in the end she implicitly indicates a direction in this research. The empathic understanding of the other's diversity could prompt a new and more satisfactory attempt in the elaboration of this definition. By underlining the significance of a person's 'self,' 'heart,' and 'soul,' all terms that usually refer to objects of empathic concern, she seems to indicate that people's deepest thoughts, beliefs, and emotions represent those elements that most profoundly constitute their individual essence. She also implicitly seems to indicate that the million people's deepest thoughts, beliefs, and emotions have a common core and that this common core might constitute the essence of what a human being is.[43]

Incidentally, these considerations seem to be perfectly in tune with Wain's point of view, when she underlines the necessity of 'A shift in focus, away from the disability and towards the person and their story, in a bid to uncover possible areas of commonality and intersection' as 'a significant step towards providing arenas for greater levels of empathy to flourish'.[44]

5. Discussion

The extract from the 14-year-old boy's essay shows a positive relationship between complex thinking and a profound interest in cultural diversity. Since a profound interest is usually characterised by the presence of complex emotions, we can reliably affirm that this interest is a significant step towards empathy. As to the extracts from the 14-year-old girl's essay, they clearly exemplify how empathic concern and complex thinking fuel each other, and that their relationship can be so close that it is practically impossible to say where one finishes and the other starts.

This implies a few important points which find resonance in research on emotions: a) an emotion is an experience constructed with a conceptual act;[45] b) consequently, emotional complexity is also a product of cognitive complexity;[46] c) emotional complexity is conducive to empathic understanding of others' feelings;[47] and d) more precisely, having a broad and differentiated repertoire of emotional experiences can help individuals understand others' feelings, 'because understanding others' feelings is presumably based partly on understanding one's own …'[48]

In sum, research findings indicate that individuals characterised by high emotional complexity are more aware of their emotions and thoughts, are more open to experience, are more cognitively complex, are more empathically involved in others' emotional and cognitive experiences, show a higher level of ego development, and are better at interpersonal interactions.[49] It therefore appears that emotional complexity, complex thinking, and empathic attitudes are closely interconnected.

At the beginning of this chapter I mentioned the importance of arts, and of literature in particular, as an instrument for shedding more light on the complexity of human mind, including its empathic abilities. In this regard, Morin underlines the role of literature, and in particular of the novel, in helping us understand the 'multiplicity of our identities ...,' which is a part of our complexity.[50] He especially mentions the importance of the internal monologue in literature, which 'reveals to us how little one knows oneself ...,' as 'We know ourselves only as an appearance of self'.[51]

An example of scarce knowledge of oneself in our data is provided by those participants who are unaware of their contradictory attitudes toward multiculturalism. The phenomenon is rather astounding. For instance, in the same essay some pupils unambiguously express two contradictory opinions about immigrants: they show a deep hostility when immigrants in general are considered, whilst they express benign, positive, and often empathetic attitudes when they refer to specific immigrants whom they know well and with whom they are sometimes friendly or even very friendly. Surprisingly, as I said above, these youths seem to be totally unaware of this contradiction. Here is a good example of this lack of coherence and integration from an essay written by a girl of 14:

> These immigrants should remain in their own countries. Only those with a work permit should be allowed to come. This way all these bad things would not happen, that also the newspapers and the TV talk about it.

> Near my home lives a Romanian family and they have lived here for almost four years. This family is numerous and all the children are very little ....

> They are a good family, but also very kind and polite, they always say 'hello' to me when they pass along, and besides, the little girl, the eldest, always plays with my sister and they get on very well together. This family came to Italy, because in Romania they could not find a job, and also because life was not very nice there and not very easy either.[52]

If the girl were capable of adequately analysing these two contradictory views, one of which is strengthened by the rather common and unjustified belief that an immigrant without a work permit is necessarily a criminal, she would probably also feel more empathetic towards immigrants in general.

6. Conclusions

It might be useful here to highlight a few points which especially address a crucial issue as far as empathy studies are concerned, namely the meaning of empathy.

Empathy can be learnt. This view is shared by other authors in this book (see, for example, Sahar, Wain, and Fairbairn, who explicitly refers to empathy as a set of skills).[53]

The other's world, which we try to 'imaginatively…inhabit'[54] through the empathic process, is 'somewhat of a mystery',[55] especially when the other is an individual very different from us, like a person with intellectual disability.[56] This kind of experience is a powerful instrument for attaining a more profound awareness and acknowledgment of the complexity of our inner and outer reality. Especially this last point supports the idea of the deep relationship between empathy and complexity, and, thus, of how appealing the search for empathy actually is. It also helps us understand how the inclusion of children with disability in mainstream classes[57] is important in order to foster the development of youths' empathic abilities and complex thinking.

It is necessary to include empathy studies within an interdisciplinary theoretical framework, where the social macro-context (power relations, in particular, and cultural worldviews) is also considered.[58] This view also belongs to complexity studies, which consider a multidisciplinary perspective to be a prerequisite in research work.

The concept of 'transformative' empathy, which Nelems discusses,[59] and the idea that the development of empathy should lead to a change,[60] are particularly useful in order to enlarge the scope of the debate regarding the meaning of empathy.

Both Larocco and Fairbairn[61] justly focus on the complexity of human empathic attitudes ('Empathy can produce feelings that are potentially destructive…,'[62] as is stated by Larocco), so that empathy might also be regarded as an ambivalent reality, a sort of Janus Bifrons.

As I said at the beginning of this chapter, here I attached a positive meaning to the concept of empathy. There may be legitimate differences in the conceptualisations regarding empathy, but it is important to specify and clarify them. Here, I would just like to suggest some tentative considerations that obviously need to be addressed in future research. As I said above, empathy implies a situation-specific affective and cognitive state, as well as the awareness both of the identification with the other and of the self-other differentiation. As a matter of fact, in some cases empathy can be blurred by negative emotions and attitudes towards the object of empathy. However, it is possible that in *true* empathy the individual experiences a 'particular' identification (and a 'particular' awareness of this identification) with the other. In this context the awareness is achieved in a mental state that is very close to mindfulness. The individual realises that 'the other' is also 'myself.' In this situation this 'myself' can only be an object of care and affection and cannot be the object of destructive feelings. It is a situation characterised by openness to and awareness of new and significant stimuli and explorations of new dimensions of experience, so that, if I become the other it goes without saying that I look for the other's good and wellbeing.

Consequently, *true* empathy can only be 'transformative' and embrace all aspects of social life, including policy making. Following these short considerations on *true* empathy, I would like to conclude with Calvino's indications, when he suggests that we should 'not only…enter into selves like our own but…give speech to that which has no language, to the bird perching on the edge of the gutter, to the tree in spring and the tree in fall, to stone, to cement, to plastic…..' and states that this was also Ovid's aim, when he wrote about the continuity of forms, as well as Lucretius', 'when he identified himself with that nature common to each and everything'.[63]

Notes

[1] See for example, Edgar Morin, *On Complexity* (Cresskill: Hampton Press, 2008); Italo Calvino, *Six Memos for the Next Millennium* (London: Penguin, 2009); Paulus Pimomo, 'Poetry of Compassionate Empathy,' *Encountering Empathy: Interrogating the Past, Envisioning the Future*, eds. Veronica Wain and Paulus Pimomo (Oxford: Inter-Disciplinary Press, 2015), 35-44.

[2] Milan Kundera, *The Unbearable Lightness of Being* (Croydon, UK: Faber and Faber, 1984), 18-19, also quoted by Charles King, 'Gays Are the New Jews: Homophobic Representations in African Media versus *Twitterverse* Empathy,' in this volume.

[3] See for example, Changming Duan and Clara E. Hill, 'The Current State of Empathy Research,' *Journal of Counseling Psychology* 43 (1996): 261-274.

[4] See, for instance, Maria Miceli, Alessandro Mancini, and Palma Menna, 'The Art of Comforting,' *New Ideas in Psychology* 27 (2009): 343-361.

[5] See Flavia Cangià, and Camilla Pagani, 'Youths, Cultural Diversity, and Complex Thinking,' *The Open Psychology Journal* 7 (2014): 20-28.

[6] See, for example, Flavia Cangià, and Camilla Pagani, 'Youths, Cultural Diversity, and Complex Thinking'; Sun-Mee Kang and Phillip R. Shaver, 'Individual Differences in Emotional Complexity: Their Psychological Implications,' *Journal of Personality* 72 (2004): 687-726; Kristen A. Lindquist, and Lisa F. Barrett, 'Emotional Complexity,' *Handbook of Emotions*, ed. Michael Lewis, Jeannette M. Haviland-Jones, and Lisa F. Barrett (New York: The Guildford Press, 2008), 513-530; Edgar Morin, *On Complexity* (Cresskill: Hampton Press, 2008).

[7] For example, Duan and Hill, 'The Current State of Empathy Research'; Miceli, Mancini, and Menna, 'The Art of Comforting'; Gert-Jan Vreeke, and Ingrid L. van

der Mark, 'Empathy, an Integrative Model,' *New Ideas in Psychology* 21 (2003): 177-207.

[8] Gavin Fairbairn, 'Reflecting on Empathy,' in this volume; Steve Larocco, 'Empathy as Orientation Rather than Feeling: Why Empathy Is Ethically Complex,' in this volume; Rebeccah Nelems, 'What Is This Thing Called Empathy?', in this volume.

[9] See, for instance, Lisa F. Barrett, 'Solving the Emotion Paradox: Categorization and the Experience of Emotion,' *Personality and Social Psychology Review* 10 (2006): 20-46; Kristen A. Lindquist, and Lisa F. Barrett, 'Emotional Complexity.'

[10] Kang and Shaver, 'Individual Differences in Emotional Complexity: Their Psychological Implications,' 687.

[11] Lindquist and Barrett, 'Emotional Complexity,' 515.

[12] Barrett, 'Solving the Emotion Paradox: Categorization and the Experience of Emotion.'

[13] See Camilla Pagani, 'Violence in Cross-Cultural Relations as the Outcome of Specific Cognitive and Emotional Processes,' *The Open Psychology Journal* 4, Suppl 1-M2 (2011): 21-27; Camilla Pagani and Francesco Robustelli, 'Young People, Multiculturalism, and Educational Interventions for the Development of Empathy,' *International Social Science Journal* 200-201 (2010): 247-261; Camilla Pagani, Francesco Robustelli and Cristina Martinelli. 'School, Cultural Diversity, Multiculturalism, and Contact,' *Intercultural Education* 22 (2011): 337-349.

[14] Małgorzata Wójcik, 'The Impact of Empathy on Ethnic Prejudice. Anti-Prejudice Intervention in School Setting' (paper presented at the First Global Conference on Empathy, Prague, Czech Republic, November 7-9, 2014).

[15] This is one of the studies we conducted within the 'Progetto Migrazioni' - Department of Social Sciences and Humanities - Cultural Heritage, National Research Council. We would like to thank the school boards and the pupils for their collaboration.

[16] See Pagani, 'Violence in Cross-Cultural Relations as the Outcome of Specific Cognitive and Emotional Processes'; Pagani and Robustelli, 'Young People, Multiculturalism, and Educational Interventions for the Development of Empathy'; Pagani, Robustelli, and Martinelli, 'School, Cultural Diversity, Multiculturalism, and Contact.'

[17] See Cecilia Wainryb, Beverly A. Brehl, and Sonia Matwin, 'Being Hurt and Hurting Others: Children's Narrative Accounts and Moral Judgments of Their Own Interpersonal Conflicts,' *Monographs of the Society for Research in Child Development* 3 (2005): 1-114.

[18] See Pagani and Robustelli, 'Young People, Multiculturalism, and Educational Interventions for the Development of Empathy.'

[19] See Shoshana Steinberg, and Dan Bar-On, 'An Analysis of the Group Process in Encounters between Jews and Palestinians Using a Typology for Discourse

Classification,' *International Journal of Intercultural Relations* 26 (2002): 199-214.

[20] See for instance Maria Miceli, Alessandro Mancini and Palma Menna, 'The Art of Comforting.'

[21] Lisa F. Barrett, 'Solving the Emotion Paradox: Categorization and the Experience of Emotion,' 24.

[22] Sono 802.844 gli alunni stranieri nella scuola italiana – Immigrant pupils in Italian schools are 802.844. 'News', *Oasisociale.it*, Viewed on 15 April 2015, http://www.oasisociale.it/news/alunni-stranieri-nelle-scuole-italiane.html

[23] In the quotations from participants' essays we did not eliminate spelling, grammatical, syntactic, and lexical mistakes or any other 'idiosyncratic' element in the form and in the content of the texts.

[24] Extract from an anonymous essay written by a boy of 16. A few of the extracts presented here were also quoted in Camilla Pagani, 'Youth's Empathy and Complex Thinking,' *Encountering Empathy: Interrogating the Past, Envisioning the Future*, eds. Veronica Wain and Paulus Pimomo (Oxford: Inter-Disciplinary Press, 2015), 177-188. In the present chapter in this volume these texts are more deeply and thoroughly analysed.

[25] Haridimos Tsoukas, and Mary J. Hatch. 'Complex Thinking, Complex Practice: The Case for a Narrative Approach to Organizational Complexity,' *Human Relations* 54 (2001): 979-1013, 1001.

[26] George Soros, *The Alchemy of Finance* (New York: Wiley, 1994).

[27] See Pagani, and Robustelli, 'Young People, Multiculturalism, and Educational Interventions for the Development of Empathy'; Pagani, Robustelli, and Martinelli, 'School, Cultural Diversity, Multiculturalism, and Contact.'

[28] Pagani, and Robustelli, 'Young People, Multiculturalism, and Educational Interventions for the Development of Empathy'; in particular, teachers' affection.

[29] Raphael S. Ezekiel, 'An Ethnographer Looks at Neo-Nazi and Klan Groups: The Racist Mind Revisited,' *American Behavioral Scientist* 46 (2002): 51-71, 64.

[30] Ibid., 58.

[31] Ibid., 53.

[32] Camilla Pagani, and Francesco Robustelli, 'Youth's Attitudes toward Racism: A Psycho-Socio-Cultural Perspective,' *Conflicts in a Society in Transition*, ed. Borisz Szegál and István András (Dunaújváros: Dunaújváros College Press, 2011), 79-95.

[33] This is another extract from the same anonymous essay written by the boy of 16.

[34] Morin, 'On Complexity,' 57.

[35] Ezekiel, 'An Ethnographer Looks at Neo-Nazi and Klan Groups,' 57.

[36] Ibid., 62 (in italics in the original text).

[37] See Flavia Cangià and Camilla Pagani, '"Youths" Racism and Levels of Complex Thinking,' (paper presented at the XXXVI CICA International

Conference 'Towards Understanding Conflicts, Aggression, Violence and Peace,' Héviz, Hungary, 23-26 June 2013).

[38] Ezekiel, 'An Ethnographer Looks at Neo-Nazi and Klan Groups,' 64.

[39] Extract from an anonymous open-ended essay written by a boy of 14. The Italian word 'straniero,' which the boy uses here, actually includes various interconnected meanings, namely: foreigner, immigrant, and stranger. In this text we decided to translate 'straniero' with 'stranger,' as it seemed that the boy used this word with a slight connotation of 'extraneousness.'

[40] See Cangià, and Pagani, 'Youths, Cultural Diversity, and Complex Thinking'; Mariapia Veladiano, 'Così Si E' Ristretto il Vocabolario,' *Repubblica*, March 29, 2013.

[41] Ezekiel, 'An Ethnographer Looks at Neo-Nazi and Klan Groups,' 53.

[42] Extract from an anonymous open-ended essay written by a girl of 14.

[43] Camilla Pagani, 'The Cross-Cultural Significance of Empathy as an Instrument to Prevent Aggression,' *Cross-Cultural Approaches to Aggression and Reconciliation*, ed. Jesus Martin Ramirez, and Deborah S. Richardson (Huntington, N.Y.: NovaScience, 2001), 191-201.

[44] Veronica Wain, 'Empathy with the Enemy: Can the Intellectually Gifted Experience Empathy with the Intellectually Impaired?' in *Encountering Empathy: Interrogating the Past, Envisioning the Future*, eds. Veronica Wain and Paulus Pimomo (Oxford: Inter-Disciplinary Press, 2015), 116.

[45] Barrett, 'Solving the Emotion Paradox.'

[46] Kang and Shaver, 'Individual Differences in Emotional Complexity.'

[47] Ibid.

[48] Ibid., 693.

[49] See for example Kang, and Shaver, 'Individual Differences in Emotional Complexity.'

[50] Morin, 'On Complexity,' 38.

[51] Ibid.

[52] Extract from an anonymous open-ended essay written by a girl of 14.

[53] Nurit Sahar, 'Cognitive Milestones on Mutual Paths towards Empathy: A Four-step Model', in this volume; Wain, 'Empathy with the Enemy'; Fairbairn, 'Reflecting on Empathy'.

[54] Wain, 'Empathy with the Enemy'.

[55] Ibid.

[56] Wain, 'Empathy with the Enemy'; Sahar, 'Cognitive Milestones'.

[57] Wain, 'Empathy with the Enemy'. In Italian schools, children with disability are actually included in mainstream classes.

[58] Nelems, 'What Is This Thing Called Empathy?'

[59] Ibid.

[60] See also Sahar, 'Cognitive Milestones'.

[61] Fairbairn, 'Reflecting on Empathy'.
[62] Larocco, 'Empathy as Orientation Rather than Feeling'.
[63] Calvino, *Six Memos for the Next Millennium*, 124.

Bibliography

Barrett, Lisa F. 'Solving the Emotion Paradox: Categorization and the Experience of Emotion.' *Personality and Social Psychology Review* 10 (2006): 20-46.

Calvino, Italo. *Six Memos for the Next Millennium.* London: Penguin, 2009.

Cangià, Flavia, and Camilla Pagani. '"Youths" Racism and Levels of Complex Thinking.' Paper Presented at the XXXVI CICA International Conference 'Towards Understanding Conflicts, Aggression, Violence and Peace,' Héviz (Hungary), 23-26 June 2013.

Cangià, Flavia, and Camilla Pagani. 'Youths, Cultural Diversity, and Complex Thinking.' *The Open Psychology Journal* 7 (2014): 20-28.

Duan, Changming, and Clara E. Hill. 'The Current State of Empathy Research.' *Journal of Counseling Psychology* 43 (1996): 261-274.

Ezekiel, Raphael S. 'An Ethnographer Looks at Neo-Nazi and Klan Groups: The Racist Mind Revisited.' *American Behavioral Scientist* 46 (2002): 51-71.

Kang, Sun-Mee, and Phillip R. Shaver. 'Individual Differences in Emotional Complexity: Their Psychological Implications.' *Journal of Personality* 72 (2004): 687-726.

Kundera, Milan. *The Unbearable Lightness of Being.* Croydon, UK: Faber and Faber, 1984.

Lindquist, Kristen A., and Lisa F. Barrett. 'Emotional Complexity.' *Handbook of Emotions*, edited by Michael Lewis, Jeannette M. Haviland-Jones, and Lisa F. Barrett, 513-530. New York: The Guildford Press, 2008.

Miceli, Maria, Alessandro Mancini and Palma Menna. 'The Art of Comforting.' *New Ideas in Psychology* 27 (2009): 343-361.

Morin, Edgar. *On Complexity.* Cresskill: Hampton Press, 2008.

Pagani, Camilla. 'The Cross-Cultural Significance of Empathy as an Instrument to Prevent Aggression.' *Cross-cultural Approaches to Aggression and Reconciliation*, edited by J. Martin Ramirez, and Deborah S. Richardson, 191-201. Huntington, N.Y.: NovaScience, 2001.

Pagani, Camilla. 'Violence in Cross-Cultural Relations as the Outcome of Specific Cognitive and Emotional Processes,' *The Open Psychology Journal* 4 Suppl 1-M2 (2011): 21-27.

Pagani, Camilla, and Francesco Robustelli. 'Young People, Multiculturalism, and Educational Interventions for the Development of Empathy.' *International Social Science Journal* 200-201 (2010): 247-261.

Pagani, Camilla, and Francesco Robustelli. 'Youth's Attitudes toward Racism: A Psycho-Socio-Cultural Perspective.' *Conflicts in a Society in Transition*, edited by Borisz Szegál, and István András, 79-95. Dunaújváros: Dunaújváros College Press, 2011.

Pagani, Camilla, Francesco Robustelli and Cristina Martinelli. 'School, Cultural Diversity, Multiculturalism, and Contact.' *Intercultural Education* 22 (2011): 337-349.

Pimomo, Paulus. 'Poetry of Compassionate Empathy'. *Encountering Empathy: Interrogating the Past, Envisioning the Future*, edited by Veronica Wain and Paulus Pimomo, 35-44. Oxford: Inter-Disciplinary Press, 2015.

Soros, George. *The Alchemy of Finance*. New York: Wiley, 1994.

Steinberg, Shoshana, and Dan Bar-On. 'An Analysis of the Group Process in Encounters between Jews and Palestinians Using a Typology for Discourse Classification.' *International Journal of Intercultural Relations* 26 (2002): 199-214.

Tam, Kim-Pong. 'Dispositional Empathy with Nature.' *Journal of Environmental Psychology* 35 (2013): 92-104.

Tsoukas, Haridimos, and Mary Jo Hatch. 'Complex Thinking, Complex Practice: The Case for a Narrative Approach to Organizational Complexity.' *Human Relations* 54 (2001): 979-1013.

Veladiano, Mariapia. 'Così Si E' Ristretto il Vocabolario.' *Repubblica*, 29 March 2013.

Vreeke, Gert-Jan, and Ingrid L. van der Mark. 'Empathy, an Integrative Model.' *New Ideas in Psychology* 21 (2003): 177-207.

Wain, Veronica. 'Empathy with the Enemy: Can the Intellectually Gifted Experience Empathy with the Intellectually Impaired?' *Encountering Empathy: Interrogating the Past, Envisioning the Future*, edited by Veronica Wain and Paulus Pimomo, 111-120. Oxford: Inter-Disciplinary Press, 2015.

Wainryb, Cecilia, Beverly A. Brehl and Sonia Matwin. 'Being Hurt and Hurting Others: Children's Narrative Accounts and Moral Judgments of Their Own Interpersonal Conflicts.' *Monographs of the Society for Research in Child Development* 3 (2005): 1-114.

Wójcik, Małgorzata. *The Impact of Empathy on Ethnic Prejudice. Anti-Prejudice Intervention in School Setting.* Paper presented at the First Global Conference on Empathy, Prague, Czech Republic, November 7-9, 2014.

Camilla Pagani is a psychologist and an associate researcher. She is mostly involved in the study of humans' relationship with diversity in various contexts within a theoretical framework where principles from socio-cognitive psychology and complexity theory are especially considered.

Reflecting On Empathy

Gavin J. Fairbairn

Abstract

Acknowledging the difficulty of saying what empathy is, this chapter reflects on empathy in three distinct, though interrelated, parts. The first section offers some observations about the important role of empathy in teaching, one of the areas in which I think strong empathic ability makes a significant difference. The second section articulates three 'problems' that arise because of ways empathy is sometimes construed: the mistake of thinking of empathy as simply being about imagining how one might feel oneself in another person's shoes, as a way of coming to know another's experience; the way in which empathy is sometimes confused or conflated with sympathy, and the adoption of a what I refer to as a 'cosy' view of empathy, in which empathy is thought always to be a good thing. Finally, the third section turns to a critical reflection of the British psychopathologist Baron-Cohen and his writings about empathy, as a way of allowing me to share some of what I think about this most valuable and yet most dangerous of human abilities. This chapter draws on the papers I presented at Inter-Disciplinary.Net's First and Second Global Conferences on Empathy.[1]

Key Words: Empathy, sympathy, bullying, torture, sexual abuse, Baron-Cohen, ethicality, problems with empathy, cosy views of empathy, moral neutrality of empathy.

*****

1. Introduction

Empathy, the ability to gain some understanding of what another person is experiencing – what they are feeling and thinking, is an attribute that anyone who relates to other people arguably possesses to at least some extent, because being able to apprehend these things at some level, is necessary for the everyday business of living in relationship with others. This is probably what Larocco is referring to when he writes, in this book, that 'Empathy *is* at the core of life together'[2]. I agree wholeheartedly with him, but I agree, also, with what he says next, that empathy:

> ...functions in complex ways: oscillating between facilitating interpersonal bonds by the sharing of feelings and minds, but also providing much of the cognitive/affective infrastructure for the manipulation of others according to their recognized dispositional vulnerabilities, as in the grooming of a child for sexual abuse...[3]

It might seem odd, in a chapter about empathy, which is (rightly in my view) widely recognised as one of the more positive human capacities, to applaud a statement that draws attention to some of its less savoury uses. That I have done so gives a clue to what is to come, because centrally important to this chapter is my rejection of the 'cosy' and overly positive views of empathy that are currently popular.

Empathy is of interest to practitioners and researchers working in a great many fields. For example, over the course of its first two conferences, the steering group for Inter-Disciplinary.Net's *Empathy* project, of which this book is a product, received abstracts from participants working in:

> History; Theology; Law; Computer Studies; Anthropology; Sociology; Psychology; Drama; Film Studies; Media Studies; Philosophy; Ethnography; Cultural Studies; Neuroscience; Literature, including Poetry; Education; Buddhism; Health and social care, including Nursing, Mental Health, Dementia Care, Social Work, Psychotherapy, Counselling, Disability and Psychoanalysis; Art and Design, including Photography, Fine Art and Industrial Design; Television; Human Rights; Teaching; Conflict Resolution; Peacemaking; Music; Dance; Theatre; Cinema; Journalism; Social Media and Computer Gaming.

Interest in empathy – in what it is, how it arises, why it is important and how it can be developed, has grown enormously since I first became aware of it in the 1970s. Nelems reports that '...more academic articles were published on empathy in 2014 alone (31,200) than were published cumulatively between 1900 and 1970 on the topic (28,840)'.[4] And whereas, when I first heard of it through the person-centred psychology of Carl Rogers, empathy was mainly of interest to professionals involved in therapy, counselling and other 'people professions', it is now, as the list above suggests, of interest to a wide range of practitioners and researchers in other areas. Not only that, but it is now integrated into the mainstream of life, as may be surmised from Nelems' report that 'The number of "empathy" google search results in the first five months of 2015 (5,860,000) alone...total more than 15 times more than those that appeared in 2010, and 65 times more than those that appeared in 2005'.[5] Despite its increasing popularity, however, empathy is difficult to pin down and in this chapter I want both to discuss what it is and why it is important, and to raise some issues that arise from the different ways in which it is construed.

As is obvious to anyone who stops to think about it, the term 'empathy' is used in many different ways and in writing this chapter I have struggled with how to refer to the phenomenon and human practice that it is used to label – as, for example, 'an ability or skill'; 'a talent'; 'a concept'; 'an aptitude', or as 'a way of coming to know'. A thorough discussion of the different ways in which people think about and use the term 'empathy', and of the ways in which the practice of empathy might be defined and described is beyond the scope of this chapter, in which I offer instead, a briefer exploration of this most important of human attributes.

I begin with some observations about the importance of empathy in teaching, one of the areas in which I think strong empathic ability makes a significant difference. After that, I turn my attention to three problems that arise because of ways that empathy is at times construed, though actually the three I have chosen are only the tip of an iceberg of problems. Perhaps the most important of these is the way in which empathy is often confused with compassion, a view that is shared by Larocco, who writes:

> Because empathy and compassion are often conflated, which I will argue is an intellectual mistake, it is often treated as obvious that a rise in compassion would also entail an extension or increase of empathy...[6]

Finally, I say a little about some of what the British psychopathologist Baron-Cohen has written about empathy and the language of empathy.

2. Empathy, Intuition and Expertise in Teaching

Asked what they believe makes for expertise in teaching, many teachers would emphasise knowledge, along with mastery of pedagogy and understanding of the ways in which people learn, including reference to both cognitive processes and 'learning styles'. As someone who has taught at all stages, from the early years to postgraduate level, I recognise the importance of all of these, along with some understanding of both personal and environmental factors, in the development of competence as a teacher. However, in my view these factors are less important in marking out the expert teacher than strongly developed empathic ability which, when combined with professional knowledge, allows her both to understand pupils or students and their needs, and to decide how best to act to meet those needs. Something similar is true of experts in other professions in which human flourishing is a major focus, such as nursing, social care; psychotherapy, counselling or physiotherapy, in which empathic ability is often crucial in allowing expert practitioners to act helpfully in relation to an individual's experienced needs and even in relation to needs that though present, have not consciously been experienced.

Many years ago, when I was involved in preparing teachers to work with young children, I published an article about 'Empathy, intuition and the development of expertise in teaching' in which I argued that everyone who is training to teach this age group should be exposed to the work of practitioners in others areas of work from whom I think they could learn a great deal.[7] The practitioners I had in mind included physiotherapists and children's entertainers, who often have skills and ways of being that overlap with what is necessary for expertise in teaching at any level, including the ability to engage and encourage others, and to communicate meaningfully with them, all of which depend on empathy.

I first had the opportunity to watch physiotherapists at work while my wife was recovering from a serious debilitating illness with the help of a physio, whose work focused mainly on helping her to walk again. Their sessions took place in a large hall, in which several other physiotherapists were also working with patients. I was impressed by what I observed and was particularly struck by the way in which the physios seemed to tailor their work with each individual, devising or selecting tasks that were not only appropriate for his or her physiological needs, but created the motivation necessary if they were to reach targets set for them, thus facilitating the development of new views of themselves and of their abilities. In that article, I wrote that:

> ...while the physiotherapist working with my wife engaged her in the attempt to walk elegantly on a very wobbly mattress, and conjured up images for her to attempt to emulate even as she stumbled from one shaky step to the next, another, who was working with rather a tough and macho-looking man with severe and unsightly scars from deep burning to his arms, worked with him on exercises that demanded little elegance but enormous strength, including rolling up a substantial gymnastic mat with his bare hands.[8]

As I watched these physiotherapists working it seemed clear that there was something more at work here than just the application of knowledge or the utilisation of technique. For example, rather than merely applying his knowledge of how useful it can be to use a water bed in helping a person who has been rendered incapable of walking for a time to develop the strength she needs to walk again, I guessed that my wife's physiotherapist had decided on this strategy because his empathic ability had allowed him to 'catch' something of who she was and what would motivate her, both to re-locate her ability to balance, and to develop the confidence to move forward under her own steam. And I think the ability of the physio working with the macho-looking man to empathise with him, allowed her to seduce him into flexing his muscles to show the world and himself that he could still exert power over a little gym mat because, despite his injuries, he was still the man he always was.

Turning now to children's entertainers, in the article to which I have already referred, I invited my readers to think:

...about the children's magician or puppeteer, the juggler or clown, who manages somehow to hold his audience, however large, however diverse in age, spellbound, to control their behaviour and their emotions, to engage their imaginations, their vocal chords and the movements of their bodies, without effort.[9]

I was so full of admiration for Mr. E, the children's magician who lived along the street from us when our son, Thomas, was little, that I once paid for a performance in Tom's school, as a way of thanking the staff for allowing me to spend some time teaching there, thus maintaining my credibility with the student teachers whose practice placements I supervised.

I had seen and admired many similar performers before. However, it was watching Mr. E – as he moved a school of perhaps three hundred children to levels of excitement so high that I thought for a moment that the head teacher would never let me cross her threshold again, then drawing them down to a quiet so soft that you could hear yourself breathing, that made me realise that all teachers could learn something from him and from people like him. It is not that I think that learning a few magic tricks will turn a bad teacher into a better one, though the ability to make small objects disappear and reappear again from odd places has been useful for me at times, when working with small children. However, Mr. E had the ability to get alongside the children for whom he performed. Somehow he knew, not only how to hold their attention, but both when it was safe to excite them and when it was necessary to calm them down and how to do so. As with the physiotherapists I have discussed, my hunch is that Mr. E's expertise in working with children probably owed as much and perhaps more, to his ability to empathise, as it did to his undoubted knowledge and skill as a magician.

I never did persuade my colleagues that we should introduce visits to watch physiotherapists at work or masterclasses by children's entertainers into the curriculum for our student teachers. It is not that that they simply found incomprehensible the idea that teachers of young children could learn something of practical relevance to teaching from people whose work was outside primary education. Rather, there were other, and in their view much more important, issues on their mind. In particular, alongside subject knowledge, most of my colleagues were keener to develop competence in classroom organisation and in the skills and disciplines necessary for conveying curriculum content and monitoring children's work, than they were to help students in developing their ability to understand their pupils as people. I think they were mistaken, because in my view, the development of the ability to empathise with one's students or pupils – with their lives; with their beliefs; with their aspirations; with their understandings and misunderstandings; with their hopes and fears, is crucial for the development of expertise as a teacher.

One way in which our ability to empathise contributes to the development of expertise in teaching is that it informs our 'intuitive' responses to everyone with whom we interact, allowing us to 'catch the moment' when a learner is ready to advance in understanding, so that we can hopefully respond appropriately.

Intuition, the faculty that most people sometimes have (and some people often have) to act intelligently for no apparent reason, is the principle characteristic of those that I would refer to as 'expert practitioners' in many areas, especially professions in which human wellbeing is centrally important, including nursing, physiotherapy, social care and psychotherapy as well as teaching. Interestingly, however, intuition is arguably also one of the principle characteristics of expert practitioners in many other areas in which empathy is not centrally important, because a person's ability to act intuitively in any situation will depend on her having had a range of prior experiences that in some way relate to the situation in which she now finds herself, whether she is a teacher, a jazz musician, a snooker player, a master carpenter, a dry stone waller, or a children's entertainer.

In my earlier article about 'Empathy, intuition and the development of expertise in teaching', I wrote:

> ...I do not conceive of intuition as most people do - as a spooky, otherwordly gift, something that emerges as the result of 'gut feelings' about situations and about people. Rather I view intuition in terms of skill in matching what one sees and hears – what one experiences in relationship with one's students or pupils, and what one observes about them – with one's previous experiences, and one's acquired knowledge, which allow one to make helpful decisions about how best to act to ensure learning. Intuition as a teacher develops as a consequence of time spent in reflection on practice.[10]

Those who act apparently intuitively often feel as if their actions have just 'come out of nowhere,' and this is just how it may look to observers. However, most often 'intuition' isn't about simple hunches that have no empirical foundation. Rather, though they might seem to onlookers to arise from 'thin air' rather than from reflection on evidence, and might even feel like this to those who perform them, 'intuitive acts' are surely rooted in a range of barely recognised reasons that draw on prior experience, acquired knowledge and as-yet-unspoken recognitions. Indeed, although when they act intuitively, they may not be conscious of why they are doing what they are doing, or even that they are doing it, when asked to justify such actions they will usually be able to give a coherent account of why they did what they did. Often this will include reference to observations about which they were not consciously aware at the time. Typically, they will also be able to relate the present situation to earlier experiences and to say how it resembles or overlaps with them.

Intuition as a teacher, like intuition in many other areas, including car driving, counselling, improvised music and the care of elderly and infirm people, develops through a process of sifting and re-sifting experience; organising and re-organising, analysing and assessing our performances; rejoicing in our successes; learning from and forgiving ourselves for our failures. Expert teachers act intuitively in their work, by continually drawing on their pool of accumulated knowledge and experience – about, for example, what they have done with learners in creating solutions to problems of different kinds that they have faced in the past.

Intuitive action involves unconscious matching of the present situation, with situations one has experienced in the past, then drawing on those experiences and the outcomes of one's actions, in deciding how to act. In other words, intuition is about making coherent pictures from partial knowledge, and those who seem intuitively to be able to act in the right way do so because they are able to assimilate a wide range of experiences – both personal and vicarious, and to draw on them in responding to situations with which they are faced.

In my earlier article, I wrote that:

> It is intuition...that allows a nurse who walks onto a ward to make a guess (an expert guess) at what is needed for a patient whether, for example, this is to arrange for some change to his treatment regime, or merely to change his position.[11]

Without giving any outward indication that she is doing so, the expert nurse might, for example, notice as she enters the room and approaches her patient, the way in which he is sitting, his complexion, what he is doing with his hands, whether he is looking round the room, the expression on his face and the tone of his voice as he responds to her questions about how he is feeling today. When, without even forming a conscious view of how she should be acting, she simply acts, she will be drawing on previous experiences of how patients looked, spoke, sat, held themselves and so on. And when an expert teacher acts intuitively, her apparently unplanned acts will arise from her ability to match what she observes about her students and what she experiences in relationship to them, with her previous experiences and acquired knowledge, in a way that enables her to make helpful choices about how best to facilitate their learning.

In the sense in which I am using 'intuition,' empathy and intuition are closely related. They often act as a team, so to speak, enabling experts to perform to the highest professional standards, because the ability to empathise – to imagine oneself into the life and experiences of another person, will inform one's 'intuitive' responses to them and one's ability to empathise is partly underpinned by intuition. In both teaching and nursing, the catalogue of experience and understanding, on

which experts draw when they act intuitively will include much that will have been
gained through the exercise of empathic skill.

3. Three Problems with Empathy

I turn now to some of the problems that arise from the difficulties in saying
what empathy is, how it arises and the part it plays in human life. Though there are
many such problems I draw attention to only three in this chapter: the mistake of
thinking of empathy as being about imagining how one might feel oneself in
another person's shoes, as a way of coming to know something about their
experience; the ways in which empathy is sometimes confused with sympathy, and
the adoption of a what I refer to as a 'cosy' view of empathy, in which it is viewed
as always being a good thing.

A. The First Problem: Imagining One's Own Experience

The first problem with empathy I want to raise relates to its being commonly
misconceived as something like:

> The ability to imagine what one might feel like, were one
> standing in another's shoes.

This view of the nature of empathy seems to suggest that there is nothing more
to empathising than imagining how we would feel were we to find ourselves in
another person's life, rather than how that person might be feeling, which sounds
similar, but is much harder. It depends on the assumption that our imagined
experience of another's situation would pretty much mirror what that person is
experiencing. If this was all there was to it, empathy would be fairly easy for
anyone who had reasonable recall about what had happened to him in the past and
of how it had affected him, along with the ability to extrapolate this information,
thus allowing informed and reasoned guesses about how he might experience other
situations and events. But empathy is surely more complicated than this. Rather
than being the ability simply to imagine what one's own experiences – one's own
perceptions and feelings would be, were one to find oneself in another person's
shoes, surely it is about the attempt imaginatively to inhabit the other's world as if
we were them, in other words to understand, to experience, and to feel things as the
other person might feel them.

Of course, since it is impossible ever to enter into another person's mind and
body and thus to feel what he feels, the attempt to imagine his world as if we are
him will inevitably involve drawing, not only on what we know about him, but on
our own remembered experiences and on the shared experiences of others.
However, it is important to avoid lapsing into the attempt merely to imagine how
we would feel were we in his situation because, among other things, the view that
empathy depends simply on imagining our own feelings in the other's situation

leads some people to believe that they know what the person feels when in fact they don't. And in the case of those (and there are many of them) who believe that the purpose of empathy is always about working out how best to help another person, this view obviously opens the door to disastrously unhelpful actions, because it may lead them also to think that they know what he needs or what would be best for him, when in fact they don't. This is especially important in circumstances where there is a great difference between us and the person who is the subject of our empathic attention. One such situation is where the recipient of attempted empathy is a vulnerable person who is in need of care, but is unable to communicate his or her needs and wishes.

Consider, for example, how difficult it might be to empathise with the situation of Mary who, following a glittering career in law, entered politics, rose quickly through the ranks to a senior post in government that she occupied for several years, until traumatic brain injuries left her profoundly disabled both physically and intellectually, unable to undertake the most basic personal care tasks or to communicate her needs and wishes. To make things even more difficult, the nature and extent of Mary's injuries led to the settled view on the part of the clinicians caring for her, that this is pretty much what the future holds for her.

In situations of this kind, my view is that if they are to treat the person for whom they are caring with respect, those who have to decide how to act in relation to her, should act, so far as is possible, in accordance with what she would choose, were she presently able to make her wishes known. Achieving this will require the attempt to empathise so far as is possible, with someone whose life not only differs greatly from their own lives, but also from the life that person once lived. Those who hold the future of someone like Mary in their hands need to remember that in attempting to empathise with her, they are thinking as people who are not disabled in the same ways and to the same extent as that individual, who has suffered such grave brain injuries that her life and potential are now wildly different from what they were before. They need to accept, for example, that though – were they to imagine themselves living a life that was so severely limited, they might perceive of it as tragic and horrid; devoid of meaning and perhaps, even, not worth living, cut off as she is from her previous life, the individual with whom they are trying to empathise, might enjoy the simple pleasures her new life brings. And whereas, for example, they might find the necessity for round the clock intimate physical care demeaning, such a person might find it enjoyable, even though her view would have been very different in her former life.

In situations of the kind I have described above, those who think they merely have to imagine themselves inhabiting the life of another to be able to know something of what that person is feeling and thinking, are likely to make mistakes in deciding how to act. Or at least this is the case if they agree with my view that the right thing to do is to act, so far as is possible, in accordance with what a severely disabled the individual would choose, were she able to make her wishes known.

B. The Second Problem: Confusing Empathy with Sympathy

Like the ability to feel sympathy, the ability to empathise with others, by imagining their experience, is arguably an indicator of our humanity. Sometimes empathy may be triggered by sympathy, as when someone who is moved by another person's upset or sadness, tries to understand it in order to be able to help and support him. However, we can also empathise with people for whom we feel no sympathy, and we can even empathise in situations in which sympathy is either inappropriate or impossible. Thus, though they are sometimes connected, empathy and sympathy do not depend on one another. Yet they are sometimes confused, and this is the second problem to which I wish to draw attention.

Sympathy is an emotional response, uninvited and unplanned. It comes from the gut; immediate and uncontrolled, and can hit us without warning. And whether the other or others for whom we feel sympathy are near us or far away, whether we become aware of their situation directly or indirectly and no matter how closely (if at all) we are related to them, it can sometimes overwhelm us, disabling our ability to help. By contrast, empathy is more complex. It is about listening and observing in the attempt to imagine how another person is feeling and what he is experiencing in the attempt to understand how life is for him, which is why it is so useful when we want to support and care for another person more fully, more effectively and more ethically. Whereas we have little control over sympathy, we do have some control over empathy. Larocco writes, for example, that '…empathy is a phenomenon of attention and focus, of what one attends to, voluntarily or involuntarily.'[12] In other words, we can decide either to employ empathy in our meetings with others, or to leave it to one side, and we can also decide how seriously we will attempt to empathise with them. Or perhaps it would be more accurate to say that we can decide to 'turn up or turn down the volume' on our empathy, intensifying or diminishing the extent to which we apply our empathic sense.

Another difference between sympathy and empathy is that unlike empathy, sympathy may be experienced in the absence of any direct knowledge of the person who is its subject. Not only that, but we can feel sympathy even when the experience of the individual for whom we are feeling it does not warrant or invite it. This would be the case, for example, if the sympathy we felt resulted from our identifying, not with that individual's actual experience, but with what we imagined or expected their experience to be. Such 'sympathy' is clearly misplaced, because it has nothing at all to do with the feelings or experience of the individual for whom it is felt or expressed.

Imagine for example, that on hearing of the death of Fay's husband, Elizabeth is overcome with sympathy and writes to Fay to express that sympathy. Imagine, further, that Fay, who Elizabeth believed had loved and cherished her husband, through thick and thin, in bad times and in good, for more than thirty years, actually despised him, and that far from being distraught, she is thus secretly elated that he has died. And so, although Elizabeth feels something and would describe what she feels as 'sympathy for Fay', it is misplaced, because it does not relate to what Fay is feeling. In other words, arising as it does, from her identification with what she imagined Fay must be feeling, and drawing on what she imagines she would be feeling if she had just lost her own husband, Elizabeth's 'sympathy' is more related to her own life and the things that move her, than it is to Fay's. It is perhaps important to note that although it would not make sense to talk of empathy being misplaced, a person might think that they have successfully empathised with another, and that they thus have a true understanding of how that person is feeling and what she is experiencing, when in fact they have no understanding at all of her or her world. It is because of this that those who focus their interest in empathy on its therapeutic and caring uses, emphasise the need for those who are attempting to empathise with another to continually check whether their understanding of how the other is feeling matches how they in fact are feeling.

Sometimes those who confuse empathy and sympathy merely use these two words in ways that suggest that they do not understand the difference between them. I am especially interested in situations where a person claims to be empathising when what is going on is more to do with sympathy. Imagine, for example, that Jane hears a story on a television news broadcast, about a man who has lost his job and is worried about how he will manage to feed his children or who, perhaps, is faced with caring for a wife, recently diagnosed with an aggressive form of cancer. When, in relating this story to a friend, Jane says that she can 'really empathise' with this man, she will clearly be well meaning. Most probably she will feel sorry for the man and sympathise with him in his plight; no doubt she will be able to imagine how she would feel were she to be in a similar situation. However, it seems likely that what is going on here is not empathy, but sympathy, because empathy is usually based on more information than Jane will have gathered from the news broadcast, about the individual with whom empathy is being claimed.

Of course it is possible and perhaps even likely, that someone with highly developed empathic skills could make a reasonable stab at imagining the experience of a person about whom she knew only as much as could be communicated in a TV news item, such as the one with whom Jane claimed she could 'really empathise', especially if he had encountered folk with relevantly similar lives in the past. However, such a person would make his guess at how the individual in question might be feeling, not as a result of having attempted to empathise with her, but because he was able to draw on his experience of individuals whose lives in some ways were similar to the individual with whose life he was attempting to identify. This relates closely to what I said, earlier in this chapter, about expertise, in which those who have highly developed skills in an area of practice and have accumulated a large store of experience, are able to act in apparently effortless and 'intuitive' way.

The mistake of believing that identifying closely with a person somehow equates with empathy, as was the case with Jane, who felt able to 'really empathise' with the person she heard about via a TV news broadcast, is arguably related to another mistake, that of believing that the ability to empathise somehow depends on a person's having had relevantly similar experience to the person with whom she wishes to empathise, so that if she has not had or perhaps could not have, such experiences, she will not be able to empathise with that person and with her experiences. Here I am thinking, for example, of the claim that only women can understand a range of experiences that women may have as a result of their capacity (or lack of capacity) to bear children. I thinking, especially, about the frequently asserted claim that men can never empathise either with a woman who finds herself pregnant when she had been trying to avoid pregnancy, or who, despite making every effort to do so, is unable to achieve a pregnancy, as if it is obvious that the lack of a womb makes men incapable of imagining what a woman might experience and feel in this area of her life. The truth, as I have argued elsewhere, is that it will often be possible to empathise with others who are living lives very different from our own.[13]

So, for example, given sufficient life experience, a well-practised imagination and sensitivity to others, I could empathise with someone who was living with a life threatening disease or in poverty so bad that he was unable to provide food for his family, even though these are things I have never experienced, and hopefully never will experience. It is even possible to empathise with people in experiences that we could never have and with people whose values and beliefs differ very much from our own. That is why, for example, I could empathise both with a woman who had just given birth to a stillborn child, and with one who was facing the reality of an unplanned and unwanted pregnancy. And it is why I could empathise with a suicidal person who sees no way out of the prison that life had become for him, other than by arranging his death, even if, as is the case, I believed that suicide is morally mistaken because of the damage it can do to others. I could even, if I tried hard enough, empathise with a self-centred person who cared so little for fairness and human care, and so much about her own welfare and satisfaction, that she was willing to harm others to gratify her own desires.

C. The Third Problem: The 'Cosy View' of Empathy

The third problem with empathy to which I wish to draw attention relates to its often being conceived, as if through 'rose-tinted spectacles', as always and necessarily a good thing, as if empathising with other people is always about human wellbeing and the intention to act towards others in life enhancing ways and about caring for and supporting them. This rather comfortable and cosy view of empathy fails to take account of its importance in areas that are not focused on human care, and the part it plays in less positive and sometimes destructive, cruel and inhumane, behaviours. For example, as I have pointed out elsewhere, it is empathy:

> …that allows a skilled salesperson to persuade you to buy something you didn't know you needed, with money you didn't know you had. And it is empathy that allows those who wish to subjugate others to decide the best tactics in order to do so, and that allows the best torturers to practice their art so well.[14]

I'll say a little about empathy in relation to torturers and bullies presently, but first let's think about salespeople, especially those who work in retail settings, who are likely to be more concerned with ensuring that customers part with as much money as possible, than with ensuring that these customers have the opportunity to buy what best fulfils their needs. Empathy is clearly helpful in developing understanding of what makes customers and potential customers tick. As a consequence, salespeople often develop a wide array of empathic gambits for eliciting responses that will allow them to form a picture of who they are dealing with, in order to decide the best way to pitch their products. Depending on one's point of view and the particular situation, such uses of empathy could be a morally neutral matter – after all, salespeople have to communicate with and understand their customers if they are to do business with them at all. However, it could be a matter for serious moral concern, as when empathy is used to persuade people to make purchases that they cannot afford, especially perhaps, if doing so means that they become encumbered by ongoing debt.

It is obvious that empathy is also utilised in many other areas of life in which the intention of the empathiser is not underpinned by benevolent concern towards the person with whom she is empathising. I am thinking, for example, about literature; advertising; theatre; cinema; fine art, and the law. In such areas, individuals have a range of other reasons for cultivating empathy, because getting alongside others by imagining the world from their point of view; trying to feel what they might feel, and think what they might think, is useful for anyone who wants to try to understand them – their feelings and beliefs; their values and fears and joys, their hopes and aspirations; what moves them and what motivates them. For example, an actor may use his ability to empathise in order to 'get inside' and begin to understand people whose lives overlap with a character that he is preparing to play, while an advertising campaign manager will probably use it in order to work out how best to persuade people to buy a product. In the law, on the other hand, the ability to empathise is clearly important, both for police officers when they are interviewing suspects in criminal cases, and for lawyers when they are examining witnesses during trials. As is the case with empathy's use in sales settings, how its use in these other settings should be morally assessed will depend on the ways in which the empathiser utilises the understandings she develops by employing it.

Even more importantly, empathy can underpin obviously destructive, cruel and inhumane behaviour towards other people. As Larocco suggests,

> Empathy *is* at the core of life together, but it functions in complex ways: oscillating between facilitating interpersonal bonds by the sharing of feelings and minds, but also providing much of the cognitive/affective infrastructure for the manipulation of others according to their recognized dispositional vulnerabilities, as in the grooming of a child for sexual abuse...[15]

For example, as has become obvious from wave after wave of stories in recent years about current and historic sexual abuse both in the UK and in other countries, empathy is an extremely useful skill for those who sexually abuse others, in particular children and young people, because abusers can employ it in 'grooming' vulnerable youngsters either face-to-face, as might happen where the abuser is a teacher, clergyman or other significant adult, or via social media. Empathy is also obviously of great value to both torturers and bullies. Thinking first of torture, it is clear that the ability to imagine how their subjects feel, and to mark out what their values are and who and what is most important to them can help torturers to plan how to approach their task with each individual. Importantly, empathic ability on the part of a torturer must be combined with the ability to 'turn off' sympathy and/or an absence of good will. In this, torture is close to bullying of all kinds because despite the common view that bullying results at least in part from a lack of empathy, it is clear that, as with torturers, the ability of bullies to bully their victims, both psychologically and physically, is enhanced by well-honed empathic skills, which enable them to understand their victims, and what will upset and harm them most.

4. What can Baron-Cohen Tell us about How to Think about Empathy?

In his book *Zero Degrees of Empathy*,[16] Baron-Cohen introduces his lifelong fascination with empathy by discussing some examples of human cruelty, beginning with personal stories about how he first became aware of the ways that human beings can objectify one another. One of these stories, which, as a child, he heard from his father, concerns the mother of his father's former girlfriend, who had survived a Nazi concentration camp, but only after her hands had been severed by scientists, who switched them round before sewing them back on, so that they were effectively back to front. He also tells how, as a medical student, he learned that the best available data about how human beings respond to extreme cold had come from experiments by Nazi scientists that involved immersing inmates of Dachau concentration camp in freezing water. He finds these two examples of human cruelty:

> ...particularly shocking, because they involve educated doctors and scientists (professions we are brought up to trust) performing inhumane experiments or operations'[17]

Baron-Cohen testifies to the fact that he does not think we should use knowledge gained through experiments such as were engaged in by Nazi scientists, but generously assumes that those who carried them out '...were not being cruel for the sake of it'.[18] Rather, he suggests, they wanted to gather medical knowledge which, in the case of the freezing experiments, could be useful in developing ways of helping victims of shipwrecks in icy seas. In other words, he allows for the possibility that however cruel, like surgeons who slice through human flesh with the intention of helping the person whose flesh is being sliced, these scientists and doctors, might in some sense, have had good intentions. Indeed, drawing attention to the political framework within which they were living and working, in which Jews were defined as being 'genetically sub-human', he argues that they might have viewed their work as 'ethical' because it had the potential of contributing something to 'the greater good'. Of course, in reflecting on his assessment of a way in which these members of the scientific and medical community might construe their abuse of other human persons in a positive ethical light, it is important to remember that the acts in which they engaged differ greatly from those of slicing surgeons. After all, surgeons cut their patients with the intention of helping them, while these Nazi experimenters did what they did with no thought for the welfare of those on whom they experimented.

Baron-Cohen then turns the spotlight on the actions of concentration camp guards, towards whom he is considerably less generous than he was towards the scientists who froze people who had not agreed to be frozen, asserting that: 'Cruelty for its own sake was a part of the ordinary Nazi Guards' behaviour'.[19]

I confess to having some difficulty in understanding why Baron-Cohen is willing to look for ways of making sense of monstrous, though well-educated physicians and scientists, while condemning ordinary concentration camp guards, for whom he seems to think cruelty was a more normal occurrence. I find unsettling the level of magnanimity he demonstrates towards people whose acts in conducting inhumane experiments clearly involved not only treating others as a means to an end, but behaving towards them in ways that amounted to torture. I find it especially unsettling that in a book about empathy and its importance, he offers no discussion, or even passing comment, about the part that empathy or its lack, played in the work of these members of the scientific community. Indeed, despite telling us that he does not think we should make use of knowledge gained by the means they employed, Baron-Cohen seems motivated to try to understand the zeal of the Nazi scientists who, in pursuing their scientific interests, were willing to expose Jews to cold water until the point of death. It is almost as if he cannot avoid empathising with them because, as a scientist, he can understand their enthusiasm to use the resources they had at hand, even though those resources were an unending supply of replaceable Jewish people that were viewed as fair game for use as experimental material, because they had been scientifically defined as 'genetically sub-human' by the Nazi regime.

Baron-Cohen, who is a fine storyteller, draws us into his discussion of the behaviour of ordinary Nazi guards, by relating an incident witnessed by Thomas Buergenthal, who survived Auschwitz concentration camp. He writes that, as a nine year old, Thomas:

> ...had to watch while an inmate was forced to hang his friend who had tried to escape. The SS guard ordered the inmate to put a noose around his friend's neck. The man couldn't fulfil the order because his hands were shaking so much, with fear and distress. His friend turned to him, took the noose and, in a remarkable act, kissed his friend's hand, and then put the noose around his own neck. Angrily, the SS guard kicked the chair away from under the man to be hanged.[20]

When I first began reading Baron-Cohen's book I was especially interested in this terrible story, because the way in which he discussed it seemed to make no sense. Let me tell you why. It is because, while noting what (in my view, probably correctly) he thinks was the importance of empathy in motivating the act of the doomed man in placing the noose round his own neck, he seemed not to understand the role that empathy probably played in the guard's act. After all, it is easy to imagine that, like all successful bullies and torturers, the guard was practiced in the art of deciding what would upset and harm his victims most, and that he had worked out that forcing one of the two men to kill his friend would allow him to inflict discomfort on both, as well as arranging the death of one.

However, far from drawing attention to the part that empathy most likely played in structuring the guard's cruel and bullying behaviour, Baron-Cohen actually refers to 'the extreme lack of empathy' that he guard showed. This surprised me very much, especially since he goes on to note that if the guard had simply wanted to 'punish or set an example' he could have carried out any punishment himself and that he had probably chosen '...this particular form of punishment because he wanted the two friends to suffer'.[21] Given this account, which seems to me to be a fair assessment of empathy's role in what the guard did, I could not understand why Baron-Cohen was talking as if the guard had shown an extreme lack of empathy, since, by his own admission, and in line with my view of the situation, the guard not only knew how to inflict great suffering, but set out to do so. Until, that is, I realised that his view of empathy is very different to mine.

At this point I should perhaps explain that I began reading Baron-Cohen's book because a number of participants in IDNET's first Global Conference on Empathy had referenced his work during their presentations. More than that, they had spoken his name in reverential tones, almost as if it is so clear that his work on empathy is of such overwhelming importance, that they believe that it is to Baron-Cohen that we must all turn, if we want to understand empathy – what it is, where it comes from and why it is important. I think they are misguided, because Baron-Cohen's views are so unclearly stated and so poorly argued as to make it very difficult to construct a coherent picture of what he actually does believe.

It might help to explain why I found Baron-Cohen's analysis of what was going on in the awful scene in which the man places the noose round his own neck, so strange, if I try say a little about how my own view of empathy differs from his. I have written elsewhere that empathy:

> …is about the attempt to understand, to experience, to feel things as another human person understands, experiences and feels them. In other words, empathy involves the attempt imaginatively to inhabit the other's world as that person, rather than the attempt to imagine one's own experiences – what one's perceptions and feelings would be, were one to find oneself in such a world.[22]

This understanding of empathy is the one with which I have grown up, and until quite recently, I think it was pretty widely accepted, though of course, others would state it differently. In it, despite the importance of empathy in contexts in which it is utilised in order to enhance human wellbeing, the empathic act of trying to understand another person's life by imagining how the world looks and feels from their point of view, is viewed as a morally neutral thing.

Larocco points out that 'Empathy towards the other can lead to concern and care' but recognises that it '…is not limited to such feelings or impulses…'[23] Of course, people often both recognise and choose to make use of their developed ability to empathise for good purposes, which often involves the attempt to support and help others. Indeed for some people, this positive use of empathic skill seems to have become the whole of empathy. It is common among people who think of empathy mainly in relation to its importance in areas in which human wellbeing and flourishing is of central importance. For example, practitioners in areas such as nursing, medicine, counselling, psychotherapy, education and social care, may embrace it because for them empathy is associated with the intention to care for others, both because the experience of being understood can be helpful in itself and because understanding can allow more informed care and support. Having first became familiar with 'empathy' through work in social, educational and health care contexts where the positive value of empathic skill was recognized, long before its use had become as common in everyday life as it is now, I believe strongly that any kind of skilled practical care depends upon the empathic ability of practitioners. I can thus understand how the idea that empathy is always about helping, supporting and caring for others, could arise. Nonetheless, I think it is important to recognise the moral neutrality of empathy and its ability to be turned to bad as well as good purposes.

It must be difficult for those who embrace a 'cosy' view of empathy, to accept that despite its central role in contexts that are dedicated to enhancing human flourishing, it also plays an important role in some of the most uncaring and undesirable of human activities, including bullying and torture, and it is easy to understand their inclination to deny that the empathic skills they use or see being used to do good are the same skills that are used in these cruel ways. However, it is more difficult to see how they could fail to comprehend that empathic skills are also useful in many settings where cruelty is not the main intention, even though the agenda is something other than human care. Many of these areas, along with human care settings appear in the list with which I began this chapter, of areas from which prospective participants in IDNET's Empathy project have come. I am thinking, for example, of academic areas such as history, anthropology, literature, film studies and philosophy and professional and practice areas such as social media, computer gaming, photography, cinema and journalism, where the main concern is not to offer care and support to others, but in all of which empathy has a crucial role to play.

Baron-Cohen's view of or definition of empathy qualifies as a member of the family of 'cosy views', even though it is unclear from what he says, exactly what he thinks empathy is. Given his enthusiasm as a scientist, for science and what he thinks it can do for us, it is not surprising that at least part of Baron-Cohen's interest in empathy is rooted in his ambition to come up with what he refers to as a 'scientific' way of speaking about the cruel ways in which people at times treat one another. His great desire seems to be to replace the use of the term 'evil' by a 'scientific' term, so that we can replace what he refers to as the 'non-explanation' that those who act in such ways are 'simply evil' with a more helpful term - one with explanatory power.

Unfortunately, Baron-Cohen is not only rather muddled about which term he wants to use to replace 'evil', but about the uses to which he is putting the terms he proposes. And so, although he seems to be suggesting that instead of 'evil' we should use the term 'empathy erosion', he also talks of replacing 'evil' with 'empathy' and of introducing the term 'empathy deficit', but offers neither clarity about how these terms are to be used, nor a satisfactory justification for the idea that whereas 'evil' is a religious term, 'empathy erosion' is a scientific one. And so, though I can understand his wish to clarify the language and conceptual apparatus that we use to talk about human cruelty, I don't feel persuaded that either 'empathy erosion' or 'empathy deficit' are any more scientific than the term 'evil'. Nor, incidentally, am I in the least persuaded that the use of scientific terms (even genuinely scientific terms, rather than pseudo-scientific terms like 'empathy erosion') will be more helpful in describing and discussing human cruelty than the term 'evil'. It is worth noting, finally, that I find Baron-Cohen's un-argued preference for scientific language surprising, given that from his discussion of the activities of Nazi physicians and scientists to which I have already referred, he clearly has some awareness of the way in which scientific terms such as 'genetically sub-human' can be used to justify inhumane acts.

I confess to being dumbfounded by how successful Baron-Cohen has been in persuading people to adopt his language and ways of talking about empathy, and so as I move towards the conclusion of what I want to say about his ideas, I will focus briefly on how he defines or describes 'empathy'. Having begun with the view that 'Empathy occurs when we suspend our single-minded focus of attention and instead adopt a double-minded focus of attention'[24] he finally settles on a very self-assured definition:

> Empathy is our ability to identify what someone else is thinking or feeling, and to respond to their thoughts and feelings with an appropriate emotion.[25]

Baron-Cohen elaborates this definition by adding the stipulation that unless a would-be empathiser is able both to identify what the other is thinking or feeling (which he refers to as 'cognitive empathy') and to respond appropriately to them (which is what he calls 'affective empathy') they cannot be said to have empathised at all. I have some problems understanding what this means, not least because it is unclear how Baron-Cohen thinks we should decide what an 'appropriate response' would be. I am intrigued by his use of the word 'identify', which seems to suggest that he does not allow of the possibility that empathy comes in gradations of acuity, so that when we try to empathise with another, sometimes we get it right and sometimes we don't. This seems strange. After all, most people – both those who recognise, with me, that empathy is a morally neutral thing and those who embrace the cosy view believing it always to be a good thing, think of empathy as being about the attempt to understand as well as they can, the experience of another person, by imagining what it might be like to be that person. In other words, they recognise that we can be more or less successful in our attempts to empathise with others. Many people also recognise that we have control over whether or not we apply whatever empathic skills we have. I have drawn attention to these points elsewhere:

> Empathy is not an all-or-nothing affair and it is found to a greater
> or lesser degree in different people. Not only that, but an
> individual may be more or less successful in empathising with
> another or others, and may be more or less inclined to do so –
> depending, for example, on whether she likes or feels
> responsibility for the other person.[26]

In relation to the first two of these points, Baron-Cohen seems to allow of the
possibility that there is some variability in empathy across different people, when
he writes that 'The key idea is that *we all lie somewhere on an empathy spectrum*
(from high to low).'[27] Unfortunately, though this seems like a fairly sensible idea,
he follows it up with a throwaway remark delivered as if it is factual one (after all,
he is a scientist) to the effect that 'People said to be "evil" or cruel are simply at
one extreme of the empathy spectrum'[28] which makes no sense at all to someone
like me, who recognises that many acts that some people might call 'evil', depend
on empathy, rather than coming about because their perpetrator lacks empathy.

Let me return, finally, to Baron-Cohen's definition and especially to his use of
the word 'identify' in describing what goes on in the act of empathising – the idea
that the empathiser 'identifies' something in the person who is the subject of her
empathy (what they are thinking or feeling). This suggests that he entertains the
idea that empathy has some certainty to it, so that, like picking out a suspect in an
identity parade the empathiser can select from a range of possible feelings and
thoughts the ones that match those felt and thought by the subject, thus allowing
her to form a pretty accurate picture of what he is experiencing. My view that by
his use of the word 'identify', he intends to suggests a fair degree of clarity and
accuracy, is supported by his claim that being able to empathise with another
means being able to understand their position 'accurately'.

> Being able to empathize means being able to understand
> accurately the other person's position, to identify with 'where
> they are at'.[29]

Despite apparently allowing of the possibility that empathy comes in a range of
qualities, Baron-Cohen does not seem to believe that it relies on the imagination,
but rather on observation of a pretty straightforward kind. He seems, in other
words, to believe that rather than merely allowing us to form hunches about what
another person might be thinking or feeling, which might be more or less accurate
and which we might be able to 'check out' in various ways, empathy can actually
allow us to know these things accurately. Perhaps, being a scientist, he feels the
need to be precise, even if precision is not justified. I find this odd, because it
implies that merely by observing others closely and attending carefully to what

they are saying, it should be possible to have a degree of certainty about what they are feeling and thinking, that most empathic people would find hard to imagine.

5. Concluding Remarks

Empathy, as I conceive it, is a skill or ability that we can nurture and grow through the exercise of the imagination in conjunction with intuition, and which we can choose either to utilise in our thinking about others and in our relationships with them, or decide instead to leave to one side. Not only that, but we can choose whether to use it for good purposes or for bad ones – in helping others, in manipulating them or, as in the case of bullies, torturers and other cruel people, in harming them. I believe strongly that any kind of skilled practical care depends upon the empathic ability of practitioners and that therefore those who engage in such care should be helped to develop their ability to empathise. Indeed, in the article on 'Ethics, empathy and storytelling in professional development' to which I have already referred, I offered some suggestions about ways of doing this through the use of imaginative storytelling. However, I do not subscribe to the cosy view that empathy is always and obviously a good thing, because there is so much evidence that at times it can be used for negative, even evil purposes, by which I simply mean 'very morally bad', with apologies to Baron-Cohen for failing to offer a full analysis of what I mean by 'evil', which must wait for another occasion, though it is perhaps worth noting that for me the term has no religious overtones of the kind to which he objects. What makes the use of empathy into a positive thing, in other words, is the presence alongside the ability, skills, aptitude or intentions that are employed in its practice, of good will, human care and the urge to respect others as persons.

Notes

[1] Gavin J. Fairbairn, 'Three Problems with Empathy,' *Encountering Empathy: Interrogating the Past: Envisioning the Future*, eds. Veronica Wain and Paulus Pimomo (Oxford: Inter-Disciplinary Press, 2015), 25-31; Gavin J. Fairbairn, 'How to Think about Empathy: The Curious Case of Simon Baron-Cohen, Part 1' (paper presented at the Second Global Conference on Empathy, Oxford, UK, September 7-9, 2015).

[2] Steve Larocco, 'Empathy as Orientation Rather than Feeling: Why Empathy is Ethically Complex', in this volume.

[3] Ibid.

[4] Rebeccah Nelems 'What Is This Thing Called Empathy?,' in this volume.

[5] Ibid.

[6] Larocco, 'Empathy as Orientation.'

[7] Gavin J. Fairbairn 'Empathy, Intuition and the Development of Expertise in Teaching,' *Analytic Teaching* 19.2 (1992): 9-18.

[8] Ibid., 10.
[9] Ibid., 9-10.
[10] Ibid., 12-13.
[11] Ibid, 15.
[12] Larocco, in this volume.
[13] Gavin J. Fairbairn, 'Storytelling, Ethics and Empathy,' *Ethical Space* 2.3 (2005): 48-55.
[14] Gavin J. Fairbairn, 'Empathy, Sympathy and the Image of the Other', *Peace Review* 21.2 (2009): 188-197.
[15] Larocco, in this volume.
[16] Simon Baron-Cohen, *Zero Degrees of Empathy: A New Theory of Human Cruelty and Kindness* (London: Penguin Books, 2012).
[17] Ibid., 2.
[18] Ibid.
[19] Ibid., 3.
[20] Ibid.,
[21] Ibid.
[22] Gavin J. Fairbairn, 'Ethics, Empathy and Storytelling in Professional Development', *Learning in Health and Social Care* 1.1 (2002): 29.
[23] Larocco, in this volume.
[24] Baron-Cohen, *Zero Degrees of Empathy,* 11.
[25] Ibid., 12.
[26] Fairbairn, 'Ethics, Empathy and Storytelling, 29.
[27] Baron-Cohen, *Zero Degrees of Empathy*, 11.
[28] Ibid.
[29] Ibid., 13.

Bibliography

Baron-Cohen, Simon *Zero Degrees of Empathy: A New Theory of Human Cruelty and Kindness.* London: Penguin Books, 2012.

Fairbairn, Gavin J. 'Ethics, Empathy and Storytelling in Professional Development'. *Learning in Health and Social Care* 1.1 (2002): 29.

Fairbairn, Gavin J. 'Empathy, Intuition and the Development of Expertise in Teaching'. *Analytic Teaching* 19.2 (1992): 9-18.

Fairbairn, Gavin J. 'Storytelling, Ethics and Empathy.' *Ethical Space* 2.3 (2005): 48-55.

Fairbairn, Gavin J. 'Empathy, Sympathy and the Image of the Other.' *Peace Review* 21.2 (2009): 188-197.

Gavin J. Fairbairn, Professor Emeritus of Ethics and Language at Leeds Beckett University, UK, is an applied philosopher and ethicist. A practitioner in special education, teacher education, mental health, professional development and learning disability, he has published widely on suicide, disability, sexuality, education and professional development, peace and reconciliation, storytelling; empathy, and academic writing.

Empathy with the Enemy: Can the Intellectually Gifted Experience Empathy with the Intellectually Impaired?

Veronica Wain

Abstract

Identification and self-identification are intrinsic to navigating one's way through life in terms of choosing a life partner, a career, where to live or even which foods to eat. They underpin the basic decisions ascribed to an average, 'normal' life in modern Western society. Some of those born with intellectual disabilities are unable to access the mechanisms to make what appear to others as the most basic of life's choices. Others require significant support and advocacy to articulate their choices, whilst many will be able to communicate quite clearly their version of what constitutes a good life, with the help of various modes of supported communication. The available research and findings reveal possible contradictions with regard to intellectual disability. Questions remain around whether it is possible for the greatest minds and intellects to empathise with those born with intellectual disability. Are they equipped to produce meaningful, empathetic findings that will inform the way in which the subjects of their enquiry might aspire to live their version of what constitutes a meaningful life? This chapter begins to explore some of these seemingly inherent contradictions that arise when those charged with researching those in the population identified as intellectually impaired, formulate and articulate quality of life measures and markers on behalf of their subjects. With a view to inspiring further scholarly debate regarding agenda setting, policy making and advocacy for those rendered vulnerable by way of intellectual difference, this chapter poses questions regarding what might constitute a quality life, who decides the measure of quality and how those quality measures might be implemented on behalf of another.

Key Words: Intellectual disability, identification, empathy, education, policy, advocacy, narrative, ethics, intercultural, power dynamics

*****

1. Introduction

As an academic and filmmaker, who is also mother to a young woman born with an intellectual impairment, I have a particular interest in the capacity of my colleagues to feel and experience empathy with my daughter and our family, given that my hopes for my daughter's future well-being will rest in the hands of others when I am no longer able to support and advocate for her.

From a personal perspective, these first twenty years of my daughter's life have been an unfolding, an undoing and an unknowing of all that I thought I knew about

© KONINKLIJKE BRILL NV, LEIDEN, 2018 | DOI 10.1163/9789004360846_006

being human and about what it is to *be happy*. It has taken time; in many respects, it has been an extended meditation of sorts, as I have discovered a different *who I am* since she arrived, and in her becoming. There are commonalities and intersections, but there exists, still, an 'unknown' between her and I. While we experience life in parallel – occupying the same space – more often than not, we are seeing, experiencing and being in different ways.

This quest to find others who embody empathy and compassion and see value in these parallel ways of being is a personal one; however, it is more than that. This desire may be seen to align with parent/advocate Eva Feder Kittay's view that the 'personal is philosophical is political'.[1]

Moreover, 'nothing about us without us'[2] has become a global catch cry for people with disability as they have collectively sought to give voice to their right to access the most basic of human rights and have a say over how they choose to live their lives. In the world of intellectual disability, giving voice to one's needs and desires is complex when the capacity to articulate one's worldview, experiences and needs does not 'fit' with traditional modes of communication or understanding. Establishing and clarifying needs and desires in this context can be a lengthy process requiring advocacy and support from trusted others where possible, a process further hampered in the absence of economic and social capital.

This chapter endeavours to inspire discussion about the capacity of those whose intellect to at least some extent has enabled their entry into positions of authority and power, to experience empathy with those with intellectual disabilities – who are subject to the effects of the former's decision making processes. Policy making, political imperatives and agenda-setting for pathways to what may constitute a 'good life' for people with intellectual disability has rested in the hands of those who do not live with an intellectual disability, and who as individuals undeniably have greater access to economic capital, the capacity and opportunity for self-expression. Thus, the question is the extent to which these individuals are able to experience empathy with those who experience the consequence of their decisions.

2. Defining Terms of Reference

Within this volume, the many faces of empathy, what it is and how it may be defined and made manifest is been explored. With reference to this chapter, the notion of access to an 'other' and their worldview looms large. If we are to take the most common and basic view of empathy as the capacity to walk in another's shoes, which in itself is contested in Nelems' chapter,[3] we must in the first instance have access to those shoes. What might they look like and how might they feel? Where might they take us and how might the steps we take in them, shape and change us? If we cannot access the shoes, can it be that empathy remains unattainable? Further, if it is unattainable, how might we proceed to a better way of being with those we are unable to empathise with, unable to gain entry into their world?

Whilst Larocco acknowledges that empathy '*is* at the core of life together' he qualifies its workings as 'ethically complex and at times, troubling'.[4] The empathic transaction is, as he points out, complex. As Taranto articulates, this complex core is set within:

> ...a set of moral sensibilities, issues and practices that arise from taking seriously the fact that care is a central aspect of human existence...a species activity that includes everything that we do to maintain, continue and repair our 'world' so that we can live in it as well as possible. That world includes our bodies, ourselves and our environment, all of which we seek to interweave in a complex, life-sustaining web.[5]

Within the world of intellectual disability, the interweaving is indeed complex and intimate, and this chapter can but only scratch the surface of the many barriers and challenges to how empathy for, and the care of, people with intellectual disability can be best achieved. As a group that has been historically herded to together as they have resisted the 'normalising' structures of the modern western world, bringing 'them' back into community, where the majority have had minimal exposure to people with intellectual disability has proven to be challenging to say the least. These challenges are widespread as is evidenced by the need for the United Nations, for example, to issue directives with their Convention on the Rights of People with Disabilities.[6]

Various terms are now used to describe people with intellectual disability including learning disability and within medical literature, the term mental retardation persists. The American Association on Intellectual and Developmental Disability definition is:

> *Intellectual disability* is a disability characterized by significant limitations in both intellectual functioning and in adaptive behavior, which covers many everyday social and practical skills. This disability originates before the age of 18.[7]

People with intellectual disability are diverse and cannot be categorised – nor can commonalities across this group be easily identified, yet broad-stroke approaches to service delivery, health care, education and employment persist as do approaches (where they exist) towards enhancing empathic engagement.

In terms of accessing the needs and desires of people within this broad group, Albrecht and Devlieger for example, explore what 'a good life' might look like when framed within disability.[8] They identify critical differences in how people with disability perceive their own quality of life in comparison to the way their service providers do, and suggest various influences contributing to a disability paradox.[9]

Those living with disability view their lives, in general, far more positively than those who support and care for them. This disparity demonstrates a lack of understanding and illustrates part of the challenge in accessing empathy within exchanges with people with intellectual disability; pre-conceived ideas about what is good for another are framed within one's personal experience and perspective. In addition to a lack of access to decision-making process which affect their lives, people living with intellectual disabilities also experience a power imbalance in the context of service provision. This lack of access has historically silenced these persons who are receiving care, affecting their ability to self-actualise in ways of their own choosing.

Power here is defined from the perspective of possessing agency to advocate for oneself – having the means to ask for that which you need or desire and having a reasonable expectation of those needs or desires being met.[10] Jordan's definition of mutuality and power offers some insight into the power differentials this chapter is concerned with and perhaps points to some of the challenges in the potential for an equal exchange between those with and those without intellectual disability:

> The capacity to respect vulnerability in each person and the ability to maintain oneself in a state of openness to influence are essential. If we respond to the vulnerability in the other with a wish to contribute to her/his growth as well as to the growth of connection, we are in the realm of love and mutuality … a decidedly open and growing process. If vulnerability in the other instead leads to exercise of unilateral personal self-interest, we have moved into a "power over" paradigm. When we are invested in a self-image of invulnerability, an aversion develops for "weakness," permeable boundaries, malleability, and affect, i.e. anything that moves us. The need to control and exercise "power over" others reduces our capacity for relationship as it contributes to closed and static intolerance of uncertainty; it further objectifies others in a way that isolates and deadens.[11]

Those creating policy and setting agendas for care are far removed intellectually, and usually also physically, from those subject to the implications of said policies and agendas. However, I am interested in how those charged with these tasks may not necessarily lack empathy but rather partake in an institutionalised lack of empathy somewhat akin to Larocco's 'groupthink'.[12] Thankfully, many academics and advocates sitting on the 'outside' have continued to knock on the door and whilst progress has been slow, some progress has and continues to be made.

3. In The Absence Of Empathy

Shut Out: The Experience of People with Disabilities and their Families in Australia,[13] a report compiled in 2009 following extensive consultation with people with disability, provides numerous examples of disability policy missing the mark in delivering necessary supports for people with intellectual disability. For example, an elderly mother who had cared for her son with an intellectual disability for over forty years was unable to access appropriate support for her son when she became unwell. The son underwent the required IQ assessment showing he had a full scale of IQ of 72, rendering him ineligible for assistance as the eligibility 'cut-off' was 70. The gentleman was unable to shop, cook, tie his shoelaces or attend to his own personal care, however, he had attended a regular school, could drive a vehicle and held a job as a cleaner. The report also stated that people such as this gentleman are 'overrepresented in the criminal justice system both as victims and offenders'.[14]

The *Shut Out* report cites numerous examples of challenges in accessing appropriate educational settings faced by those with intellectual disabilities, including the case of a 13-year old boy whose only option was home-schooling following numerous challenges within mainstream environments, in spite of the education standards demanded under the Disability Discrimination Act. The boy's mother in her submission stated:

> Our experience has found that an education professional's inability to act appropriately to behavioural responses in children with special needs stems from a lack of knowledge of the needs of those with a disability and/or attitudinal beliefs.[15]

There appears to be a substantial abyss between those who write the policies and drive the agendas and those whose lives are governed by said policies and agendas. Most importantly, where there are instances of good, person-focussed policy, strategies to *implement* evidence-based, best practice are missing. Is it possible for the intellectually gifted to facilitate creative pathways for people with intellectual disability when they may not have the capacity to enter into or empathise with their subjects' unique worlds?

The above examples and countless others demonstrate how those with intellectual impairment still occupy the unenviable position whereby they are subject to, and dependent upon, their historical oppressors - those possessing average or above average intelligence, for survival. 'Oppressors' may appear to be a strong term in a contemporary context where many decision-makers have no such intent, however, the institutions, governance and policies (where governance and policy actually *existed*) upon which our current institutions are built were founded in a failure to value people with intellectual disability, evidenced by the very language that was used to describe people with impairment – 'imbeciles', 'idiots' and 'feebleminded'.[16]

This is not to say that academic enquiry or activism challenging the status and institutionalisation of the intellectually impaired has not occurred. However, the fact that to this day, institutionalised 'care' facilities are still being dismantled, that the language and terms of reference for people categorised as intellectually impaired continues to be contested, and that how support is provided for people with disability continues to be a challenge echoes of the ongoing struggle for this sector of our society in collectively accessing the most basic of their human rights.

Since the disability movement took root in the 1960s,[17] a growing number of scholars have challenged the deficit-laden discourse within which people with intellectual disability have been devalued and situated,[18] citing instances ranging from gross abuse and injustice and the absence of a human rights-based approach in creating appropriate support and frameworks for community-based living for those rendered vulnerable due to their alternate ways of being in the world. The case of Winterbourne View[19] and the abhorrent neglect and abuse of people placed 'in care' demonstrates the prevailing lack of insight that exists, still in how to best support those whose intellectual capacity has rendered them powerless.

However, a chasm exists also between academics and the intellectually disabled, adding another layer of complication or distance. The academic's life, identity and career is predicated upon his or her capacity to learn, interpret and communicate complex texts, situations and environments. The intellectually impaired have been historically categorised as incapable of understanding complexity and their lives have been constructed and governed by those who have sought to control, manage or moderate their lifestyle and behaviour.[20] By way of their intellectual identities, each are as shut out of one another's worlds as the other.

The distance between the academic and the intellectually impaired can be seen as a veritable cultural chasm where empathic understanding of one another's world view could be, well-nigh impossible. How then might the chasm be bridged?

Inherent contradictions within the realm of academic enquiry with reference to intellectual impairment have, for instance, become more evident in recent years as representatives of the greater disability community, including parents of children with intellectual disabilities, have sought entry into the world of academe in a bid to counter the devaluing and dehumanising narratives of intellectual disability.

Whilst academics such as Peter Singer and Jeff MacMahan could be viewed as 'easy' targets to focus upon to highlight what may be seen as a deficit in empathy towards people with disability, their exchange with fellow academic and parent of a person with profound intellectual disability, Eva Feder Kittay, is worthy of discussion. The three entered into a spirited public discussion at a conference at the Stony Brook University, New York, in 2008. The ensuing conversation illustrated both Singer and MacMahan's diminished valuing of people with intellectual disability as well as a lack of respect for the capacity of Kittay to engage in a robust, academic discussion outside her role as mother. Kittay's views were relegated by the scholars to those of a parent whose role as advocate was a barrier to her being able to grasp and understand their more 'learned' points of view.[21]

Whilst Singer may not engage directly in policy creation, his influence cannot and should not be underestimated in terms of shaping public opinion. Listed as one of Australia's top 40 public intellectuals[22] in 2006, his writing and philosophies regarding the euthanizing of babies born with disability have been widely disseminated and in some quarters, are held in high regard. Whilst his intellectual capacity is remarkable and his viewpoint could certainly be viewed positively by some in terms of displaying empathy, his opinions regarding life and death decisions, in the absence of lived experience raising a child with intellectual disability need to be challenged. It is perhaps too great a stretch for polar opposites to be able to walk in each other's shoes.

It could be argued that a parent, acting as advocate, may in many instances be the person most able to experience and articulate, or empathise with, their son or daughter's way of being in the world and what may constitute their versions of a 'good life'. The intimacy in the relationship between parent and child within the context of intellectual disability is in certain contexts potentially heightened. Where a parent is so completely involved with the ongoing survival of child, finding a way through is paramount. Creativity, intuition, education and a thirst to 'know' the child, in ideal circumstances become the currency of their day to day existence. A particular empathy is borne within these day to day transactions and new ways of being in the world emerge for both the parent and the child. This is of course, somewhat of an idealised scenario and does not address the oftentimes difficult journey that is so much a part of the modern day narrative of intellectual disability.

However, what I am endeavouring to highlight is how counterproductive it is to reduce the opinion of a learned scholar, such as Kittay, who has lived experience and draws upon informed research, to an emotional, parental reaction to issues that are of concern to us all. That is, if our concern for the continuation of community, understanding, compassion and empathy are of any import.

4. The Possibility and Promise of Empathy within the World of Intellectual Disability

Interest in disability studies has grown since the first disability activists and scholars gave voice to the dehumanisation and devaluing of people with congenital and acquired disability[23] and demanded appropriate societal recognition. Issues ranging from the creation of accessible physical spaces and the dismantling of institutionalised care have seen those living with disability begin to realise significant changes in their environments. There is evidence of these shifts in everyday life in the West from the most basic and obvious provision of disability parking spaces and accessible toilets to the inclusion of children with disability in mainstream classrooms.

These changes have been slow and have come about as a result of lobbying by citizens with physical disabilities who have been able to articulate their needs and advocate for those changes themselves. Legislating, creating building codes and enforcing rules and regulations are the stuff policy makers are made of and car parking spaces and accessible bathrooms are significant advances, however legislating with a view to creating empathic pathways for working with people with intellectual disability and ensuring rules of engagement are enforced presents a much more complex arena.

As is demonstrated in this volume, empathy has garnered attention across multiple disciplines, particularly in medicine and education, where the training and education of professionals has evolved to include and embrace this quality within their ranks. This has led to a description of one's capacity to experience empathy, that quality enabling one human being to be able to imagine the world from the perspective of another, as a desirable trait. The development of teaching and learning resources within disciplines, however, appears to have lacked adequate exploration[24] in terms of two logical starting points – understanding how a person with intellectual disability may view their own life and how empathy may or may not be acquired by the professionals and carers charged with supporting people with intellectual disability.

In his interrogation of such differences in perception between care providers and those living with disability, Couser writes:

> One of the major obstacles to the delivery of health care to disabled people is the well-established disparity between the quality of life of disabled people as they report it and the estimates of their quality of life by medical professionals. In survey after survey, disabled people rate their quality of life almost as highly as *non*disabled people rate theirs. But nondisabled ***health care professionals*** render significantly ***lower*** estimates of the quality of life of disabled people – even lower estimates than those rendered by the general nondisabled population.[25]

Supposed innovations in training and education for medical and education professionals have been designed to encourage and inspire the development of empathy for those working with people with disability. The practice of simulating the experience of physical disability, particularly within educational contexts, has gained popularity and inspired investigation with seemingly positive results in spite of scholars, including Couser, who challenge the value of the practice.[26] Whilst these practices are designed to inspire, facilitate and develop students' awareness so that they may develop empathy towards their future students, patients and clients, Couser argues that this approach is flawed by way of focusing participants' attention upon the simulated disability and succeeds in embedding a skewed experience of disability rather than a holistic view. This approach may thus prove to be counterproductive; accessing and simulating the intellectually impaired experience is significantly problematic and it is unclear how this might be achieved and what benefit could be derived from such an exercise.

It may be argued that the vacuum of opportunity for people with intellectual disability to self-actualise and navigate their own versions of a 'good life' in adulthood can be attributed to a lack of empathy for the world as they experience it, from those who have been charged with the representation of their needs in public agenda setting, policy making and academic enquiry.

Other academics have also entered into the arena to contest the formulation of policy and agenda-setting affecting the lives of people with intellectual disability. For example, Cameron[27] has identified fundamental flaws in the most basic of premises whereby policies in the United Kingdom have been created to support social inclusion, without a clear articulation of what social inclusion is, beyond being the opposite of social exclusion. From this weakened premise, it is not surprising that progress in this area is impossible to properly assess and gauge whether or not people's situations have improved.

Some parallels can be drawn here with Nelems' assertions with regard to the creation and introduction of educational resources concerning empathy; without concrete articulations of what empathy is, questions about how it may be taught and for what purpose and hoped for outcomes, remain.[28] Instinctively, it seems empathy and social inclusion are 'good', but without adequate interrogation and meaningful research, progress will at best, be haphazard.

In his critique of the policies governing inclusion in the UK, Edward Hall challenges the focus on granting people access to the *same* opportunities with respect to employment, education and housing, rather than addressing the distinctive needs and wider social conditions required to facilitate these opportunities.[29] He also notes these policies have not been based upon an assessment of whether these changes are what are required, possible or needed.

It may be that the bases for some of the policy approaches are grounded in the principles of normalisation prevalent within Wolfensberger's Social Role Valorisation (SRV).[30] With the push in recent times for inclusive education, scholars such as Culham and Nind[31] have called for the deconstruction of notions of normalisation associated with SRV in a bid to ensure that the mistakes of the past are not repeated. Whilst they concede that SRV provided some valuable in-roads for people with intellectual disability to enter into society more fully, they echo Ferri and Gregg's assertion that 'individuals are encouraged to change themselves to gain access to society, rather than calling into question their exclusion in the first place.'[32]

Perhaps this disparity reflects Larocco's assertion that 'the 'empathizer's emotional repertoire and conditioned dispositions and other learned forms of social orientation and behavior'[33] have significant impacts upon the potential for a positive and transformative encounter. In this light, the vastly different life experience of the policy maker, service provider or academic may pose distinctive challenges for each of these to experience a meaningful empathetic connection and understanding with the intellectually impaired 'Other'. Within these relationships, unequal power relations also exist.

Were we to reverse the transaction and discussion, what might we find? Is it possible for the intellectually impaired to experience empathy for the academic, the service provider or the policy maker? Is it necessary or useful to view the transaction from this perspective? If we are to believe in the transformative power of an empathic encounter, what this new vantage point offers is the opportunity to re-examine how we enter into an encounter with a person with an intellectual disability. Perhaps rather than taking the historical view of deficit with us, a position of openness and enquiry for what we might learn – rather than what we might fix or repair – opens the way for a different encounter. Perhaps too, we may open the door for the 'other' in our encounter to learn more about us, or to perhaps access us in a different way. Psychologist Judith Jordan, in her exploration of mutuality and power offers some possibilities to be considered:

> One is both affecting the other and being affected by the other; one extends oneself out to the other and is also receptive to the impact of the other. There is openness to influence, emotional availability, and a constantly changing pattern of responding to and affecting the other's state. There is both receptivity and initiative toward the other. Both the wholeness and the subjectivity of the other person are appreciated and respected. One joins in the similarities with the other and also values the qualities that make that person different. When empathy and concern flow both ways, there is an intense affirmation of the self and paradoxically a transcendence of the self, a sense of the self as part of a larger relational unit.[34]

Given the historical grounding of disability within a medicalised model that still persists, it is not surprising that the drive to intellectualise the value of one life *style* over another, according to a generalised summation of what constitutes a 'good' life rests in medicalised terms: distant, deficit-driven, sterile, and devoid of emotion. The above offers a new entry point into how the medical, education fields and disability service sector can re-frame the conversation.

If there is an inherent misrepresentation and de-valuing of individuals living with disability and how they live their lives, could it be that the values and frameworks that inform the supports and decisions surrounding the intellectually impaired need to be reflected upon and challenged? Developing modules addressing the need for empathy within these professional fields, and the seeking of new ways of understanding and engaging with people of diverse abilities, has revealed a deficit within the traditional education and medical fields, and by inference, a lack of understanding of how to engage with those individuals.[35]

If there is a distinct mismatch between the views of the supervising medical practitioner and their patient, the service provider and the service user, the teacher and the student, the researcher and the subject, how can appropriate and meaningful outcomes be achieved?

How can we best elicit, interpret and actualise the information necessary for supporting people with intellectual disability to attain their version of quality of life? In exploring the notion that the quality of empathy is a desirable trait for people working with people with intellectual disability, within the context of emerging work in the field, there is increasing evidence across various disciplines linking the sharing of testimony as a way forward.[36] The contribution of scholars such as Rebecca Garden are now challenging dominant discourses and power relations with practical approaches within the bioethics and humanities arenas wherein practitioners are encouraged to embrace self-reflection as part of their practice.[37] Self-reflection is another theme that has emerged in this volume, as a pathway whereby passive empathy may be avoided and a more transformative experience might occur.[38]

If we are to take the commonly held view that this quality we call 'empathy' may be a way that academics and policy makers come to more fully understand the needs of people with intellectual disabilities, an examination of the workings of an ethical, empathic encounter and how this may inform one group about another becomes necessary. However the assumption that experiencing empathy is in and of itself a way to embrace and understand the 'Other' is, within the context of this volume, a contentious one.

Is empathy necessary in the formation of appropriate policy-making or are there alternative frameworks that may be created to safeguard the well-being and quality of life that parents may desire for their children who lack the capacity to advocate for themselves? How can empathy be learned, facilitated and achieved amongst professionals such as academics and policymakers, who may have minimal or no contact with those their work affects?

5. Determining Quality of Life for People with Intellectual Disability

Sunderland, Catalano and Kendall have begun to make valuable inroads in challenging the dominant negative views associated with living with disability.[39] In their work, which deals with people with acquired disability, they explore how the way in which dialogue is constructed with people with disability has a marked influence on the way in which people are able to respond and engage with one another. They found that interview-style formats and focus group discussions, where interaction and sharing of life stories amongst participants was facilitated, a 'full (and 'normal') range of positive, negative and in-between emotions, experiences and aspirations'[40] was consistent. This stood in contrast to engagements based on the use of closed questions and survey-style research, whereby the former modes of enquiry appear to allow a more holistic view for how people view their own lives and serve to enable positive and humorous dialogue in the shared articulation of life experiences. The article opens and concludes with a challenge to policy makers and researchers to re-examine the way in which research is conducted and reported, citing the absence of aspirational language within disability policy writing as opposed to the affirming and positive language used in documents such as *Backing Australia's ability* policy suite for example.[41] *Backing Australia's ability* was a document targeted at average Australians, inspiring positive future directions. However, whilst the document obeys the conventions of a policy-driven format, 'it confirms that policy-makers and politicians are capable of producing broad and intense aspirations for human flourishing within the policy genre, but they choose not to in the case of disability policy.'[42]

What is at issue in this particular research and does in fact resound within disability discourse, is the continued practice of commencing dialogue and discussion regarding disability from a position of deficit – whereby the lack or absence of intellectual ability is the navigational point from which all movement begins. This position presumes that something within the individual is lacking, and fails to recognise or capitalise upon the abilities and attributes upon which to build a holistic view of person and their desires. Hence, the negative connotation and intonation in disability policy writing prevails. Available narratives addressing life with disability continue to support the view that disability is a condition to be overcome, the ultimate goal being the attainment or approximation of normalcy and the achievement of a heroic outcome.[43]

Quality of life is the subject of ongoing debate and discussion across multiple disciplines. Frameworks for conceptualising and measuring quality of life and juxtaposing these with various social systems have been created. These include nine core domains coupled with the social system within which an individual may live. This work emanates from the following definition of intellectual disability:

Intellectual disability is a condition that in practice affects people's ability to make self-determined choices. Living a life that is judged as one of quality frequently requires support beyond that typically needed by others at a similar age and stage of life.[44]

This definition is significant due to the reference to self-determined choices and the level of support required by others to ascertain those choices. The core domains: emotional well-being, interpersonal relationships, material well-being, personal development, physical well-being, self-determination, social inclusion and rights have been established. The expert knowledge and experience informing the study, however, could differ significantly from the lived experience and knowledge of the subjects of the study.

The study's findings emphasise the necessity of informed agenda setting and policy-making, and the work presents as sound and informative. In some cases it would be difficult to ascertain the level of importance that the core domains and social systems might hold for people with intellectual disability. It is here that the question of empathy arises in terms of assessing what may or may not be deemed as necessary or important in determining quality of life for these individuals. With the barriers to communication that affect people with intellectual disability, confirmation of what they deem as necessary is often difficult and may be viewed as a contributing barrier when considering the notion of empathy with an individual's particular situation.

At a personal level, the challenge presented to me and perhaps other parents, is accessing what my daughter may view as markers of a quality or good life for her, let alone conveying these to the policy makers. I am challenged to continually revisit my own frameworks, assumptions and values as I endeavour to imagine her version of a good life; one that exists outside my aspirations and version of a good life, all the while harbouring a deep sense of fear that the releasing of my will over hers will render her vulnerable in the absence of a safe and secure future. The world of intellectual disability is a complex labyrinth that cannot be easily resolved.

6. Towards an Empathic Future

If empathy can be taught and learned, how do we now move forward to determining best practice within the world of intellectual disability? My answer to this question is: Cautiously – as one does with the unknown, the unchartered and the extraordinary, for this is the world of intellectual disability. Nelems' discussion of pedagogical approaches to teaching empathy, most particularly passive versus transformative, are evidence of steps in the right direction.[45] So are studies, such as Brunero, Lamont and Coates' review of empathy education in nursing,[46] which indicate a drive towards improving the way in which care givers' capacity to acquire the necessary 'tools' of empathy are heartening.

Incorporating specific criteria pertaining to empathetic approaches within ethics guidelines on academic or policy research may be a helpful step. Similarly establishing a manager or front line service provider's propensity to act ethically and empathetically via the introduction of the Empathy Construct Rating Scale (ECRS)[47] might be considered. Would those already entrenched in positions of power be willing to be subject to a redress of their authority to speak on behalf of another?

In the absence of being able to access a version of an individual's vision of a good life, how do we ascertain what quality of life means to those whose minds and needs lay beyond our understanding at this point in time? Constraints in terms of available, sustainable resources and opportunities to engage with people with intellectual disability mean that students and scholars lack opportunity to engage and develop enhanced levels of empathy. Couser suggests that

> ...medical education needs to address the gap head on. Pun intended: closing the gap may be less a matter of changing attitudes than a matter of changing *minds*. That is, the process may require a cognitive shift, rather than an emotional one. And perhaps it is respect for disabled people, more than empathy, that medical education needs to inculcate. The study of narrative can be invaluable in that project.[48]

There continues to be tension in the area of medical intervention. Continued promotion and distribution of alternate narratives that celebrate diverse ways of being in the world is an important component in challenging hearts and minds, inspiring shifts in perceptions, and making incremental shifts toward an empathetic impulse. The alignment of disability studies with those concerned with power relations, race, gender and queer studies – in terms of redressing and affirming alternate states of being in the world as valuable, valid and not requiring remedy – is also useful in furthering necessary dialogue. The growth of autobiography in literature and film provides greater access to diverse narratives of people with disability that can be shared with the wider community, offering time and space to explore a more holistic, authentic version of life lived with disability.[49]

Clearly there is a need for further exploration and research regarding empathy in and of itself and the ways in which empathy, in the context of disability can be taught and learned within diverse institutional settings.

To look into the face of intellectual disability is to confront fear of vulnerability and powerlessness. It is to realise both the incredible frailty and majestic beauty of all that being human is and can be. We will all, should we be fortunate to live long enough, be confronted with our well-being and safety in being subject to another's care; potentially an unknown other in an unknown environment. However, our internal frames of reference will dictate how we meet these fears. Our impulse or reaction to these realities are to some extent dictated by our individual life experiences. Some will fight; some will ignore, some will find love or compassion; and some will be compelled to act out of care or nurture.

Can we legislate compassion and can we govern with a *care-full* hand? If empathy depends purely on imagining what it is like to walk in another's shoes or imagining how we might feel or 'be' in a similar situation, then we are in a world of trouble. For those whose reason for being, self-worth, and purpose in life, rely upon intellectual prowess, the imagined loss of this capacity would, in the absence of alternate world views, quite likely mean the end of their life and result in their desire to cease being. Perhaps it is necessary to relinquish the intellectually imagined lines that separate us and that which we think we know so that we may enter, together, into the unknown. I, for one, cannot speak on behalf of another, particularly when I too am challenged in my capacity to imagine how my life might be in the absence of my intellect.

Notes

[1] Eva Feder Kittay, 'The Personal Is Philosophical Is Political,' *Cognitive Disability and Its Challenge to Moral Philosophy*, ed. Eva Kittay and Licia Carlson (United Kingdom: Blackwell Publishing Ltd and Metaphilosophy LLC, 2010), 97-110.

[2] See for example, J. I. Charlton, *Nothing about Us without Us: Disability Oppression and Empowerment* (Berkeley: University of California Press, 1998); and 'International Day of Disabled Persons, 2004 - Nothing about Us without Us,' Viewed 22 July 2014, http://www.un.org/disabilities/default.asp?id=114.

[3] Rebeccah Nelems, 'What Is This Thing Called Empathy?,' in this volume

[4] Steve Larocco, 'Empathy as Orientation rather than Feeling: Why Empathy is Ethically Complex,' in this volume.

[5] Joan C. Tronto, *Moral Boundaries: A Political Argument for an Ethic of Care* (London: Routledge, 1994), 12.

[6] United Nations Convention on the Rights of Persons with Disabilities, viewed 8 June 2014, http://www.un.org/disabilities/convention/conventionfull.shtml.

[7] American Association on Intellectual and Developmental Disabilities, viewed 3 September 2015, http://aaidd.org/intellectual-disability/definition#.VhUgNsuqqkp.

[8] Gary L. Albrecht and Patrick J. Devlieger, 'The Disability Paradox: High Quality of Life against All Odds,' *Social Science and Medicine* 48.9 (1999): 977-988.

[9] Ibid.

[10] Michael J. Kendrick, 'Historical Contributors towards Increasing Respect for the Voices of People with Disabilities in Western Societies', *Social Role Valorization.com*, (2010), viewed 10 June 2014,

http://www.socialrolevalorization.com/articles/kendrick/respect-for-people-with-disabilities.html.

[11] Judith V. Jordan, *The Movement of Mutuality and Power*. Work in progress # 53. Wellesley, MA: Stone Center Working Paper Series (1991).

[12] Steve Larocco, in this volume.

[13] Kirsten Deane, 'Shut Out: The Experience of People with Disabilities and Their Families in Australia', *Australian Government, Department of Social Services.gov.au*, viewed 2 September 2014,
https://www.dss.gov.au/our-responsibilities/disability-and-carers/publications-articles/policy-research/shut-out-the-experience-of-people-with-disabilities-and-their-families-in-australia?HTML#foreword.

[14] Ibid.

[15] Ibid.

[16] Anne Digby and David Wright, *From Idiocy to Mental Deficiency: Historical Perspectives on People with Learning Disabilities* (New York: Routledge, 2002).

[17] David Frum, *How We Got Here: The '70s* (New York: New York Basic Books, 2001), 250-251.

[18] See for example Mitchell, *Special Educational Needs and Inclusive Education: Systems and Contexts;* and Anne Digby and David Wright, *From Idiocy to Mental Deficiency: Historical Perspectives on People with Learning Disabilities* (London: Routledge, 2002).

[19] 'Winterbourne View: Summary of the Government Response', *UK.gov*, viewed 10 June 2014,
https://www.gov.uk/government/uploads/system/uploads/attachment_data/file/213221/4-page-summary.pdf.

[20] Digby and Wright, 'From Idiocy to Mental Deficiency.'

[21] Kittay, 'The Personal Is Philosophical'.

[22] Richard Nile, 'First Cohort for Thought', *The Australian.com*, (2006), viewed 9 January 2015,
http://www.theaustralian.com.au/news/first-cohort-for-thought/story-e6frg6n6-1111112254409 .

[23] Michael Oliver, 'The Politics of Disablement,' (Leeds: University of Leeds Disability Archive, 1990), viewed 10 September 2014,
http://www.leeds.ac.uk/disability-studies/archiveuk/Oliver/p%20of%20d%20oliver4.pdf.

[24] Nelems, in this volume.

[25] G. Thomas Couser, 'Narrating Disability Inside and Outside the Clinic: Or, Beyond Empathy,' *Academia.edu*, viewed 10 June 2014,
https://www.academia.edu/4427582/Narrating_Disability_Inside_and_Outside_the_Clinic_Or_Beyond_Empathy.

[26] Ibid.

[27] Angus Cameron, 'Geographies of Welfare and Exclusion: Initial Report', *Progress in Human Geography* 29 (2005): 194-203.

[28] Rebeccah Nelems, 'The Horizons of Empathic Experience', *Encountering Empathy: Interrogating the Past, Envisioning the Future*, eds. Veronica Wain and Paulus Pimomo (Oxford: Inter-Disciplinary Press, 2015), 165-176.

[29] Edward Hall, 'Spaces of Social Inclusion and Belonging for People with Intellectual Disabilities, *Journal of Intellectual Disability Research* 54.1 (2010): 48-57.

[30] Wolf Wolfensberger, 'A Brief Overview of Social Role Valorization', *Mental Retardation* 38.2 (2000): 105-123.

[31] Andrew Culham and Melanie Nind, 'Deconstructing Normalisation: Clearing the Way for Inclusion', *Journal of Intellectual & Developmental Disability* 28.1 (2003): 65-78.

[32] Beth A. Ferri and N. Gregg, 'Women with Disabilities: Missing Voices', *Women's Studies International Forum* 21 (1998): 435

[33] Larocco, in this volume.

[34] Jordan, 'The Movement of Mutuality and Power'.

[35] G. Thomas Behler, Jr. 'Disability Simulations as a Teaching Tool: Some Ethical Issues and Implications (Ferris State University).

[36] See Ann-Louise Davidson's work for example with new approaches to collaboration with people with intellectually disability – whilst the notion of empathy is not used, the process driven approach demonstrates respectfulness and flexibility in developing mutually satisfying results. Ann-Louise Davidson, 'Community and Residential Integration, and Paid Employment Go Hand-in-Hand – A Collaborative Inquiry, *Journal of Developmental Disabilities* 15.2 (2009): 27-37.

[37] Rebecca Garden 'Expanding Clinical Empathy: An Activist Perspective', *Journal of General Internal Medicine* 24.1 (2009): 122-125.

[38] Nelems, in this volume.

[39] Naomi Sunderland, Tara Catalano and Elizabeth Kendall, 'Missing Discourses: Concepts of Joy and Happiness in Disability,' *Disability and Society* 24.6 (2009): 703-714.

[40] Ibid., 713.

[41] Commonwealth of Australia, *Backing Australia's Ability.com*, Prime Minister's Message, (2004), Viewed 10 May 2015, http://backingaus.innovation.gov.au/pm_message.htm.

[42] Sunderland, 'Missing Discourses', 712.

[43] Couser, 'Narrating Disability.'

[44] Robert L. Schalock, Ivan Brown, Roy Brown, Robert A. Cummins, David Felce, Leena Matikka, Kenneth D. Keith, and Trevor Parmenter, 'Conceptualization, Measurement, and Application of Quality of Life for Persons with Intellectual

Disabilities: Report of an International Panel of Experts,' *Mental Retardation* 40.6 (2002): 457-470.
[45] Rebeccah Nelems, 'The Horizons of Empathic Experience.'
[46] Scott Brunero, Scott Lamont and Melissa Coates, 'A Review Of Empathy Education In Nursing,' *Research Gate.com,* Viewed 5 April 2015, http://www.researchgate.net/profile/Scott_Brunero/publication/41411646_A_revie w_of_empathy_education_in_nursing/links/09e4150b578bac62d1000000.pdf.
[47] E. L. LaMonica 'Construct Validity of an Empathy Instrument', *Research in Nursing and Health* 4 (1981): 389-400.
[48] Couser, 'Quality-of-Life Writing: Illness, Disability, and Representation', *Teaching Life Writing Texts,* eds. Miriam Fuchs and Craig Howes (New York: MLA, 2008), 350-58.
[50] See G. T. Couser, *Signifying Bodies: Disability in Contemporary Life Writing* (Michigan: University of Michigan Press, 2009); and Sarah Brophy and Janice Hladki, *Embodied Politics in Visual Autobiography* (Toronto: University of Toronto, 2014).

Bibliography

Admunson, Ron. 'Quality of Life, Disability and Hedonistic Psychology.' *Journal for the Theory of Social Behaviour* 40.4 (2010): 374-292.

Albrecht, Gary L., Katherine D. Seelman, and Michael Bury. *Handbook of Disability Studies.* London: Sage Publications, 2001.

Albrecht, Gary L. and Patrick J. Devlieger. 'The Disability Paradox: High Quality of Life against All Odds.' *Social Science and Medicine* 48.9 (1999): 997-988.

American Association on Intellectual and Developmental Disabilities. Viewed on 3 September 2014. http://aaidd.org/intellectual-disability/definition#.VhUgNsuqqkp.

Behler, Jr., G. Thomas. *Disability Simulations as a Teaching Tool: Some Ethical Issues and Implications.* Ferris State University.

Brophy, Sarah and Janice Hladki, eds. *Embodied Politics in Visual Autobiography.* Toronto: University of Toronto, 2014.

Brunero, Scott, Scott Lamont and Melissa Coates. 'A Review of Empathy Education in Nursing.' *Research Gate.com.* Viewed on 5 April 2015, http://www.researchgate.net/profile/Scott_Brunero/publication/41411646_A_revie w_of_empathy_education_in_nursing/links/09e4150b578bac62d1000000.pdf.

Cameron, Angus. 'Geographies of Welfare and Exclusion: Initial Report'. *Progress in Human Geography* 9 (2005): 194-203.

Campbell, Jennifer, Linda Gilmore and Monica Cuskelly. 'Changing Student Teachers' Attitudes towards Disability and Inclusion.' *Journal of Intellectual & Developmental Disability* 28.4 (2003): 369-379.

Charlton, J. I. *Nothing about Us without Us: Disability Oppression and Empowerment.* Berkeley: University of California Press, 1998

Commonwealth of Australia. *Backing Australia's Ability* Prime Minister's Message. (2004), Viewed 10 May 2015.
http://backingaus.innovation.gov.au/pm_message.htm.

Couser, G. Thomas. *Signifying Bodies: Disability in Contemporary Life Writing.* Michigan: University of Michigan Press, 2009.

Couser, G. Thomas. 'Quality-of-Life Writing: Illness, Disability, and Representation.' *Teaching Life Writing Texts*, edited by Miriam Fuchs and Craig Howes, 350-358. New York: MLA, 2008.

Couser, G. Thomas. 'Narrating Disability inside and outside the Clinic: Or, Beyond Empathy.' *Academia.edu.* 2014. Viewed 10 June 2014.
https://www.academia.edu/4427582/Narrating_Disability_Inside_and_Outside_the_Clinic_Or_Beyond_Empathy.

Culham, Andrew and Melanie Nind. 'Deconstructing Normalisation: Clearing the Way for Inclusion. *Journal of Intellectual & Developmental Disability* 28.1 (2003): 65-78.

Davidson, Ann-Louise. 'Community and Residential Integration, and Paid Employment Go Hand-In-Hand: A Collaborative Inquiry. *Journal of Developmental Disabilities* 15.2 (2009): 27-37.

Digby, Anne and David Wright. *From Idiocy to Mental Deficiency: Historical Perspectives on People with Learning Disabilities.* New York: Routledge, 2002.

Dunst, Carl J., 'Effects of Puppetry on Elementary Students' Knowledge of and Attitudes toward Individuals with Disabilities.' *International Electronic Journal of Elementary Education* 4.3 (2012): 451-457.

Dykens, Elisabeth M. 'Toward a Positive Psychology of Mental Retardation.' *Research Gate.net*. Viewed 5 April 2015. http://www.researchgate.net/profile/Elisabeth_Dykens/publication/7062295_Toward_a_positive_psychology_of_mental_retardation/links/00b4952862ac55ffe8000000.pdf.

Einfeld, Stewart L., Andrea M. Piccinin, Andrew Mackinnon, Scott M. Hofer, John Taffe, Kylie M. Gray, Daniel E. Bontempo, Lesa R. Hoffman, Trevor Parmenter and Bruce J. Tonge. 'Psychopathology in Young People with Intellectual Disability.' *The Journal American Medical Association* 296.6 (2006): 1981-1989.

Ferri, Beth A. and N. Gregg, 'Women with Disabilities: Missing Voices'. *Women's Studies International Forum* 21 (1998): 429-439.

Frum, David. *How We Got Here: The '70s*. New York: New York Basic Books, 2001.

Garden, Rebecca. 'Expanding Clinical Empathy: An Activist Perspective'. *Journal of General Internal Medicine* 24.1 (2009): 122-125.

Hall, Edward. 'Spaces of Social Inclusion and Belonging for People with Intellectual Disabilities.' *Journal of Intellectual Disability Research* 54.1 (2010): 48-57.

'International Day of Disabled Persons: Nothing about Us, without Us.' *UN.org*. Viewed 22 July 2014. http://www.un.org/disabilities/default.asp?id=114.

Jordan, Judith V., 'The Movement of Mutuality and Power'. Work in Progress # 53. Wellesley, MA: Stone Center Working Paper Series, 1991.

Kittay, Eva Feder. 'The Personal Is Philosophical Is Political.' *Cognitive Disability and Its Challenge to Moral Philosophy*, edited by Eva Feder Kittay and Licia Carlson, 97-110. UK: Blackwell Publishing Ltd and Metaphilosophy LLC., 2010.

LaMonica, E. L. 'Construct Validity of an Empathy Instrument.' *Research in Nursing and Health* 4 (1981): 389-400.

McDonnell, Andrew, Emma Breen, Roy Deveau, Eimear Goulding and John Smythe. 'The Slippery Slope to Abuse'. *Studio3.org*. Viewed 10 August, 2014. http://www.studio3.org/wp-content/uploads/2014/04/A-Mac-The_Slippery_Slope.pdf

Michelmore, Karen, Nick McKenzie and Richard Baker. 'Calls for Inquiry into Victoria's Disability Sector amid Allegations Care Provider Yooralla Failed to Act on Assault Warnings'. *ABC.Net*. Four Corners. Viewed 24 November 2014. http://www.abc.net.au/news/2014-11-24/inquiry-push-into-disability-sector-after-yooralla-abuse-claims/5912010.

Nelems, Rebeccah. 'The Horizons of Empathic Experience'. *Encountering Empathy: Interrogating the Past, Envisioning rhe Future*, edited by Veronica Wain and Paulus Pimomo, 165-176. Oxford: Inter-Disciplinary Press, 2015.

Nile, Richard. 'First Cohort for Thought'. *The Australian.com.au*. 2006. Viewed 9 January 2015. http://www.theaustralian.com.au/news/first-cohort-for-thought/story-e6frg6n6-1111112254409.

Oliver, Michael. 'The Politics of Disablement,' *The Disability Archive UK*. University of Leeds, 1990, Viewed 10 September 2014, http://www.leeds.ac.uk/disability-studies/archiveuk/Oliver/p%20of%20d%20oliver4.pdf.

Phelvin, Andrew. 'Winterbourne View Hospital and the Social Psychology of Abuse.' *Art and Science Workplace Culture* 17.10 (2014): 25-29.

Rillota, Fiona and Ted Nettleback. 'Effects of an Awareness Program on Attitudes of Students without an Intellectual Disability towards Persons with an Intellectual Disability.' *Journal of Intellectual and Developmental Disability* 32.1 (2007): 19-27.

Schalock, Robert L., Miguel A. Verdugo, C. Jenaro, M. Wang, M. Wehmeyer, X. Jiancheng and Yves Lachappelle. 'Cross-Cultural Study of Quality of Life Indicators.' *American Journal of Mental Retardation* 110.4 (2005): 298-311.

Schalock, Robert L., Ivan Brown, Roy Brown, Robert A. Cummins, David Felce, Leena Matikka, Kenneth D. Keith, and Trevor Parmenter. 'Conceptualization, Measurement, and Application of Quality of Life for Persons with Intellectual Disabilities: Report of an International Panel of Experts.' *Mental Retardation* 40.6 (2002): 457-470.

Sellers, Heather. *Recovering Bodies: Illness, Disability, and Life Writing*. Madison: University of Wisconsin Press, 1997.

Shakespeare, Tom. *Disability Rights and Wrongs Revisited*. London: Routledge, 2013.

'Shut Out: The Experience of People with Disabilities and their Families in Australia', Australian Government, Department of Social Services.Viewed 2 September 2014. https://www.dss.gov.au/our-responsibilities/disability-and-carers/publications-articles/policy-research/shut-out-the-experience-of-people-with-disabilities-and-their-families-in-australia?HTML#foreword.

Sunderland, Naomi, Tara Catalano and Elizabeth Kendall. 'Missing Discourses: Concepts of Joy and Happiness in Disability.' *Disability and Society* 24.6 (2009): 703-714.

Tronto, Joan C. *Moral Boundaries: A Political Argument for an Ethic of Care*. Routledge: London, 1994.

'United Nations Convention on the Rights of Persons with Disabilities'. *UN.org*. Viewed on June 8, 2014. www.un.org/disabilities/convention/conventionfull.shtml.

'Winterboure View: Summary of the Government Response'. *UK Government*. Viewed 10 June 2014. https://www.gov.uk/government/uploads/system/uploads/attachment_data/file/213221/4-page-summary.pdf.

Wolfensberger, Wolf. 'A Brief Overview of Social Role Valorization.' *Mental Retardation* 38.2 (2000): 105-123.

Yazbeck, Marie, Keith McVilly and Trevor R. Parmenter. 'Attitudes toward People with Intellectual Disabilities: An Australian Perspective.' *Journal of Disability Policy Studies* 15 (2004): 97-111.

Veronica Wain is an independent filmmaker and academic who works with the Disability Service Organisation Equity Works Assoc. in Australia. She is mother to her nineteen-year old daughter who was born with a rare genetic condition located on the 18th chromosome, resulting in physical and intellectual disability.

Cognitive Milestones on Mutual Paths towards Empathy: A Four-Step Model

Nurit Sahar

Abstract

Empathy is often described as a socio-emotional ability that develops over the lifespan, a foundation for human interactions and relationships, and an essential attitude and tool in the work of the therapist while working with patients. Research findings have established that empathy follows a developmental course in which cognitive and emotional factors play a major role. There is wide range of evidence supporting the effectiveness of interventions to foster empathy through a variety of dimensions. Based on the developmental course of empathy, a question arises regarding the effectiveness of such interventions, whether applied in groups or in personal therapy, when cognitive and emotional development does not develop in what is often described as the 'normal' course of development. In this chapter, the concept of empathy is explored with respect to children and adolescents who have been diagnosed with Autistic Spectrum Disorder (ASD), particularly those in the high functioning end of the spectrum. A four-step model for acquiring empathy is presented, based on guiding questions that lead patients to cognitive and affective explorations of situations, of themselves, and of others to the point of developing empathy. The model is presents through moments of therapy sessions conducted with adolescents, which allow for some insight into therapeutic processes that can foster empathic abilities with High Functioning ASD (HFASD) adolescents.

Key Words: Empathy, Autistic Spectrum Disorder (ASD), High Functioning Autistic Spectrum Disorder (HFASD), autism, psychotherapy, Asperger syndrome, cognition, Cognitive Behavioural Therapy (CBT), social skills.

*****

1. Introduction

Empathy has been perceived to be a desirable socio-emotional ability, which serves as the basis for human interactions and prosocial behaviours.[1] Facilitating empathic abilities has become a goal and focus of educational and intervention programmes,[2] including target-groups such as high-school students,[3] and medical professionals.[4] Educational and intervention programmes have also been devised to enhance the social skills of young people with autism.[5] The developmental character of empathy,[6] comprising both cognitive and affective components,[7] made me wonder about the potential – and effectiveness – of interventions that aim to enhance empathy when development does not follow what is typically referred to in the literature as a 'normal' course,[8] especially in individual psychotherapy.

© KONINKLIJKE BRILL NV, LEIDEN, 2018 | DOI 10.1163/9789004360846_007

A theoretical framework of empathy will serve as the basis for thoughts and insights on stories and moments from therapy of three adolescents with autism. Drawing on such moments as well as research findings that indicate a need for mutual inquiry and clarification regarding the degree of extant empathy, I have formulated a four-step model which indicates how the acquisition of empathy might be facilitated.

2. Empathy: Definition and Development

Psychiatric notions of empathy were first introduced in 1959 by Heinz Kohut, an Austrian-born American psychoanalyst best known for his development of *Self-Psychology*. Empathy was presented as a scientific tool that defines the field of psychology. Kohut consistently referred to the construct of empathy until his last lecture in 1983, when he explicitly declared it a curative element in human beings, noting that the enactment of empathy is a therapeutic tool in itself.[9] Empathy, according to Kohut, is the force that connects human beings even more than love itself. Not only is it the force that instils peace between individuals and groups, it is also the boundary between the destructiveness of individuals towards others.

As Fairbairn highlights, empathy is an ability that can lead to destructive, cruel, and negative behaviours, as well as positive ones.[10] From this point of view, bullies and torturers, as well as salesmen, must have and implement empathic abilities and understandings of others' needs and feelings, in order to achieve their goals.[11] Empathy can also provide the affective foundation for the kinds of contagious groupthink that lead to hostility towards those who are not considered part of the collective, while aggressively sanctioning members of the in-group.[12] In order for empathy to lead to positive behaviours, it must be accompanied by goodwill, kindness, and awareness of others as people who have hopes, fears, wishes, and values that matter to them.[13]

The amazing power of empathy is within us at birth, claimed Kohut, but when we grow, it is obscured by non-empathic affinities towards others, which we accumulate through our interactive existence in the world. Returning to an empathic stance at any chosen moment requires a deep and complex process in which all of the accumulated forms of non-empathic references must be peeled; which means to say that the narcissism of the individual existence must be emptied in favour of non-individual existence in the lives of others.[14]

In its most strict definition, empathy extends beyond the mere understanding of the other. Rather, it is an internal viewpoint that eliminates the duality between two individuals.[15] Empathy refers to one's ability to perceive and fully and deeply understand the other's feelings, or, as Kohut put it, 'empathy is the capacity to think and feel oneself into the inner life of another person.'[16] In the state of empathy one does not 'identify' with or 'become' the other, so that one is 'flooded by' the intensity of another's feelings; rather, this state allows the individual to be aware of the other's feelings and emotions, while simultaneously still being aware of their own feelings and emotions.

Both the clinical setting and the social world rely on an underlying assumption that empathy, when it occurs, will lead to a change – a shift in one's attitudes and feelings, or a shift in the interaction and relationship between individuals and groups due to internal-emotional processes. Studies demonstrating the impact of empathy support this assumption.[17] Empathy has a negative correlation with violence and the tendency to discriminate,[18] and positive correlations with socially desirable traits such as leadership or conflict-resolution skills.[19] It is also a predictor of adult social competencies.[20] These traits underpin educational interventions designed to facilitate change in students' attitudes and behaviour. One such intervention aimed to evaluate prejudice in adolescents in Poland following an educational intervention targeting feelings and opinions toward the Ukrainian minority in the country.[21] Although no change was recorded following this intervention in students' opinions regarding Ukrainians, a change in reported feelings of students towards this minority indicated a decrease of negative perceptions.

In a therapeutic process, empathy serves as a tool for the therapist with which to gain a glimpse into the inner world of the patient, and to understand him or her. It also serves as a tool for the patient to deepen their understanding of themselves and their environment. In therapeutic relationships, therapists regard empathy as an important socio-emotional ability, and a factor that affects the individual's behaviour, including responses of both the individual and others. Therapists try to assess, develop, and use empathy in the process of encouraging self-awareness and change.

An antecedent of the experience of empathy seems to be the individual's ability to handle complex cognitive processes, including multiple perspective-taking, creativity, self-awareness, acceptance of uncertainty, and contradiction. Another quality of empathy is the ability to experience emotional complexity, and particularly, simultaneously experience both negative and positive emotions, each well-defined and distinguished.[22] These are developmental abilities, which, as do most developmental processes, interact with each other and are affected by both environment and nurture.

Many theoreticians refer to empathy as a rather stable trait of human personality and define it as the person's capacity to feel another person's emotions, and, accordingly, display compassion and assimilate emotional states of other people.[23] Today, it is widely accepted that empathy is bi-dimensional, entailing both cognitive and affective abilities. *Cognitive empathy* refers to the ability to infer another's emotions by adopting their perspective while *affective empathy* refers to the emotional response to another's emotion that is congruent with the emotion of the other.[24]

The lifespan development of empathy as a socio-emotional ability begins in early childhood. Empathy is evidenced as early as a few days after birth, when newborns show signs of distress in response to hearing other babies crying.[25] Also, very early in life, children experience the affective dimension of empathy through their vicarious experiencing of another's emotional state.[26] During the first years of life, empathy develops in tandem with the emergence of self.[27] Empathy is considered essential for distinguishing the self from others while the awareness of the self is the foundation for one's consciousness of one's own feelings and thoughts that are separated from those of others.

Factors that affect the development of empathy are genetics, neuro-development, temperament, parenting, and the quality of parent-child relationships. Recent research shows that neuro-mechanisms that evolve over time are involved in the acquisition of one's ability to assume the other's perspective. The literature refers to this mechanism as *Theory of Mind* (ToM).[28] ToM capacity, a component of the cognitive dimension of empathy, requires complex cognitive functions, including perspective-taking and mentalising.

Cognitive empathy, in this context, is the ability to 'imagine' the other's experience, as mentalising allows the individual to draw explicit inferences about the mental states of other people.[29] By better attaching one's empathic feelings to a conceptualisation of the other's experience rather than one's own, ToM facilitates the transformation of the early developing affective experience of empathy to a more sympathetic, other-focused experience

Longitudinal research shows that empathy may be conceptualised as part of a larger prosocial personality trait that develops in children and motivates helping behaviours into young adulthood.[30] Children would engage in more effective helping strategies as they increase their ability to identify with another's experience presumably because they are viewing the situation more accurately.[31] Empathy thus contributes to the internalisation of rules, prosocial, and altruistic behaviour, social competence, and the quality of relationships. What happens, however, when empathy does not develop due to developmental deficits, such as Autistic Spectrum Disorder (ASD)?

3.   Fostering Empathy: Foci and Interventions

A variety of intervention programs have been developed and implemented in the past decade aiming to foster empathy. In light of research findings that highlight the importance and vast positive influence empathy has on a variety of social behaviours and outcomes, it is understandable why fostering empathy has become a focus of academic and educational attention. Many intervention programs emerged against the popularising view that empathy is an invaluable human asset that can be both taught and learned.[32] Some programs focus exclusively on empathy training, while others address empathy training as part of a wider set of abilities such as general social skills. Some programs are implemented in schools, while others are designed for special groups such as children and adolescents with autistic spectrum disorders, mainly with Asperger Syndrome, now referred to as High-functioning Autism Spectrum Disorder (HFASD) (see below).[33]

Nelems discusses the typology set forth by Boler, distinguishing between passive and transformative empathy.[34] *Passive empathy* is experienced without any actual involvement and entails a projection of the self, its fears, worldviews, and accompanying assumptions onto the other. *Transformative empathy*, on the other hand, necessitates an openness and willingness to be self-reflective and to critically examine one's own assumptions, views, and beliefs so that one might encounter others with their own distinct views and beliefs. As such, transformative empathy is the empathy that can produce action or change.

These qualities of empathy present implications for interventions, both educational and therapeutic. Abstract exposure to situations might lead to passive empathy at best, and it might also result in the misinterpretation of a person's empathic abilities, since it does not produce a change in empathy behaviours. In contrast, exposure to real-life stories and situations that foster empathy may lead to a desirable change in feelings and behaviours, due to transformative empathy that occurs and produces a change of attitudes and behaviours. The narrative approach has the power to facilitate empathy as described by Wain:

> As experience and engagement with people with intellectual disability indicates, greater time needs to be taken in facilitating communication between the intellectually gifted and the intellectually impaired, to enable the sharing of stories of their life, their whole life... A shift in focus, away from the disability and towards the person and their story, in a bid to uncover possible areas of commonality and intersection, may be a significant step towards providing arenas for greater levels of empathy to flourish.[35]

Such re-focusing on the power of story is found in an intervention initiative that aimed to engage healthcare staff in the experiences of an elderly woman suffering from dementia, where the use of an ethnodrama was tested for positive effects on providing healthcare, especially through enhancing empathy, both cognitive and affective.[36] Results demonstrated that watching a film, which enabled the staff to see the experience through the patient's eyes (rather than by didactic education), led to an increased understanding of her feelings, a change in attitudes, and a change in behaviour towards patients in her condition. Based on the above, it seems that it was the personal context offered by this intervention that enabled the shift that transpired.

In her review of empathy research and findings, Cotton identified specific training components that are related to desirable outcomes, including training in interpersonal perception and empathic response; focus on one's own feelings as a point of departure for relating to the feelings of others; focus on similarities between oneself and others; role-taking/playing activities; sustained practice in imagining others' perspectives; exposure to emotionally arousing stimuli; expression of positive trait attribution; modelling of empathic behaviour; and learning about the lives of famous empathetic persons.[37] Some adaptations may be required when teaching social skills to specific target groups.

4. Social Deficits and ASD

ASD is a neuro-developmental disorder characterised by persistent impairment in reciprocal social communication and social interaction and restricted and repetitive patterns of behaviour, interests, or activities, which are present by age three.[38] Asperger Syndrome, or HFASD, describes individuals who have ASD but show no cognitive-intellectual impairments, and who are characterised by the main feature of social deficits alongside high verbal functioning and a broad range of interests and activities compared to other ASDs. Due to the limited ability to empathise, the autistic disorder has often been described as an *empathy disorder*.[39]

Despite significant evidence that individuals with ASD display empathic impairments, relatively little is known about the exact nature of these impairments. Research to date has focused primarily on the cognitive component of empathy, and only few studies have examined the behavioural component of empathy; that is, whether children with ASD behave empathically in response to the emotions of others.[40] The behavioural response is assumed to be the overt expression of affective or emotional empathy.

Some evidence emerges that adults with Asperger have deficits in cognitive empathy but not in emotional empathy.[41] This finding is consistent with the ToM understanding of ASD, which purports a central role of deficits in the ability to 'read' others' minds or understand the perspectives of others in contributing to the overall social and communication deficits present in ASD.

Therapists, educators, parents, researchers, and other professionals working with individuals who have ASD, must rely on outsiders' inferences regarding empathic skills based on observations, laboratory-situations, and simulations. It is thus assumed that we can make inferences regarding an abstract construct such as empathy by examining actual response, both affective and cognitive or behavioural. As a reflection of empathy, such responsiveness has been found to vary as a factor of age.[42] The summary offered by Scheeren and colleagues shows that young children with ASD have difficulty understanding others' emotions and mental states whereas school-aged children with ASD and normal intelligence quotient (IQ) show relatively adequate perspective-taking skills and emotional understanding, despite their social interaction problems.[43]

Similarly, parents of adolescents with ASD report overall improvement in empathic responsiveness from middle-school to late adolescence.[44] Auyeung and colleagues found that in comparison with non-ASD adolescents, individuals with ASD scored significantly lower on an affective-empathy scale, which described a tendency to identify another person's emotions and thoughts and to respond to these with an appropriate emotion.[45] Notwithstanding, these children scored exceptionally high on a systemising scale, which described a tendency to analyse or construct rule-based systems with regards to perceiving and responding in the social world as a representation of cognitive empathy.

Mazza and colleagues examined affective and cognitive empathy in adolescents with ASD as reflected in mentalising and experience-sharing abilities.[46] These researchers found that adolescents with ASD exhibited deficits in all mentalising measurements to the point where they were incapable of interpreting and understanding the mental and emotional states of other people. In contrast, on experience-sharing measures, which indicate the extent to which people experience the internal states of others, these adolescents were able to empathise with the emotional experience of other people when the latter expressed emotions with positive valence but not when the emotions were negative, such as anger or sadness. Another study showed that HFASD adolescents exhibiting low severity of autistic symptoms expressed higher empathic responsiveness to sadness simulated by the interviewer, compared to expressions of happiness or pain. No correlation between verbal IQ and empathic responsiveness was found in either the HFASD group or the normally developed control group.[47]

5. Assessing Empathy in ASD

Empathic responsiveness in individuals with ASD was both tested in laboratory conditions and estimated by self-reports of adolescents and their parents. In the assessment of empathy, several questions are explored: Do responsiveness ratings vary across different sources of information? If so, to what should they be attributed?

Self-reports of children and adolescents with HFASD, together with research findings based on observations in laboratory situations, show that in some circumstances, children both with and without HFASD may behave similarly in response to the emotional state of an unfamiliar adult. The authors concluded that for this to occur, circumstances must be kept rather simple with fairly few social stimuli to consider and the emotion expressed must be clear.[48] In contrast, compared to non-ASD children's development, parents' reports regarding the empathic responsiveness of their HFASD children yielded reduced everyday empathic responses, especially for children with more severe autistic symptoms. These ratings were also lower than the parents' coding of their children's empathic responses in the laboratory situation. It thus seems that parents of HFASD children expect some empathic responses from their child.[49] These findings require an explanation of the difference between the records of parents and self-reports of the HFASD children and adolescents themselves.

The discrepancy between the perceptions of parents compared to perceptions of their HFASD children was also evident in studies concerning social skills and quality of life.[50] In the evaluation of a social group intervention aimed at enhancing social skills among HFASD adolescents, such as making and keeping friends and handling peer conflict and rejection, results suggest that ratings of social functioning by the adolescents were higher than ratings of parents regarding their child's social functioning. This is a key finding for therapists who rely on adolescent patients' self-reports as well as the reports of their parents. For treatment outcomes, parents reported less change in social anxiety, social engagement, and empathy compared to the children's self-reports.[51] This discrepancy should therefore caution professionals who work with HFASD populations when designing interventions and setting goals.

Similarly, in a study of the quality of life (QoL) across the lifespan of individuals with autism, van Heijst found that self-reports of individuals with autism reflected higher quality of life than evaluations offered by the parents.[52] The researcher suggested some explanations for the discrepancy. Firstly, the fact that parents of children with health problems tend to report lower QoL than the children themselves may be attributed to the notion that it is easier to evaluate observable functioning (e.g., physical capability) than non-observable functioning (e.g., emotional responses or social skills). Secondly, the difficulties of people with autism to report inner emotional structures due to deficits in self-representations and ToM might influence their self-report regarding abstract concepts such as mood and emotions. Thirdly, possibly, limited social and emotional functioning may not be perceived as a problem by autistic children although the parents perceive it as such.

These discrepancies suggest that what an HFASD adolescent might consider as an empathic response might not be perceived as such by others, at least not immediately, before further inquiry and clarification are implemented. Individual psychotherapy processes can serve as the setting in which such exploration can be achieved, provided that the therapist bears in mind the need to lead a gradual step-by-step interaction that allows patients to explore and better understand their own feelings, thoughts, and motives as a starting-point to understanding those of the others.

When teaching social skills to adolescents with ASD, specific adaptations are required. These include increasing the structure and predictability of therapy sessions, incorporating visual aids, using explicit verbal cues and feedback, drawing explicit attention to important social cues, including parents in treatment, and providing multiple opportunities for rehearsal of skills.[53]

My experience as a therapist supports this theoretical knowledge, and I would suggest the application of these principles in the context of individual therapy sessions, to achieve better outcomes regarding empathy learning and fostering with youth with HFASD, as described below. The traditional belief that by merely experiencing the empathy of a therapist, a patient would be able to feel and behave empathically in real-life situations does not usually apply with HFASD patients, and a more direct approach is needed. I also suggest that HFASD adolescents should participate in setting the goals of any intervention, thus promoting self-awareness and a sense of self-agency.

6. A Four-Step Model for Acquiring Empathy

The trigger for my explorations of empathy development among HFASD adolescents was a dialogue I had with one of my patients, E, a 16 year-old boy, who had been diagnosed in childhood with HFASD. Through my dialogues with E and other AFASD patients, I formulated a model for the mutual exploration of empathy in different situations. More specifically, the model can lead patients to a broader and more flexible view and understanding of the situation, which in turn allows them to acquire the ability to empathise.

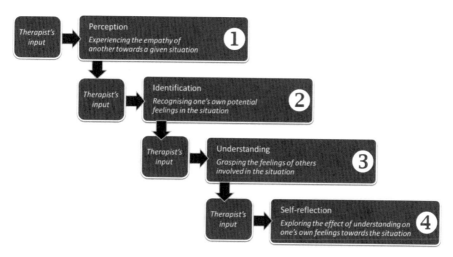

Figure 1: *The four-step model for fostering empathy in HFASD patients.*
© 2016. Courtesy of the author.

The model comprises four steps (Figure 1). The first step is that of *perception*: the patient experiences the empathy of the therapist as emerging from their understanding of a given situation. The second step is that of *identification*: through a cognitive process offered by the therapist, the patient recognises and understands the emotions they might have felt had they been in the other's shoes. The third step is that of *understanding*: through a process facilitated by the therapist, the patient develops a grasp of the other's feelings and motives in the given situation. Finally, the fourth step is that of *self-reflection*: the therapist guides the patient to self-reflection in order to explore whether understanding the other's feelings and motives affected their own feelings regarding the given situation.

E and I had been meeting for two years, almost every week, and he had arrived at our meetings willingly, recognising the benefits of our discussions in many areas of his life. On one particular day, E arrived feeling very emotional, telling me he had a big fight with his mother (whom I had also been seeing every week for the past three years). This is how he described what happened:

> I don't understand why she keeps telling me that I'm violent like my father was!!! They've been divorced for 12 years now!! What does it matter what happened in the past?? Besides, I don't remember him as a violent man, so why does she say he was??

These painful, angry words, offered with signs of tears in his eyes, nearly broke my heart, and yet came as a bit of surprise to me. While being empathic towards his pain and frustration, I thought to myself 'Is it not obvious that the past affects the present? Can't he understand what it was like for her?' I suddenly wondered: 'Do most adolescents of this age think like this? Is this typical of adolescents at large, or is it the result of E's impairment in understanding the other's perspective, which is characteristic of HFASD?' After we had discussed his pain and other feelings to the point where he relaxed, the remainder of the meeting dealt with that incident:

E: She [mother] says that my father was violent towards her before the divorce. I do not think that is true.

Me: How can you know? You were a little boy then.

E: Okay, so maybe he was violent to her, but I do not remember him as a violent man. What does that have to do with me? I had a fight with her and I yelled at her and she yelled at me, and then she told me I'm like Dad, who was violent. What does the past have to do with what is going on today?

Me: There is no connection?

E: No! What was in the past is over! Now is the present!

Me: You do not think that things you went through in the past affect you today?

E: No!...maybe yes...all the bullying I suffered, I won't be silent about it anymore! [Shouting] Today I will shout out all the shouts that I did not shout back then, when they used to hit me... Do you think that I yell at Mom because when she yells at me I feel like a victim? Like what I felt then?

Me: What do you think?
E: Well... [Leans back on the couch silent for a few minutes] I have
        an insight! Maybe, just like I'm affected by what happened to me
        in the past, and when I fight with my mother, I react as if the
        person in front of me are all the kids who used to hit me... maybe...
        when I yell at Mom, she doesn't see it's me? She sees it is my
        father from the past, who used to be violent towards her.

E's starting point was to ask why he should be implicated in his father's
actions, or his father in his. A gentle steering of the focus from his father to himself
and the exploration of the connection between past events and the present led him
to understand that his emotions, attitudes, and behaviours are shaped and affected
by past experiences. This insight allowed me to further guide him towards an
understanding of factors that might affect the behaviours of others (in this case, his
mother).

This dialogue was the first of many, a few of which are presented below, that
accentuated the need to enable, join, and lead a spiral, mutual process that allows
the patient to reach a deeper level of understanding of himself and others. By
directing E to explore his own life-experiences and emotions connected to them, he
identified an internal emotional process that has an effect on his behaviours and
feelings and that led to a different understanding of the other's motives and
behaviours. An emotional response led to a cognitive process, which, in turn,
enabled an emotional process regarding self and other, which can be seen as an
empathic process that was not evident before.

A different conversation I had with E just a few months after this one serves as
an example of how cognitive empathy can lead to affective empathy, given a set of
cognitive milestones with which he could guide himself through the process. It is
also another example of the spiral process from self to other, which E had utilised
when feeling he needed help in clarifying emotional issues to himself:

E: I can't believe my trip to Poland [a journey in Israeli high schools
        to concentration camps in memory of the Holocaust] is coming
        soon! It's very important to me because of Grandpa [who is a
        Holocaust survivor]. I know everyone will be crying there, but I
        never cry. I don't feel anything. It's strange.
Me: When you think about what went on there, you feel nothing?
E: It interests me, but I don't feel anything. I think I want to feel, but I
        don't know how to do it [looks sad and confused].
Me: Do you think there is something that can make you feel?
E: Maybe if I knew or thought about what they went through, I could
        feel it, too.

Me: From our previous conversation, do you remember what you can
        do to understand what someone else is feeling?
E: Yes. If I think about what it would be like for me if I had to live
        like they did, and how I would feel, then I will understand what it
        was like for them. But, you know, I think imagining it will not be
        as close as to actually living it. So I guess I can only feel a small
        part of their suffering, and still it would be horrible, but it's better
        than not feeling it at all ... I think I might cry when in Auschwitz.

I met E on the day he returned from Poland. He told me that what eventually
made him cry were the stories that he had heard first hand from the Holocaust
survivor who accompanied the students on their journey. E brought to life the
intervention described above regarding the usefulness of a personal story to elicit
empathy. He said about the Holocaust survivor who accompanied the class to
Poland that 'her stories made it [the experience] real.' Another session with E,
before he went to Poland, went as follows:

E: I heard that three soldiers were killed today in a terrorist attack. I
        felt very sad, I cried when I heard about it.
Me: Yes, it was very sad. I read about it.
E: I cannot understand. Why is it that I feel sadness and I cry when I
        hear about those three soldiers, but when I hear and learn about the
        Holocaust, I feel nothing? Only curiosity? In the Holocaust, six
        millions were killed and here only three soldiers, and yet I cannot
        feel?
Me: Do you have any idea why is that?
E: When I think of the soldiers, they died with a purpose, their death
        had a meaning, and they died defending our country. I cannot find
        any meaning, purpose or sense in the six million that were
        murdered. I think it is too much for me to understand so I cannot
        feel the sadness.

E expressed his distress for not being able to feel and react as he expected
others would with a growing sense of uneasiness concerning his impairment.
Apparently, he could see the suffering and horrors of the Holocaust – he had an
everyday reminder of it with his grandfather – yet he feared he would not cry,
which is the response he cognitively assessed as most appropriate.

The disparity, regarding the evaluation of empathic ability between parents and
their HFASD adolescents,[54] indicates that the adolescent's response (verbal or
behavioural) would not necessarily immediately be considered as empathic.
Therefore, a careful inquiry on behalf of non-HFASD individuals, and particularly

therapists, is necessary in order to interpret it as such. Once again, a conversation with E comes to mind:

E: Did I tell you that I have a blog on the internet?

Me: No, what is it about?

E: It is about bullying. I write about the bullying I suffered at school. I want everyone to know what I went through.

Me: Doesn't it embarrass you to expose your personal life to others? Even to people you do not know?

E: No. I feel good about it. I cannot explain why but I know I feel good when I write about it.

Me: Can you think of reasons why this makes you feel good?

E: First, I feel better when I write about it; it makes it easier to handle. I hate those memories. I hate those boys. Second, I feel that if others will know that it is okay to talk about it, maybe other children who suffer from bullying will also talk about it. It is better to talk about it than to keep it a secret about which you feel ashamed. If they will tell, they will get help and will feel better about their lives. I want to help other children. I think that my writing about it will help others. So, I write in my blog to help myself as well as others.

E's empathic ability was not obvious at first, but knowing him and taking into account his need for guidance in trying to understand his feelings and motivation for actions, enabled this mutual process of understanding and the exposure of his empathy. Without this mutual process, his blog might have been understood (by himself as well as well as by others) as only a self-centred way to alleviate his pain.

A dialogue I had with M, a 16 year old girl, who has also been diagnosed with HFASD, further demonstrates the application of the four-step model. In our conversation, M explored her tense relationship with her younger sister.

M: I am very angry with my sister. She thinks she can tell me with whom I should be friends.

Me: Tell me what had happened.

M: She had a fight with a girl who is a good friend of mine, and she told me that since she is not talking to her anymore, I should not be talking to her, either. She cannot tell me that!! She always does it!!

Me: Why do you think she asked you not to talk to her?

M: I have no idea [looks confused]. I cannot think of any reason she would do this. She has no right telling me what to do!!

Me: Can you understand her feelings? What she might feel if you will talk to that girl?

M: No! She has no right ... I do not know how she feels. How can I know? We are different people.

Me: Try to imagine if it was you. If she would be best friend with W [a boy in her class she dislikes]. How would you feel?

M: But why should she be his friend? He is not a nice boy.

Me: Look into your heart. How would you feel?

M: I would be very angry with her!! But I will never tell her not to talk to him! She has no right!

Me: I can see that you are angry. Let us try to separate the emotions and the behaviours. They are not the same thing. We have thoughts, emotions and behaviours. Try to look at each of them separately.

M: I would be hurt! And frustrated... and disappointed... She is my sister! She is supposed to be on my side!!! He might turn her against me... [looking sad, sitting quiet for a minute]. I think I understand! She asked me not to talk to that girl because she wants to feel that I am on her side, maybe she also fears that she would turn me against her. But I will never tell her not to talk to someone. I will let her know how I feel and hope she will understand that I prefer that she will be on my side. She should also think about me. I do not have many friends. She should try not to fight with my friends because they might not want to be my friends. She makes friends easily, it is harder for me. I know now that I should behave like a sister should, but I am afraid that then I will be alone again.

Me: What do you feel now? Do you feel different about her?

M: Yes, I am not so angry anymore, I can understand her, but now I also understand that my fear of being alone might influence my behaviour, so it will be different from what I believe is the right way.

M needed my guidance in the process of understanding and assuming her sister's point of view. She succeeded in doing so only when she could recognise her own feelings in a similar or opposite situation. This led to her ability to distinguish between thoughts, emotions, and behaviours, which allowed her to focus on each element separately, thus reaching a wider understanding of herself in this situation. She was now able to be aware of and understand the complex emotions she was experiencing and understand her sister's point of view. By applying cognitive empathy, M could make the first step towards affective empathy through her own cognitive process.

An additional dialogue exemplifying the model was conducted with N, a 14 year old girl, also with HFASD. Her parents had divorced when she was two years old, and her relationship with her father had been unstable. She avoided meeting him, since she felt that he was less interested in her than in her brothers. At the time, I had been meeting her for therapy over a period of four years. The following session pursued an interview with an education placement committee (a professional forum that decides whether the child is entitled to special education), which we both attended as part of her case. Her father, whom she had avoided seeing for months, also attended the interview, as did her mother. Her father spoke openly about the high possibility that he might also be suffering from HFASD although he was never diagnosed. N and her father had not exchanged a single word during the hour in which we all sat together before, during, and after the interview.

Me: How was this experience for you? It was your first time...
N: It felt okay, not too strange. It was strange that my father was there. He is never around.
Me: I think it was important for him to be there, don't you?
N: Important? He does not care about me, he is not interested in me. That is why I don't want to meet him. He always talks about himself, how he got high grades in school. He expects us to be perfect students. He does not know me at all, and he doesn't want to get to know me better! If he wanted to, he would have asked me about my feelings and my hobbies, and maybe we would have found shared interests. That is how you make a social connection; you have to look for shared areas of interest. However, he only speaks of himself.
Me: You are angry, frustrated, and disappointed with him.
N: Yes! Did you see what he talked about with you? His health! You didn't ask, and he didn't ask any of us if we want to know about it! He just talked!
Me: Why do you think he did it? Can you think of a reason?
N: Maybe he wanted to feel part of the conversation, but that is not how it is supposed to be done! If you want to be part of a conversation, you have to listen first and then join it with the same subject; you do not try to join a conversation talking about yourself!
Me: And how did you come to learn this?
N: We talked about it here and I learned how to do it, and I watch other girls do it, so I learned.
Me: Can you try to imagine how you would act at present, if you didn't have a mother who cared about you and took you to a psychologist?

N: Oh! I would have never been the same as I am now. I would still be the quiet, scared girl, who doesn't understand the world and doesn't know how to act in social places. However, my father never got help; no one knew he has Asperger. That is why he doesn't know how to behave socially.

Me: Do you remember what he said at the committee interview?

N: Yes, he talked about how he was as a child, that he felt lost in big schools and classes, and that a small class was better for him.

Me: Do you think he tried to tell you something by sharing that with everyone?

N: Maybe he tried to tell me that we are alike, that we have this in common, that he can understand my feelings [she smiles]. I am not so angry with him now that I understand him better. So, if I will meet with him again, I will try to remember to not only listen to his words, but to also try and understand what is it that he is trying to tell me. I know how to do it now, and I have to remember that he didn't receive any help. Maybe in time I can help him.

Through questions that directed N to attempt to cognitively understand her father's motives and feelings, she could empathise with him emotionally, thus reaching affective empathy. That, in turn, allowed her to feel his empathy towards her, which led her to feel less hurt and angry and more willing to try to renew her relationship with him.

7. Conclusions and Implications

This chapter has explored the concept of empathy from both the theoretical and developmental perspectives, focusing mainly on the empathic abilities of children and adolescents with HFASD. This condition is often referred to as an *empathy disorder* since the core dysfunction is in the ability to recognise mental and affective states and respond in an appropriate manner. Research shows that adolescents with HFASD can experience and express empathy in a variety of simple social situations. When, however, these situations are more complex, spanning multiple dimensions, empathy is not immediately experienced or expressed by these individuals.

Due to the developmental nature of empathy, a wide range of possibilities emerges for both individual and group interventions that may enhance empathic abilities and behaviours. In fact, evidence suggests that fostering empathy in and of itself in social and educational systems has the potential to enhance the well-being of both individuals and society.

Fostering empathy has become a major educational goal due to the positive influence of empathic abilities on prosocial behaviours. Intervention through individual psychotherapy offers a broad scope for deliberating on empathic emotions and behaviours. Specifically, I propose a four-step model for acquiring the ability to empathise.

The dialogues presented in this chapter, conducted during sessions with my HFASD adolescent patients demonstrate the way by which the four-step model assisted these patients in fostering empathy. Through guiding questions, both cognitive and affective, directed at enhancing the understanding of the other's perspective, my HFASD patients became increasingly aware of their own feelings and motivations, which then led to empathy towards both the self and the other. My patients were able to analyse given situations from a broader and more flexible perspective, which led to a better understanding of their own emotions and drives, as well as those of others, and thus enabled an emotional shift in them, following which they experienced empathy towards both themselves and the other. Cognitive pathways of empathy lead the way to affective empathy in a process that is mutually shared by both therapist and patient.

Psychologists and other professionals working with ASD youth and their parents should be aware of the complexities involved in fostering empathic abilities. The journey to empathy is long for these individuals, but I believe that we can facilitate the goal by accompanying them and taking turns in the mutual paths towards empathy. When the process is successful, these are magical moments, for therapist and patient alike, mutually experienced and shared by both.

Notes

[1] Lambros Lazuras, Jacek Pyzalski, Vassilis Barkoukis, and Haralambos Tsorbatzoudis, 'Empathy and Moral Disengagement in Adolescent Cyberbullying: Implications for Educational Intervention and Pedagogical Practice', *Studia Edukacyjne* 23 (2012): 57-69.

[2] Rebeccah Nelems, 'What Is This Thing Called Empathy?,' in this volume.

[3] Malgorzata Wojcik, 'The Impact of Empathy on Ethnic Prejudice: Anti-Prejudice Intervention in School Setting' (paper presented at the First Global Conference on Empathy, Prague, Czech Republic, November 7-9, 2014).

[4] Leslie Baillie and Eileen Sills, 'The Use of an Ethnodrama with Healthcare Staff to Prompt Empathy for People with Dementia', *Encountering Empathy: Interrogating the Past, Envisioning the Future*, ed. Veronica Wain and Paulus Pimomo (Oxford: Inter-Disciplinary Press, 2015), 99-110.

[5] Crystal Ferrendelli, Jessica Hopkins, Cecilia Costa, and Elizabeth Laugeson, 'Distinct Perceptions of Social Functioning and Treatment Outcome across Parents and Adolescents Following the UCLA PEERS Intervention [Research Poster]'. Semel Institute, UCLA, 2014.); Elizabeth A. Laugeson and Mi N. Park, 'Using a CBT Approach to Teach Social Skills to Adolescents with Autism Spectrum Disorder and Other Social Challenges,The PEERS Method', *Journal of Ratio-Emotional Cognitive-Behavioral Therapy* 32 (2014): 84-97.

[6] Nicole M. McDonald and Daniel S. Messinger, *The Development of Empathy: How, When, and Why* (2009), Viewed on 15 April 2016, http://www.psy.miami.edu/faculty/dmessinger/c_c/rsrcs/rdgs/emot/McDonald-Messinger_Empathy%20Development.pdf.

[7] Frans B. M. de Waal, 'Putting the Altruism Back into Altruism: The Evolution of Empathy', *Annual Review of Psychology* 59 (2008): 279-300.; Lazuras et al., 'Empathy and Moral Disengagement'.

[8] Such as McDonald and Messinger, *The Development of Empathy*.

[9] Raanan Kulka, 'How Does Analysis Cure?' *Between Tragedy and Compassion*, ed. Heinz Kohut (Tel Aviv, Israel: Am Oved Pub. Ltd., 2005).

[10] Gavin Fairbairn, 'Reflecting on Empathy,' in this volume; Steve Larocco, 'Empathy as Orientation Rather than Feeling: Why Empathy Is Ethically Complex,' in this volume.

[11] Fairbairn, in this volume.

[12] Larocco, in this volume.

[13] Fairbairn, in this volume.

[14] Ibid.

[15] Ibid.

[16] Heinz Kohut, *How Does Analysis Cure?* (Chicago: The University Press, 1984), 82.

[17] Mathias Allemand, Andrea E. Steiger, and Helmut A. Fend, 'Empathy Development in Adolescents Predicts Social Competencies in Adulthood', *Journal of Personality* 83 (2015): 229-241; Leslie S. Greenberg, Jeanne C. Watson, Robert Elliot, and Arthur C. Bohart, 'Empathy', *Psychotherapy* 38 (2001): 380-384; Ari Kaukiainen, Kaj Bjorkvist, Kirsti Lagerspetz, Karin Osterman, Christina Salmivalli, Sari Rothberg, and Anne Ahlbom, 'The Relationships between Social Intelligence Empathy and Three Types of Aggression', *Aggressive Behavior* 25 (1999): 81-89; Isaac E. Mostovicz, Nada K. Kakabadse, and Andrew P. Kakabadse, 'A Dynamic Theory of Leadership Development', *Leadership & Organizational Development Journal* 30 (2009): 563-576.

[18] Kaukiainen et al., 'The Relationships between Social Intelligence Empathy and Three Types of Aggression'.

[19] Mostovicz et al., 'A Dynamic Theory of Leadership Development'.

[20] Allemand et al., 'Empathy Development in Adolescents Predicts Social Competencies in Adulthood'.

[21] Małgorzata Wójcik, 'The Impact of Empathy on Ethnic Prejudice: Anti-Prejudice Intervention in School Setting' (paper presented at the First Global Conference on Empathy, Prague, Czech Republic, November 7-9, 2014).

[22] Camilla Pagani, 'Empathy, Complex Thinking, and Their Interconnections', in this volume.

[23] Lazuras et al., 'Empathy and Moral Disengagement'.

[24] de Waal, 'Putting the Altruism Back into Altruism'; Jean Decety and Meghan Meyer, 'Emotion Resonance to Empathic Understanding: A Social Developmental Neuro-Science Account', *Development and Psychology* 20 (2008): 1053-1080.

[25] McDonald and Messinger, *The Development of Empathy.*

[26] Ibid.

[27] Ibid.

[28] Ibid.

[29] Simone G. Shamay-Tsoory, 'The Neural Bases for Empathy', *Neuroscience* 17 (2011): 18-24.

[30] Nancy Eisenberg, Ivanna K. Guthrie, Bridget C. Murphy, Stephanie A. Shepard, Amanda Cumberland, and Gustavo Carlo, 'Consistency and Development of Prosocial Dispositions: A Longitudinal Study', *Child Development* 70 (1999): 1360-1372.

[31] McDonald and Messinger, *The Development of Empathy.*

[32] Nelems, in this volume.

[33] Kathleen Cotton, *Developing Empathy in Children and Youth* (Northwest Regional Educational Laboratory, 2001.); Laugeson and Park, 'Using a CBT Approach to Teach Social Skills to Adolescents with Autism Spectrum Disorder and Other Social Challenges,The PEERS Method'; Nelems, 'Horizons of Empathic Experience'; Wójcik, 'Impact of Empathy'; American Psychiatric Association, *Diagnostic and Statistical Manual of Mental Disorders*, 2013.

[34] Nelems, in this volume.

[35] Veronica Wain, 'Empathy with the Enemy: Can the Intellectually Gifted Experience Empathy with the Intellectually Impaired?' *Encountering Empathy: Interrogating the Past, Envisioning the Future*, eds. Veronica Wain and Paulus Pimomo (Oxford: Inter-Disciplinary Press, 2015), 116.

[36] Baillie et al., 'The Use of an Ethnodrama'.

[37] Cotton, *Developing Empathy in Children.*

[38] American Psychiatric Association, *Diagnostic and Statistical Manual of Mental Disorders.*

[39] Decety and Meyer, 'Emotion Resonance.'

[40] Anke M. Scheeren, Hans M. Koot, Peter C. Mundy, Larissa Mous, and Sander Begeer, 'Empathic Responsiveness of Children and Adolescents with High-functioning Autism Spectrum Disorder', *Autism Research* 6 (2013): 362-271.

[41] Simon Baron-Cohen, Alan M. Leslie, and Uta Frith, 'Does the Autistic Child have a Theory of Mind?', *Cognition* 21 (1985): 37-46.

[42] Scheeren et al., 'Empathic Responsiveness of Children and Adolescents with High-Functioning Autism Spectrum Disorder'.

[43] Scheeren et al., 'Empathic Responsiveness.'

[44] Corina W. McGovern and Marian Sigman, 'Continuity and Change from Early Childhood to Adolescence in Autism', *Journal of Child Psychology and Psychiatry* 46 (2005): 401-408.

[45] Bonnie Auyeung, Carrie Allison, Sally Wheerlwright, and Simon Baron-Cohen, 'Brief Report: Development of the Adolescent Empathy and Systemizing Quotients', *Journal of Autism and Developmental Disorders* 42 (2012): 2225-2235.

[46] Monica Mazza, Maria C. Pino, Melania Mariano, Daniela Tempesta, Michele Ferrara, Domenico De Berardis, Francesco Masedu, and Marco Valenti, 'Affective and Cognitive Empathy in Adolescents with Autism Spectrum Disorder', *Frontiers in Human Neuroscience* 8 (2014): Article 791.

[47] Scheeren et al., 'Empathic Responsiveness.'

[48] Ibid.

[49] Ibid.

[50] Ferrendelli, et al., 'Distinct Perceptions of Social Functioning'; Barbara F.C. van Heijst, 'Quality of Life in Autism Across the Lifespan' (M.A. thesis, University of Amsterdam, 2013).

[51] Ferrendelli, et al., 'Distinct Perceptions of Social Functioning'.

[52] van Heijst, 'Quality of Life in Autism Across the Lifespan'.

[53] Laugeson and Park, 'Using a CBT Approach'.

[54] Cotton, *Developing Empathy in Children and Youth.*; Ferrendelli, et al., 'Distinct Perceptions of Social Functioning'; van Heijst, 'Quality of Life in Autism Across the Lifespan'.

Bibliography

Allemand, Mathias, Andrea E. Steiger, and Helmut A. Fend. 'Empathy Development in Adolescents Predicts Social Competencies in Adulthood'. *Journal of Personality* 83 (2015): 229-241.

American Psychiatric Association. *Diagnostic and Statistical Manual of Mental Disorders*. 2013.

Auyeung, Bonnie, Carrie Allison, Sally Wheerlwright, and Simon Baron-Cohen. 'Brief Report: Development of the Adolescent Empathy and Systemizing Quotients'. *Journal of Autism and Developmental Disorders* 42 (2012): 2225-2235.

Baillie, Leslie, Eileen Sills, Deborah Parker, Nicola Thomas, Mala Karasu, and Nicola Crichton. 'The Use of an Ethnodrama with Healthcare Staff to Prompt Empathy for People with Dementia'. *Encountering Empathy: Interrogating the Past, Envisioning the Future*, edited by Veronica Wain and Paulus Pimomo, 99-110. Oxford: Inter-Disciplinary Press, 2015.

Baron-Cohen, Simon, Alan M. Leslie, and Uta Frith. 'Does the Autistic Child have a Theory of Mind?' *Cognition* 21 (1985): 37-46.

Cotton, Kathleen. *Developing Empathy in Children and Youth*. Northwest Regional Educational Laboratory, 2001.

de Waal, Frans B. M. 'Putting the Altruism Back into Altruism: The Evolution of Empathy'. *Annual Review of Psychology* 59 (2008): 279-300.

Decety, Jean, and Meghan Meyer. 'Emotion Resonance to Empathic Understanding: A Social Developmental Neuro-Science Account'. *Development and Psychology* 20 (2008): 1053-1080.

Eisenberg, Nancy, Ivanna K. Guthrie, Bridget C. Murphy, Stephanie A. Shepard, Amanda Cumberland, and Gustavo Carlo. 'Consistency and Development of Prosocial Dispositions: A Longitudinal Study'. *Child Development* 70 (1999): 1360-1372.

Ferrendelli, Crystal, Jessica Hopkins, Cecilia Costa, and Elizabeth Laugeson. 'Distinct Perceptions of Social Functioning and Treatment Outcome Across Parents and Adolescents Following the UCLA PEERS Intervention [Research Poster]'. California: Semel Institute, UCLA, 2014.

Greenberg, Leslie S., Jeanne C. Watson, Robert Elliot, and Arthur C. Bohart. 'Empathy'. *Psychotherapy* 38 (2001): 380-384.

Kaukiainen, Ari, Kaj Bjorkvist, Kirsti Lagerspetz, Karin Osterman, Christina Salmivalli, Sari Rothberg. 'The Relationships between Social Intelligence Empathy and Three Types of Aggression'. *Aggressive Behavior* 25 (1999): 81-89.

Kohut, Heinz. *How Does Analysis Cure?* Chicago: The University Press, 1984.

Kulka, Raanan. 'How Does Analysis Cure?'. *Between Tragedy and Compassion*, edited by Heinz Kohut. Tel Aviv, Israel: Am Oved Pub. Ltd., 2005.

Laugeson, Elizabeth A., and Mi N. Park. 'Using a CBT Approach to Teach Social Skills to Adolescents with Autism Spectrum Disorder and Other Social Challenges: The PEERS Method', *Journal of Ratio-Emotional Cognitive-Behavioral Therapy* 32 (2014): 84-97.

Lazuras, Lambros, Jacek Pyzalski, Vassilis Barkoukis, and Haralambos Tsorbatzoudis. 'Empathy and Moral Disengagement in Adolescent Cyberbullying: Implications for Educational Intervention and Pedagogical Practice'. *Studia Edukacyjne* 23 (2012): 57-69.

Mazza, Monica, Maria C. Pino, Melania Mariano, Daniela Tempesta, Michele Ferrara and Domenico De Berardis. 'Affective and Cognitive Empathy in Adolescents with Autism Spectrum Disorder'. *Frontiers in Human Neuroscience* 8 (2014): Article 791.

McDonald, Nicole M., and Daniel S. Messinger. *The Development of Empathy: How, When, and Why* (2009), Viewed on 15 April 2016. http://www.psy.miami.edu/faculty/dmessinger/c_c/rsrcs/rdgs/emot/McDonald-Messinger_Empathy%20Development.pdf.

McGovern, Corina W., and Marian Sigman. 'Continuity and Change from Early Childhood to Adolescence in Autism'. *Journal of Child Psychology and Psychiatry* 46 (2005): 401-408.

Mostovicz, Isaac E. , Nada K. Kakabadse, and Andrew P. Kakabadse. 'A Dynamic Theory of Leadership Development'. *Leadership & Organizational Development Journal* 30 (2009): 563-576.

Nelems, Rebeccah. 'The Horizons of Empathic Experience'. *Encountering Empathy: Interrogating the Past, Envisioning the Future*, edited by Veronica Wain and Paulus Pimomo, 165-176. Oxford: Inter-Disciplinary Press, 2015.

Scheeren, Anke M., Hans M. Koot, Peter C. Mundy, Larissa Mous, and Sander Begeer. 'Empathic Responsiveness of Children and Adolescents with High-Functioning Autism Spectrum Disorder'. *Autism Research* 6 (2013): 362-271.

Shamay-Tsoory, Simone G. 'The Neural Bases for Empathy'. *Neuroscience* 17 (2011): 18-24.

Tyink, Scott. *Teaching Empathy to Young Adolescents*. Origins-Online: The Origins Program, 2008.

van Heijst, Barbara F.C. 'Quality of Life in Autism Across the Lifespan'. M.A. thesis, University of Amsterdam, 2013.

Wain, Veronica. 'Empathy with the Enemy: Can the Intellectually Gifted Experience Empathy with the Intellectually Impaired?' *Encountering Empathy: Interrogating the Past, Envisioning the Future*, edited by Veronica Wain and Paulus Pimomo, 111-120. Oxford: Inter-Disciplinary Press, 2015.

Wójcik, Malgorzata. 'The Impact of Empathy on Ethnic Prejudice: Anti-Prejudice Intervention in School Setting'. Paper presented at the First Global Conference on Empathy, Prague, Czech Republic, 7-9 November 2014.

Nurit Sahar is an educational psychologist, serving as the Director of the North Jerusalem unit for Psycho-educational Services at the Jerusalem municipality. She runs a private practice, working with children, adolescents and their parents, focusing on cognitive-behavioural, self and narrative psychotherapy.

Part III

Exploring Empathy in the Media, Arts and Culture

Empathic New(s) Orientations in Narratives about Sexuality

LJ (Nic) Theo

Abstract

Journalists writing anti-homophobic news articles often do not recognise how their narrative structures might inadvertently fail to encourage an empathic engagement of readers, who then persist in their pre-existing homophobic biases. This is because journalists use a semiotically subjectivised language which does not convince readers to engage emotionally with real people in a real world. This engagement takes place through a semantic (and therefore emotional) distanciation of readers from interviewees subjected to homophobia, and a concomitant focus on the narrator, whose voice becomes the consciousness with whom the reader engages. Instead of encouraging empathic engagement, the narrative structures serve merely to rhetorically engage with readers' cognition, in terms of a (identity) politics of anti-homophobic discourses to which such readers already do not subscribe. In order to obviate this, journalists should incorporate narrative frames of (empathic) engagement that represent people beyond the identity-based categories of 'the homosexual,' thereby giving them voice as complex individuals. A more compelling metatheoretical framework for writing news about sexuality lies in complex notions of 'queerness,' which enables a journalist to act as both agent of socio-political critique and as pedagogue. This paradigm is consonant with narrative construction paradigms of Russian Formalism, via notions of empathy as orientational.

Key Words: Semiotics, narratology, journalism, news, sexual orientation, gay, queer, identity politics.

*****

> [A]ll quotation, from direct to indirect, is a re-voicing. To quote someone is always to re-voice previous speech at some temporal distance from its original utterance.[1]

1. Introduction

As most news-aware people probably know, the authorities of Uganda continue to aggressively denounce homosexuals, whom they claim destabilise a purportedly coherent (Christian) national morality.[2] Such simplistic religious rhetoric forms part of the political landscape in many sub-Saharan African countries, where politicians, the right-wing press and other leaders regularly whip up homophobia.

South Africa is not immune to this public discourse. For example, Jon Qwelane, who (ironically and unfortunately) was subsequently appointed the country's ambassador to Uganda, publicly voiced his opinion in crystal-clear

© KONINKLIJKE BRILL NV, LEIDEN, 2018 | DOI 10.1163/9789004360846_008

terms: 'There could be a few things I could take issue with Zimbabwean President Robert Mugabe (sic), but his unflinching and unapologetic stance over homosexuals is definitely not among those.'[3] Qwelane damns the move amongst churches to accept homosexuals and ordain women, and likens homosexuality to bestiality, hoping that

> some day a bunch of politicians with their heads affixed firmly to their necks will muster the balls to re-write the constitution of this country, to excise those sections which give license to men "marrying" other men, and ditto to women.[4]

Fortunately, the liberal constitution promises protection on the basis of sexual orientation – a cover that sadly remains wholly imperative in the context of persistent homophobic discrimination and violent sexuality-based hate crimes that serve as evidence of a deeply conservative and homophobic society.[5]

In furtherance of the anti-homophobic agenda, and in their watchdog role as the 'Fourth Estate,' the mainstream South African news media periodically publish articles by way of response to discrimination.[6] One such example is Skosana and Moyo's 2014 *Mail and Guardian* article entitled 'Double Stigma Leaves Gay Men with Little Hope,' which calls attention to homophobia in the public health system, and decries '[s]tereotyping [that] prevents men who sleep with other men from accessing proper treatment and prevention of HIV infection.'[7]

Unfortunately, however, it seems unlikely that such articles will, on balance, shift prevailing homophobic attitudes. As research by Zillmann and Knobloch indicates, news readers seem to display 'consistently greater enjoyment after news revelations of detrimental happenings to action groups toward whom negative affective dispositions were held than to such groups when met with favorable dispositions.'[8] There thus appears to be a correlation between the affective dispositions of audiences towards news items and those audiences' pre-existing notions of the 'deservingness' of the good or bad fortunes of those people around whom the reports revolve. As will be discussed later, these people are thereby linguistically conceived as objects whose agency is attenuated, rather than as autonomous subjects who are narratorially imbued with choices. This implies that although Skosana and Moyo are perhaps mostly preaching to the converted (the largely liberal readership of the *South African Mail and Guardian*), their readers who are already homophobic are likely to feel that those subjected to institutionalized homophobia within the South African health care system in some way deserve it.

This begs the question: how can journalists who write to an unabashedly anti-homophobic agenda circumvent and/or disarm readers' pre-existing biases? The immediate choice might be to proffer more explicitly political rhetoric. However, Zillmann and Knobloch's research implies that this is a fool's errand. Instead, through a close inspection of their research, an alternative and potentially more effective solution emerges, which is implicit in their methodological research paradigm which addresses how media affects readers.

2. Unpacking (In)Appropriate Research Methodologies

Much contemporary inquiry on audiences explores the effects of media on groups, rather than individuals, through socio-political research paradigms such as Framing, Agenda Setting and Priming theories.[9] These frameworks are relevant to those driving changes on a macro or systemic level, whose activities in political and legal administration are consonant with what Bernstein refers to as 'political goals': the achievement of policy change and legal reform.[10]

Skosana and Moyo's article is partly consistent with such socio-political research paradigms and their goals, in so far as it implicitly exhorts the administrators of South Africa's public health system to intercede and prevent/curtail homophobic discrimination. However, within the same article, the journalists seem to prioritise a more complex and bigger task: to address the underlying opinions that drive homophobia. They do this by attempting to personalise the debate, focusing on the effects of homophobia on named and identified individuals, rather than on the legalities of the public health service administration that allows/condones institutionalised homophobia.

Applying questions about the effects of articles such as theirs on readers is therefore a more complex task, since two distinct kinds of discourse are at play, which reference two very different research paradigms and strains of thought: one is focused on the (macro-) social level, while the other is focused on the (micro-) interpersonal level. However, paradigms focused on the (macro-) social level often fail to take account of how people relate to others on the (micro-) interpersonal level. On this latter level, complex individuals interact through subjectively-conceived meanings based on experiential orientations lodged in their bodies as vehicles through which they apprehend and comprehend the phenomenal world - where objectivity and subjectivity meet.[11] Macro-focused paradigms therefore generally reveal little about how subjective feelings and opinions inform people's behaviour.

In contrast, research that focuses on phenomenologically-conceived subjectivities enriches an understanding of social processes, by exploring how opinions and decisions are built and maintained by individuals-in-society. Such research is almost by definition complex, cross- and inter-disciplinary in its reliance on psychology, sociology, anthropology, political science and a host of other epistemological resources – consonant with what Bernstein refers to as 'cultural (or social change) goals.'[12]

Based in psychology, Zillmann and Knobloch's article is one such example of a more subjectively-oriented research enterprise which, through multiple points of contact with the complexity of social practice, seeks to reveal intersections between inner and outer worlds.[13] Their research, however, is limited in that it merely calls attention to an apparent correlation between pre-existing bias and the effects of media (or lack thereof) on readers. It does not explain the psychological or interpersonal mechanisms by which this occurs. Nor does it address how or why attempts to shift paradigms for a socially developmental purpose might fail. In the present instance, it does not illuminate why homophobic readers may not feel compelled to relinquish their pre-existing negative biases when reading articles such as Skosana and Moyo's revelations of discrimination in the public health system.

This lacuna implies that exploring media messages is insufficient if it fails to deal with questions of how instances of media engage simulacra of real-world relationships between writer and (individual) reader. These real-world relationships hinge on individual readers' prior experiences of interpersonal communications, a large proportion of which is based on non-verbal communication elements, such as body language or facial expression.[14]

By recalling that stories are not to be understood outside of the experiential relationship between reader, message and writer, and thereby calling on phenomenological conceptions of how mass media communications affect individuals rather than groups, it becomes clear that the semiotics by which meaning is conveyed is an important part of the equation, and must form part of the exploration.[15] In mass media theory a necessary linkage between the intended message and the form that it takes is well-established, as articulated by Marshall McLuhan's famous dictum that 'the medium is the message.'[16] In terms of this notion, it is clear that research into the complex interplays between intended message (for example how devastating homophobia is) and the semiotic construction of this message can better reveal the effects of (anti-homophobic) messages on audiences as a collective. Such research can also shed light on how communication architectures can confound or be mobilised to challenge discriminatory opinions within broader society, through focusing on how mass media engages with individuals rather than with groups.

In gender- and sexuality-focused research, semiotic explorations are not new, and often take the form of discourse analyses.[17] However, these tend to rely on a socio-linguistic teasing out of the speech patterns of sexual minorities. Despite best intentions this can result in a problematic specularising of marginalised people, rather than a treatment as complex individuals with their own polyvocalities. In any case, such methods are not relevant to questions of how journalists, as those with some element of discursive power, purport to 'speak for' those marginalised or discriminated against because of their sexuality. Research approaching such questions is scarce, and there remains a paucity of research exploring the semiotic mechanisms engaged in journalistic narrations.

The re-orientation of the research in this complex and subjectivity-oriented direction productively turns the methodological spotlight away from the specularised minorities and towards the mediating voices. It also implicitly breaches two gaps that often remain inherent in discipline-specific explorations. The first is the historically sedimented distinction between (sexual) political studies and (non-discourse-based) psychology, which is helpfully complicated by three main questions:

> First, how is sexuality shaped, how is it articulated with economic, social, and political structures, and how, in a phrase, has it been invented? Second, how has the domain of sexuality achieved such a critical organizing and symbolic significance in … culture, and why do we think it is so important? Third, … how is sex gendered and made hierarchical, and what is the relationship between sex and power?[18]

The second is the gap between research on cognition and that on text - a gap that is narrowed by the revelation of 'the construction of meaning in the interplay between textual features and their reception,' and 'the crucial role of the reader in the process of making sense of black marks on white pages.'[19]

3. A Deeper (Semiotic) Look at Narrative Form

Narratology has historically primarily been applied to fiction, the narratives of which are generally considered to be constituted at minimum by a series of causally linked events in a linear time sequence. On the face of it, news is not subject to the same kind of scrutiny, since, as non-fiction, it is not always constructed in the same way: it often represents events in non-linear ways and/or without necessarily clear causative linkages or conclusions. As a result, semiotic explorations of journalism, which rely on simple styles and techniques of reporting actuality, require particularly considered research methodologies appropriate to the research outcome sought.[20]

A more accommodating framework is Genette's rendition of narrative, which does not rely on necessary causal linkages for an utterance to qualify as a narrative. Additionally, a narrative for Genette includes any statement of an action or event that *implies* (though not necessarily in a linear or causal fashion) a transformation or transition in state over time.[21] Such a paradigm conceives of three parts of narrative reality in a text: story (the chronological order of events that the narrative contains or implies), narrative (the text itself), and narrating (the act of producing a text).

I will discuss how, viewed through this paradigm, journalistic narratives (including those such as Skosana and Moyo's) are not the objective accounts of the world they aspire to be in terms of the professional standards of writing which prioritise narrative modes that respect impartiality, accuracy and balance. Instead, they are carriers of subtle messages that, through subjectivised narrations, encourage an inherent narratorial distance between readers and those who are the focus of the reports. This discourages readers from understanding marginalised sexual choices in terms beyond their own paradigms, instead of through an empathic lens that affords a complex cartography of subjectivities and human experience. In turn, this discourages the growth of potentially socially transformative paradigms.

A. Subjectivised News Narration and Pathos

In literary fiction, the subjectivities of characters are rendered through a combination of speech narration and a reporting of internal, subjective experiences, including perceptions, thoughts, and feelings. This so-called 'narratorial position' can be framed and/or understood in terms of an 'objective' ('third-person') narration, or a 'subjective' ('first person') narration.[22] The third-person narrator is either omniscient (free to describe all characters' thoughts, feelings and actions) or partial (only capable of reflecting the consciousness of selected characters), while the 'first-person' narrator can only express the subjective experiences of one character since he/she cannot enter the consciousness of anyone other than his/her own character.

In news journalism, however, there is no such range of possible narratorial options, since news reporting is an enterprise touted as exclusively non-fiction, in which professional standards of objectivity are pursued in the name of impartiality.[23] In linguistic-semiotic terms, journalists use both implicit and explicit rhetorical tools to make their stories seem accurate, truthful and verifiable.[24] These tools serve to render the voices of their interviewees through largely invisible narrations.[25] Written as if 'objective', these accounts use quote-based narratives that (inaccurately) imply that the writers have no vested interest in the content and ideologies they reflect, or are not themselves emotionally oriented, whether towards or against the interviewees.[26]

Contrary to their intentions of appearing authoritative and purely representational (rather than poetic or symbolic, as in literature), these narratives have an unintended effect of failing to create a personal rapport between readers and interviewees, thereby countervailing any potential attempts at shifting readers' pre-existing homophobia.

This effect is achieved through forms of narration that discourage (socially transformative) notions of empathy in readers. Unfortunately, however, despite journalists' intentions of maintaining professional distance from the interviewee in order to convey impartiality, the mechanisms of journalistic quotation instead serve to entrench a greater or lesser pre-existing narrative proximity to the interviewee: a 'feeling for' or 'feeling against,' to call on constructions of pathos on which I will elaborate later.[27] This semiotic placement of the reader 'closer to' or 'further from' the interviewee takes no account of an allied but different notion: orientation towards or away from the interviewee, in a side-to-side movement that acknowledges both interviewees' and readers' choices, worldviews and perspectives.

In other words, through such mechanisms, readers are drawn into the life of the interviewee to a greater or lesser extent, but never close enough to hear the interviewee's unmediated voice, as if the interviewee were a real person 'in front of' them. The reader is also not presented with a narration that acknowledges the reader's own opinions and feelings: the narration is always oriented towards the interviewee in the way mandated or at least approved by the narrator.[28] I argue that, using a phenomenological lens, this is a problem because it does not encourage the reader to encounter the interviewee in a virtual relationship of mutuality, and discourages a socially transformative experience of empathy that could transcend the boundaries of the narration. Instead, it invites a relationship between reader and interviewee that is either based on sympathy (which homophobic readers refuse), or possibly a reverse-empathy (where homophobic readers empathise with their emotional counterparts - other homophobes). This all takes place through the news writing language, which distances readers from those reported on.

B. Subjectivised Language and Narratorial Distance

Journalistic quotation is part of a series of speech-act signs which reveal symbols that, in terms of subjectification theory, entrench a semiotic positioning of reporters in relation to the people about whom they report.[29] Such speech-act signs indicate the extent to which the journalist inserts his/her own viewpoint by means of imputed perspectives on the part of interviewees.[30] The more 'subjectivised' the language, the more the journalist's voice (and therefore own subjectivity) is present in the narration and, as I argue, the less the voice and consciousness of the interviewee appears, with concomitant implications that centre on the rendering of those about whom reports revolve as 'interviewees', semiotically-marked objects whose choices are mediated by both social forces and the journalist reporting on them, rather than autonomous subjects with their own agency.

These speech-acts are made through three types of reported speech: 'neutral language,' 'non-subjectivised but evaluative language,' and 'subjectivised re-assertions.'[31]

Neutral language lacks 'overt evaluation of what someone else said,' and is often constituted by value-neutral factual statements with little in the way of adjectival or adverbial elaboration, and into which is incorporated direct quotation.[32] It nevertheless almost always incorporates *covert* evaluation in the form of a distanciating directive to readers. In Skosana and Moyo's article, there is liberal use of direct quotes, such as '"I put on a golf T-shirt and black pants and avoided the wig and make-up",' and '"I didn't want to attract unnecessary attention to myself".' The apparently value-neutral language of '[t]hat day, he had made a deliberate effort to "look normal" and abandoned his usual flamboyant attire,' which is spoken through the voice of the journalist, indicates a relatively wide narrative distance between the journalist and the interviewee. However, although the voice of the interviewee is accommodated in the narration by means of direct quotes, it is nevertheless mediated through the journalists' narration, which references phrases that (homophobic) others might use, such as 'over the top' attire, and the subtler, yet still marginally value-laden if not overtly judgmental term 'flamboyant.' When taken in the broader context of the rest of the article and the liberal political agenda of the publication, this seemingly neutral language is not as neutral as it appears: by positioning the narrator in relation to both the interviewee and reader, it implies that homophobic judgement is inappropriate, whilst nevertheless calling attention to what is commonly perceived as an essential focus for gay men: cross-gender clothing.

Non-subjectivised but evaluative language is 'in quotational terms, relatively reporter-neutral,' and is often rendered by means of free-indirect quotation.[33] 'Cele sits at a table in a deserted, dimly lit restaurant in Durban's Gateway mall' might appear to be neutral and free of an obvious narratorial presence. However, the mood-inflected description of a deserted, dimly-lit space reflects a more subjectivised style of writing, one which intones a sense of solitude and isolation that the journalists aim to associate with the interviewee, but which is not explicitly present in Cele's own words that follow: 'He had delayed seeking medical attention for two weeks until the "terrible pain in my anus became unbearable" because he was afraid of the treatment he would receive at a clinic.' This example presents the interviewee in terms that construct a closer narratorial relationship between the journalist and the interviewee. Like the previous example, the interviewee's voice is mediated in a way that does not represent him negatively, but nevertheless creates associative connections between his sexuality and an emotional isolation.

Subjectivised language is highly interpretive, and results in semantically transformed language primarily by means of indirect quotation. For example, Skosana and Moyo explicitly editorialise about the interviewee's intentions, in narrating the voice of Sphelele Msimango, an outreach worker: 'One of his clients, he says, was reduced to tears at a government clinic when he told nurses that he was gay and was experiencing pain, like Cele, in his anus.' This provides a less obvious, but nevertheless notable distance between the narrator and the interviewee while at the same time failing to reflect the voice of Cele directly. In this instance Cele's voice is twice mediated: once by Msimango and a second time by the narrator, which attributes greater legitimacy or authority to Msimango than to Cele, which has the effect of further distancing him from the reader.

This three-tiered narratorial distance is constructed with the best of intentions: to counter homophobia by reporting in terms of professional standards of 'objectivity' and 'impartiality,' since journalists are expected to recount facts as if they are objectively determinable. The journalist cannot be seen to be narrating as if from the 'inside' of the story since such a close narration might be seen as a technique of fiction, and would not be taken seriously.

These aspirations are, however, semiotically misdirected, since no narrative can objectively imitate a purported reality: 'Narrative does not "represent" a (real or fictive) story, it recounts it – that is, it signifies it by means of language [...]. There is no place for imitation in narrative [...].'[34] This means that all narrative representation, including news writing, is one or other form of the telling of something (*diegesis*). This in turn implies that the narrator is always, without exception, intimately involved in the narration, and is the active constructor of new meaning rather than the objective and impartial purveyor of some existing meaning (*mimesis*) that can be 'found' somewhere 'out there.'

The original circumstance/thing that the narrator seeks to 'mime' cannot be copied. Instead, the narrator engages in a 'two-step compositional process, using language that, from a linguistic/semiotic perspective, constructs verbal (i.e. linguistic) signs interpretable as the immediate 'voice' or the more distant 're-voicing' of what someone else supposedly said.'[35]

To narrate is therefore to render a new set of meanings which serve to represent those being written about as less than entirely autonomous subjects, whose voices are at worst (as in Qwelane's article) completely redacted, and at best (as in Skosana and Moyo's article), somewhat abstracted. Interviewees are always linguistically mediated, whether invisibly (through subjectivised narration reflected through direct quotations), covertly (through subjectivised re-assertions reflected by indirect quotations), or overtly (through non-subjectivised but evaluative assertions reflected by editorialising statements). In the version of narrative construction in which journalists render purportedly objective yet inherently subjectivising narrative mediation, interviewees are denied the narrative agency to represent themselves, and thereby are denied full authority over their own voices by being represented at arm's length, as 'out there,' and as relatively unapproachable and unknowable.

C. Subjectivised Narration = (Identity-Based) Narrative Orientation

The effect on readers of this subjectivisation and linguistic mediation is, I suggest, a product of more than merely an interesting but relatively unimportant linguistic distanciation of the reader from the interviewee. Instead, the subjective perceptions of the reader render such a narration as a tool to be used by the reader to re-produce for him/herself his/her expectations of what counts as the 'usual' (and therefore morally assessable) behaviour of the interviewee and people like him/her. In this way, the semiotic placement of the reader closer to or further away from the interviewee is influenced by the reader's prior homophobic bias. In other words, the important element is not merely that journalists write in ways that have a distanciating effect, but that readers' norms/paradigms are reinforced through this distanciation. Because of this, they are not invited or even able to encounter alterity; readers' positionality in relation to the interviewee is thus predetermined by their worldviews, which remain wholly intact.

In terms of Zillmann and Knobloch's argument, non-homophobic readers are likely to agree with the anti-homophobic tenor of the article, while homophobic readers are likely to disagree with it. This is because, if read in a phenomenological way, the reader is engaging as a virtual member of the conversation not with the interviewee, but with the journalist as mediator. As if speaking to a prisoner through a prison warder, the reader is separated from any direct, unmediated access to the interviewee by the journalist's representation, which thereby acts as an obstruction rather than a channel to personal connection, as is intended.

By denying direct, unmediated access to the interviewee, this obstruction serves merely to endorse the reader's predilections towards or against the interviewee, through engaging their pre-existing assumptions as to the characteristics of the interviewee: if the reader is homophobic, he/she will assume (on the basis of the limited interaction the narrative provides with the interviewee, *qua* 'homosexual') that the interviewee is inherently bad or at fault. And, of course, vice versa for an already-anti-homophobic reader.

This takes place by means of the assumptions on which the writing lies: explicitly categorised constructions of the interviewee, described in identity-based terms, as 'homosexual' *qua* separate species.[36] Bolstered by headlines such as 'Double stigma leaves *gay men* with little hope' (my italics), journalists, by means of a narratorial mirror, reflect the pre-existing biases of (homophobic) readers who respond to terms that are deeply lodged in the liberalist ideals which are foundational to the modern moral, political, and legal vocabulary.[37]

Such terms bring with them presumptions of an essential human nature that transcends specific local historical and social differences, and is projected both backwards and forwards in time.[38] The terms imply a singular identity and 'truth' to experience which, when read by the already-homophobic reader, confirms the 'homosexual' interviewee as having, in some unexplained deterministic way, a pre-defined lifestyle or set of characteristics that characterise a fixed, binarised, unitary and coherent sexual identity,[39] which is '...full of implications, however confusing, for even the ostensibly least sexual aspects of personal existence.'[40]

Implicit in the subjectivising narrative, these terms constitute an appropriate basis for claiming political rights, such as calls for medical authorities to address homophobic practices in public health systems. Since rights are collective things, they can only be granted or refused to groups of people who share categorically distinguishable identities.

However, such terms are wholly inadequate in efforts to convince readers to relinquish homophobic beliefs, since they call on a social paradigm that, although foundational to the legal system, is one to which homophobes do not subscribe: one which prioritises commitment to individual over collective claims, a commitment to equality motivated by rational reform and progress,[41] and the right to privacy over public morality.[42] Unfortunately, such a paradigm is not morally compelling to Western conservatives (who very often subsume the rights of the individual under a presumed transcendental set of rules, often based in religion) or African traditionalists like Qwelane who often firmly believe that cultural precedent and collective decision-making under a (traditional) community leader should supersede individual (sexual identity) rights. Such conservatives and traditionalists expect the public to restrain their activities and stick to the social rules, and cannot accept any public rejection of normative sex roles and of the fundamental religious beliefs which are assumed to reside in non-normative sexuality.

D. Journalist/Interviewee Narrative Framing = Discouraging Empathy

Principled homophobes are unlikely to change their worldviews if faced with subjectivised narrations whose persuasive efforts against homophobia rely on essentialising identity-politics-based categorical labels for sexuality. This is because such representations engage the reader primarily with the priorities, perspective and worldview of the journalist (an engagement which will fail where the reader is already homophobic), rather than the interviewee.

This framing fails to consider how news writing is a multi-directional communication process – a virtual conversation between reader, narrator and interviewee. It thus fails to take account of the reader's worldviews, and therefore also to encourage an emotive representation of the interviewee in terms that enable the (homophobic) reader to (semiotically) become part of the discussion. While this narrative framing may encourage a cognitive-and-affective response in the already-not-homophobic reader (whose pre-existing worldview the narration inherently reflects), it encourages merely a cognitive response in the already-homophobic reader who has no vested interest in entering the (virtual) discussion in any emotional way.

The semiotic representation positions the (homophobic) reader outside of a place of knowing anything more of the interviewee than that their label is that of a mere cipher – 'a homosexual' who, in terms of the reader's pre-existing biases, is automatically assumed to behave 'like all homosexuals' in some essentialist and determinist way. It orients and invites the reader to turn towards the journalist and away from the interviewee, whose subjectivity is obfuscated by the inherently overshadowing narrative mediation.

This notion of semiotic emotional positioning is consonant with Steve Larocco's compelling argument of pathos as an orientation rather than an emotion.[43] Viewed in this way, the narration discourages the homophobic reader from assuming an empathic orientation towards the interviewee, an empathy which, according to Coplan, involves (cognitive and affective) caring about another individual and feeling *with* them, while imaginatively sharing in their experience or imagining the world from their perspective.[44] Instead of semiotically orienting readers towards the lived experience of the interviewee, and thereby engaging a sense that the interviewee is someone like the reader, the narration serves to orient the reader towards the journalist who, because of their obviously anti-homophobic message, is perceived to be someone 'unlike' the (homophobic) reader. In this way, the reader is encouraged to engage with the journalist's point and implicitly anti-homophobic agenda (rather than the interviewee's person), with which the reader has already formed an in-principle disagreement.

A fertile space for further research is the psycho-social mechanisms by which this process might take place subjectively, including whether such processes are indeed forms of empathy. In this exploration Gavin Fairbairn's consideration of the three problems with empathy are instructive: viewing empathy in exclusively positive terms while not acknowledging its negative potential, constructing empathy as no more than a process of imagining being in someone else's shoes, and confusing empathy with sympathy.[45]

Once these concerns are better addressed, it might emerge that the semiotic processes serve to encourage a kind of reverse empathy, whereby the homophobic reader is semiotically encouraged to feel empathy for the homophobes mentioned in the article rather than for the interviewee subjected to homophobia, in ways akin to how Nelems, in this volume, discusses 'passive empathy' based on fear for the 'Self' instead of care for the 'Other.'[46]

This 'passive empathy' can, in terms of Nelems argument,[47] serve as a way of understanding what Coplan phrases as sympathy, which

> involves caring about another individual – feeling *for* another. It does not as such involve sharing the other's experience. While sympathetic emotions are typically triggered by and related to a target individual's emotions, they need not be qualitatively the same.[48]

If engaged on sympathetic ground, the homophobic reader might therefore semiotically be discouraged from feeling pity or sympathy for the interviewee, and thereby be discouraged from engaging something like what Eisenberg speaks of as 'altruistic motivation.'[49] This means that they may 'feel against' the interviewee and be inclined to feel that homophobia is justified and that they should actively avoid assisting or contributing to the well-being of those subjected to homophobia. Readers with a pre-existing positive bias, correlatively, would be semiotically encouraged to 'feel for' the interviewee, and feel encouraged to engage altruism.

Either way, the narrative mediation results in a linguistic failure to engage readers in a sense of sharing in the complexity of the real lives of the interviewees *qua* complex humans worthy of either sympathy, empathy or merely respect. This, in turn, implies the resultant effect described in terms of Zillmann and Knobloch's logic, and therefore to the resultant findings that

...all stories featuring victimization were markedly more enjoyed by persons harboring resentment toward the victims than by those liking them. This relationship reversed for reports of benefaction. Those with negative dispositions toward the recipients of good fortunes found it more difficult than the more positively inclined ones to enjoy the outcome.[50]

4. Beyond Subjectivised Reporting: Encouraging Empathy to Counter Pre-Existing Homophobia

There can be no prescription for how, if at all, a journalist might actively challenge or disengage a reader from their pre-existing homophobia. Clearly the arguments and exhortations of generations of sexual activists have not done away with it. Perhaps journalists can only hope to avoid unintentional complicity with homophobia by refusing to engage some of the (semiotic) bases for it in the construction of their narratives.

A. Empathy and Non-Essentialist and Non-Determinist Discourses

Dealing with the distanciating effects of the subjectivising language built into news narrations must entail a process of engaging semiotic practices that attempt to connect with readers both cognitively and affectively, thereby enabling them to simulate experiences of interviewees (rather than of other homophobes), while retaining their own thoughts, emotions and desires (rather than merely engaging sympathetic altruism). This, in turn, will potentially allow readers to engage with the objects of homophobia as being similar-and-equal to themselves, and yet at the same time individual-and-different, by means of a complex imaginative process which entails taking up the subjective perspective of the people being reported on.

This kind of approach is akin to Coplan's view of empathic engagement, which she elaborates in the context of fiction but is equally apposite for news.[51] In terms of this notion, readers are caused to 'become deeply involved in characters' experiences without relinquishing their separate identities,' thereby having 'a wide range of psychological experiences during engagement with a single narrative,' and neither being 'forced to mirror exactly the characters' experiences nor forced to observe the characters' experiences from the outside.'[52]

By engaging, on a semiotic level, more complex notions of narrative construction which interact with the shared humanity of those subjected to homophobia, journalists can implicitly acknowledge narration as diegetic, rather than mimetic,[53] and encourage a sense of 'empathic engagement' amongst readers who would 'feel with' those subjected to homophobia.[54]

This kind of engagement seems consonant with notions of how reading fiction influences empathy,[55] and in the context of news reporting, could enable readers to simulate the news object's experience of homophobia, while at the same time retaining their own thoughts, emotions and desires. It would enable them to engage in *both* cognition *and* emotion, whilst retaining a separate sense of self as distinct from that of the other, whilst incorporating imaginative experience of the circumstances of that other.[56]

This complex process of self-other differentiation would in principle enable the reader 'to observe the boundaries of the other as well as his- or herself, and to respect the singularity of the other's experience as well as his or her own.'[57] This might also enable the reader to by-pass the narrator as intermediary and orient him/herself towards the interviewee, allowing the reader to identify with the whole-life experiences of the interviewee as someone whose life (including sexual preferences) is complex and valuable.

B. Semiotic Narration of Subjectivities: 'Queer Locations'

The first step to a more socially transformative paradigm requires a recognition that gender and sexual categories are overly pragmatic and simplistic ways of differentiating between people. 'Homosexuality' cannot be pinned down in any useful way, and, as with 'heterosexuality,' is not unitary and coherent.[58]

Instead, sexuality (as with any identity) is constructed of a proposition adopted by individuals, one which suggests that each 'ought to take a particular identity as part of [their] script' and to 'take this identity to project normatively into the future.'[59] Correlatively, others 'ought to assign social priority to facilitating one's living according to the resulting narrative unity of the various [competing] scripts' adopted as the constituent parts of a complex personality.[60] This implies that 'consciously claimed or denied identity is not simply or transparently congruent with sexuality.'[61] In this way *identity*, as 'a subject's more or less conscious allegiance to a particular social position,' and *identification*, as allowing for 'recognition and investigation of conflicting affiliations that may both structure and disrupt a person's claim to a particular identity' are different from each other.[62]

A clearly demarcated journalistic orientation towards sexuality as *identification* rather than *identity* will always be elusive. It is one thing to consider disruptions and inconsistencies, and to advise journalists to better reflect the complexity of subjective experience of interviewees, and with that their bodies, sexual acts and sexual objects, all of which mean different things to different people, even within the same sexual identity 'category.'[63] But how to overcome the pitfalls of the inherent subjectivizing discourses of journalistic practices is quite another.

However, to consider how difficult it might be to identify an alternative narrative paradigm might, paradoxically, be just the mechanism by which such an enterprise is begun: by taking the 'ought' propositions of both sexuality and journalistic practices, and constructing some guidelines for narration that focus on an 'ought not' proposition. This implies that news reports might adopt narrative forms which suggest that 'homosexuals' be *excluded* from what is 'proper' and socially acceptable, rather than *included* into the approved or disapproved discourses of either liberal rights or moralistic religio-conservative discourses. In other words, articles such as Skosana and Moyo's could find ways to narrate the lives of people subjected to homophobia in ways that allow for such lives to be validated through the mere fact of their presentation, and abstracted from consensus notions both of whether they are socially valuable or are morally objectionable. To engage this would require semiotic mechanisms with which to represent all lives as important, and thereby to avoid specularising some (e.g. 'homosexuals') as either extra worthy of support or of moralistic judgment. This would require a paradigm in which people are viewed in ways other than through the lenses of either politics or journalistic best-practices which currently duck and dive around notions of social acceptability of non-normative sexualities, either supporting or judging them.

A compelling starting-point for this lies in both Steve Larocco's and Rebeccah Nelems' notions of empathy as orientation rather than as content, that enables one to projectively feel beyond oneself.[64] This projection of the self beyond the self, which engages both cognition and affect, is curiously consonant with a view of sexual orientation that entails conceptions of the self and others that are neither essentialist nor determinist: 'queerness.' This view of sexuality enables a view of people not as 'sexual identities,' but as people who are (mutually) constructed 'in relation to' others, whether comfortably or abrasively.[65] But it also invites a caveat that such an exclusionary narrative proposition should call only on versions of Queer theories which open up the debate to possibilities for lifestyles and diversity, rather than merely dis-identifications with identities. Such strains of theory incorporate more than the reactionary 'ought-not' notions of 'queer' as merely another discrete identity in the 'LGBTI(Q)' discourses of sexual orientation, where 'transgender,' 'intersex' and 'queer' are labelled as somehow different to 'lesbian,' 'gay' and 'bisexual,' and in binary opposition to 'heterosexual.'

A complex phenomenological notion of orientational selves matches notions of sexualities that look beyond the binaries of gay/straight essentialist and determinist categorical injunctions, and towards notions of embodied people.[66] While not a new approach as a way out of the conundrum of representation, it is underutilised in questions of how to re-write the relationships between readers and those subjected to homophobia *qua* real people, within the paradigms of news writing that prioritises a restrictive semiotic adherence to notions of impartiality. However, re-orienting the relationship between reader (via narrator) and news object gives voice to those subjected to homophobia while enabling the writer to appear impartial in line with the professional expectations.[67]

This allows writers, in principle, to engage a narratorial voice that more accurately reflects the complexity of sexuality and identifications, without falling into the obvious diatribes of opposition-politics that are the current tools of journalists. Such strains, if thoughtfully invoked, combine in a dual function of both subversive reaction and pedagogical pro-action in the ways that RuPaul's Drag Race combines drag as subversive gender-challenging performance with contemporary reality-tv norms as a way to encourage the mainstreaming of non-normative lives.

a. Queerness as Subversive

Whereas 'gay identity' replicates the discourses of difference between heterosexual and homosexual, and therefore re-inscribes the idea of 'difference,' queerness is a 'parodic replication and resignification of heterosexual constructs within non-heterosexual frames.'[68] This parodying subverts expectations by shifting the frame of reference from the forward-looking 'ought' proposition of homo- or heterosexuality to an 'ought not' (reactive) proposition.[69] In other words, queerness parodies (hetero-)norms by denying the identity-based assumptions that people 'ought' to be 'heterosexual,' failing which they 'ought' to be 'homosexual.' This notion of queerness says that people aren't inescapably bound to being anything in particular, which in turn enables journalists to retreat from the historical, backward-looking bounds to notions of 'homosexuality'. In this version, queer semiotic representations in news reporting might act as 'a set of possibilities produced out of temporal and historical difference,' where the manipulation of time becomes a way of producing both 'bodies and relationalities,' or perhaps a porous and productive non-relationality.[70]

This implies that if certain strains of queer theory are used to ground a politics of (meta)linguistic choices for journalists, the linear and causational thinking of the 'ought' propositions can be manipulated to implicitly counter homophobia, through a revised view of the role of language in journalistic writing. Assumptions around time and space implicit in both the practices of journalism and identity politics could thereby be rephrased. Such a construction could acknowledge that there is no necessary causational link from now into the future between historic socio-cultural influences and people's (sexual) performances and self-identifications. As such, people could be represented at a deep level as choosing social performances moving forward in time, based both on the dominant discourses *and* on their experiences (rather than deterministically bound by essentialist characteristics). Such a narrative paradigm could serve to re-orient readers.

In the present example, journalists might refuse to represent non-normative sexualities through either setting out or implying a necessarily causal sequence of events between activities and their consequences as expected in mainstream narrative progression. They might be able to reflect the lives of people like Cele in ways that do not make explicit the expected correlation between the putative (morally unacceptable) lifestyle of 'the homosexual' and visits to a clinic for sexually transmitted disease, correlations which would not necessarily be made for others in the community attending a clinic for a pain in the anus.

b. Queerness as Pedagogy

This kind of off-centre rendition of both sexual identity and semiotic construction could also serve as a self-perpetuating pedagogy against homophobia, through its challenge to essentialist notions that 'homosexuals' are merely passive objects of discrimination, and through suggestion that these are instead, valid subjects who are powerful, active contributors to the world.

Such a queer pedagogy entails risking the self by engaging with multiple identifications (rather than identities), which implies, '[n]ot that anyone might be queer, but that something queer might happen to anyone.'[71] This is perhaps related to Nelems' conception of 'transformative' (as opposed to 'passive') empathy, which is based on a refusal to collapse the other into known categories in the acknowledgement and acceptance of the 'Other' as necessarily inscrutable and incomprehensible.[72] With the concomitant happiness to acknowledge and critically examine one's own perspectives, the 'Other's' specific worldviews and beliefs can be approached without fear. As a foundational precept for reporting on sexuality and in particular on homophobia, queerness engages this as possible through proffering 'a technique or a peisis which does not make the world familiar or comfortable ... but which defamiliarises, or makes strange, queer or even cruel what we had thought to be a world.'[73]

C. Queer (Orientational) Formalism

At the same time, however, such a queer pedagogic offering must come with the same caveat that Nelems, in this volume, offers in relation to the shaping of the empathic experience: it is not the pedagogy itself that changes the world, but rather 'the sociological worldview or phenomenological horizon within which student and teacher are immersed that establishes the parameters of their empathic experience.'[74]

Pertaining to journalism, this seems to imply that in order to serve as a (virtual) pedagogical agent of change, woolly political abstractions must be put aside in favour of pragmatic solutions to concrete circumstances. In the interests of professionalism, this in turn implies that the semiotic structures engaged for reporting must necessarily be both useful in terms of the social change desired and pragmatic in terms of how the world of news reporting actually functions – taking into account the authority bestowed upon the journalist. The post-structuralist, anti-identitarian, non-normative, stream-of-consciousness writing identified with some non-normative queer theory might be great for poetry and prose, but makes for poor news copy in the face of the demands of the global news machine. Journalism requires unusual approaches to a revised semiotics of narrative representation that moves beyond the mere subversion of dominant tropes. It requires mechanisms to both report facts and encourage a discourse of human interaction: the practices of friendship and relationships, the body and pleasure.[75]

Although by no means a formula for narration, the work of Russian Formalists seems to hold some promise in this regard.[76] Although often colloquially billed as a school of thinking, Formalism was instead 'a heterogeneous trend in Russian criticism, a cluster of ideas about literature rather than an organized school or method.'[77] Its loose foundations are attributed to a 'clear-cut departure from the literary-theoretical tradition in Russia,' rather than 'centripetal forces within Formalism itself.'[78] This implies that Formalism is not burdened with a dogmatic, peremptory set of instructions about the distinctions between 'good' and 'bad' form. Instead, (depending on the strain one attaches to), Formalist criticism has built into it a semiotically-oriented notion of narrative representation, which is particularly appropriate for journalistic writing given that 'the difference between literature and non-literature [is] to be sought not in the subject matter, i.e., the sphere of reality dealt with by the writer, but in the mode of presentation.'[79] At the same time, it relies on the disruption of language and representation in the way that James Joyce and surrealism challenged dominant ideologies, and therefore the economic and political (and, I suggest, the socio-cultural) relations which they secured.[80]

This somewhat paradoxical combination of structure and challenge is particularly relevant for journalistic practices, which themselves straddle the two contradictory functions. Firstly, they are all acts that formalize one or other representation of the world through the use of language. In terms of Genette's proposition, they are all *diegetic* not *mimetic.*[81] Secondly, in their provision of political commentary in their capacity as 'the Fourth Estate', they also serve as mechanisms of speaking 'truth to power.'

If explicitly calling on a complex constructionist framework, journalists can arguably both disrupt (or perhaps que(e)ry) socio-political continuities while focusing on representations of subjectivities that contribute to (anti-homophobic) social change that is consonant with postmodern emphases on 'fractured identities, multiple subjectivities, performance, and representations as markers for ever-shifting cultural formations and social practices.'[82]

This is possible if the connecting point between these two apparently incongruent notions of structure and anti-structure are related to one another by means of the confluences between Formalism's morphological construction[83] and Larocco's complex notion of empathic engagement[84], as well as Nelems' framing of transformative empathy.[85] Making these connections perhaps enables both structure and anti-structure to co-exist in (non)harmony by means of the intentional (phenomenological) placement of embodied human consciousness.

5. Conclusion: Beyond Sociology and Psychology; Towards Pragmatic Positional Representations of Subjectivities

Insisting on the inadequacy of 'identity' in journalistic and other formal mass media writing is one thing. Calling attention to the subversive, pedagogic associations of queer orientations is another. Journalism and queer theory seem to be at odds with one another, but a queer semiotics might not be so incongruent for the journalistic voicing of subjectivities, if this proposition is considered not as an opposite alternate, but instead a complex relational alternative-and-complement. This calls on arguments around the simultaneous need and opportunity for identity categories to be strategically used.[86]

As Butler notes,

> ...particular identities are being produced as contested zones within political discourse all the time, and this is being done in part by right-wing political forces.... [I]t would be perilous ... to claim or call for the surpassing of particular identities on the Left, since that would be to give over such identities to a reactionary constitution. In the face of the prospective silencing or erasure of gender, race or sexual minority identities by reactionary political forces, it is important to be able to articulate them, and to insist on these identities as sites of valuable cultural contest .... [I]t is imperative to assert identities, at the same time that it is crucial to interrogate the exclusionary operations by which they are constituted.[87]

Manifesting this kind of 'both-and' proposition through strategies to counter homophobia in news reporting enables journalists to utilise relatively pragmatic mechanisms to focus on what they deem important, through a choice of complex narratorial positioning that uses – rather than discards – form. Not so much by focusing on the words themselves in a mechanistic way, for example by refusing to use subjectivised narrations or assiduously avoiding 'gay' as a noun or adjective in a news headline. Rather, journalists can focus on the question of identity and subjectivity, the historic present (i.e. 'after Foucault,' where we are actors), and questions of ethics and values that underlie the specific narratorial/semiotic choices made.

This orientational complexity can be used pragmatically to counter homophobia in ways that transcend essentialist views of sexuality, not only in terms of the intended meanings of journalistic communications, but also in their diegeses. Journalists should re-consider their assumptions that writing objectively to reflect a purportedly representable world is semiotically possible as a way to reflect impartiality, or indeed helpful in countering homophobia. This assumption clearly serves readers' pre-existing biases, since it prevents them from empathetically engaging with the people being reported on.

A metatheoretically more coherent view is to look to queer sexual orientation as a foundation for the forms of journalistic writing that seek to engage an empathetic (cognitive and emotional) orientation on the part of readers, thereby engaging both the subversive and pedagogical potentialities of sexuality, news and emotion. By using this type of framework, journalists can make strategic choices about how to counter homophobia through the narration of subjectivities - practise which are implicit in the metanarratives of both queer theory and queer narratives.

Reporting through semiotically 'queer lenses' and engaging some of the tools implicit in Russian Formalist thinking opens up a more relational reading of the news *object* as a news *subject*, through enabling that subject to be represented in his/her complexity rather than through oppositional identity-politicking.

Notes

[1] Joseph C. Harry, 'Journalistic Quotation: Reported Speech in Newspapers from a Semiotic-Linguistic Perspective,' *Journalism* 15.8 (2014): 1041-1058, 1042.

[2] *Stephen Fry: Out There, episode 1*, dir. Stephen Fry. UK: BBC Productions, 2013. Uganda has passed the Uganda Anti-Homosexuality Act, 2014, which came into law in 2014 and prescribes life in prison for those convicted.

[3] John Qwelane, 'Call Me Names, but Gay Is NOT OK,' *The Sunday Sun*, South African Edition, July 20, 2008.

[4] Ibid.

[5] For more context see Ben Roberts and Vasu Reddy, 'Pride and Prejudice: Public Attitudes toward Homosexuality,' *HSRC Review* 6.4 (2008): 9-11; Marc Epprecht, *Hungochani: A History of a Dissident Sexuality in Southern Africa* (Quebec: McGill-Queen's University Press, 2004); Marc Epprecht, *Heterosexual Africa* (Ohio: Ohio University Press, Durban: University of Kwa-Zulu Natal Press, 2008).

[6] By which is meant a quasi-political watchdog role speaking truth to institutional power. See Julianne Schultz, *Reviving the Fourth Estate: Democracy, Accountability and the Media* (Cambridge: Cambridge University Press, 1998); Matthew Gentzkow, Edward L. Glaeser and Claudia Goldin, 'The Rise of the Fourth Estate: How Newspapers became Informative and Why It Mattered,' *Corruption and Reform: Lessons from America's Economic History* (Chicago: University of Chicago Press, 2006), 187-230.

[7] Ina Skosana and Thandeka Moyo, 'Double Stigma Leaves Gay Men with Little Hope,' *Mail and Guardian Online*, July 31, 2014. Viewed on 15 April 2016, http://mg.co.za/article/2014-07-31-double-stigma-leaves-gay-men-with-little-hope.

[8] Dolf Zillmann and Silvia Knobloch, 'Emotional Reactions to Narratives about the Fortunes of Personae in the News Theatre,' *Poetics* 29 (2001): 189-206.

[9] Dietram A. Scheufele and David Tewksbury, 'Framing, Agenda Setting, and Priming: The Evolution of Three Media Effects Models,' *Journal of Communication* 57 (2007): 9.

[10] Mary Bernstein, 'Identities and Politics: Toward a Historical Understanding of the Lesbian and Gay Movement,' *Social Science History* 26.3 (2002): 531-581.

[11] See Michele F. Epstein, 'The Common Ground of Merleau-Ponty's and Wittgenstein's Philosophy of Man,' *Journal of the History of Philosophy* 13 (1975): 221-234; Maurice Merleau-Ponty, *Phenomenology of Perception*, trans. Colin Smith (New York: Humanities Press, 1962).

[12] Bernstein, 'Identities and Politics: Toward a Historical Understanding of the Lesbian and Gay Movement.'

[13] Noting, however, that there is no clarity in psychology theory about what constitutes the boundary between subjectivities and the outer world.

[14] See Stephen Nowicki Jr. and Marshall P. Duke, 'Individual Differences in the Nonverbal Communication of Affect: The Diagnostic Analysis of Nonverbal Accuracy Scale,' *Journal of Nonverbal Behavior* 18 (1994): 9-35.

[15] Katharine Young, 'Frame and Boundary in the Phenomenology of Narrative,' *Narrative across Media: The Languages of Storytelling*, ed. Marie-Laure Ryan (Lincoln: University of Nebraska Press, 2004), 76-107.

[16] Marshal McLuhan, *Understanding Media: The Extensions of Man* (New York: Mentor, 1964; Re-issued Cambridge, Massachusetts: MIT Press, 1994).

[17] Deborah Cameron, 'Gender, Language, and Discourse: A Review Essay,' *Signs* 23 (1998): 945-973.

[18] Jeffrey Weeks, 'Remembering Foucault,' *Journal of the History of Sexuality* 14 (2005): 188.

[19] Roy Sommer, 'Beyond (Classical) Narratology: New Approaches to Narrative Theory,' *European Journal of English Studies* 8 (2004): 5.

[20] Brian Richardson, 'Recent Concepts of Narrative and the Narratives of Narrative Theory,' *Style* 34 (2000): 168.

[21] Gérard Genette, *Narrative Discourse: An Essay in Method*, trans. Jane Lewin (Ithaca: Cornell University Press, 1980).

[22] Dorrit Cohn, *Transparent Minds: Narrative Modes for Presenting Consciousness in Fiction* (Princeton, New Jersey: Princeton University Press, 1978); Coplan, 'Empathic Engagement with Narrative Fictions,' *The Journal of Aesthetics and Art Criticism* 62 (2004): 141-152.

[23] Harry, 'Journalistic Quotation: Reported Speech in Newspapers from a Semiotic-Linguistic Perspective,' 1042.

[24] Ibid.

[25] Ibid.

[26] Teun A. Van Dijk, *News as Discourse* (Hillsdale, NJ: Lawrence Erlbaum, 1988); Weeks, 'Remembering Foucault,' 186-201.

[27] See the argument around an orientational view of empathy in Steven Larocco, 'Empathy as Orientation Rather than Feeling: Why Empathy Is Ethically Complex,' in this volume. See also Coplan, 'Empathic Engagement with Narrative Fictions,' 141-152.

[28] Whether it is linguistically/semiotically/narratologically possible to acknowledge the subjectivity of the reader is moot, and links with arguments around narrative techniques to represent 'second-person' narrations. See Cohn, *Transparent Minds: Narrative Modes for Presenting Consciousness in Fiction.*

[29] Harry, 'Journalistic Quotation: Reported Speech in Newspapers from a Semiotic-Linguistic Perspective,' 1042.

[30] Ibid., 1046.

[31] Ibid.

[32] Ibid.

[33] Ibid.

[34] Gérard Genette, *Narrative Discourse Revisited* (Ithaca: Cornell University Press, 1988).

[35] Harry, 'Journalistic Quotation: Reported Speech in Newspapers from a Semiotic-Linguistic Perspective,' 1042.

[36] Michel Foucault, *The History of Sexuality*, trans. Robert Hurley (New York: Pantheon, 1978).

[37] Jonathan Goldberg, *Sodometries: Renaissance Texts, Modern Sexualities* (NY: Fordham University Press, 2010).

[38] Ibid., 5.

[39] Eve Kosofsky Sedgwick, 'Axiomatic,' *Queer Theory*, ed. Ian Morland and Annabelle Willox (Hampshire and New York: Palgrave MacMillan, 2005), 81.

[40] Eve Kosofsky Sedgwick, *Epistemology of the Closet* (Berkeley: University of California Press, 1990), 2.

[41] Goldberg, *Sodometries: Renaissance Texts, Modern Sexualities*, 19.

[42] Rhoda E. Howard, 'Gay Rights and the Right to a Family: Conflicts between Liberal and Illiberal Belief Systems,' *Human Rights Quarterly* 23 (2001): 73-95.

[43] See Larocco, 'Empathy as Orientation.'

[44] Coplan, 'Empathic Engagement with Narrative Fictions,' 141-152.

[45] See Gavin Fairbairn, 'Reflecting on Empathy,' in this volume.

[46] See Rebeccah J. Nelems, 'What is This Thing Called Empathy?' in this volume.

[47] Ibid.

[48] Coplan, 'Empathic Engagement with Narrative Fictions,' 141-152.

[49] Nancy Eisenberg and Paul A. Miller, 'Empathy, Sympathy, and Altruism: Empirical and Conceptual Links,' *Empathy and Its Development,* ed. Nancy Eisenberg and Janet Strayer (Cambridge: Cambridge University Press, 1990), 292-316.

[50] Zillmann and Knobloch, 'Emotional Reactions to Narratives about the Fortunes of Personae in the News Theatre,' 200

[51] Coplan, 'Empathic Engagement with Narrative Fictions,' 149.

[52] Ibid.

[53] Genette, *Narrative Discourse Revisited.*

[54] Coplan, 'Empathic Engagement with Narrative Fictions,' 149.

[55] Matthijs P. Bal and Martijn Veltkamp, 'How Does Fiction Reading Influence Empathy? An Experimental Investigation on the Role of Emotional Transportation,' *PloS One* 8 (2013): e55341.

[56] Coplan, 'Empathic Engagement with Narrative Fictions,' 149

[57] Ibid., 144. As Coplan notes, there is some dispute in the psychological literature over whether self and other can be distinguished in empathy, and certain developmental and experimental psychologists indicate a requirement for it, so this view is dominant in clinical psychology thinking.

[58] Judith Butler, *Gender Trouble: Feminism and the Subversion of Identity* (New York: Routledge, 1990).

[59] Mark Norris Lance and Alessandra Tanesini, 'Identity Judgments, Queer Politics,' *Queer Theory*, ed. Iain Morland and Annabelle Willox (Hampshire and New York; Palgrave MacMillan, 2005), 171-186.

[60] Ibid.

[61] Deborah Cameron and Don Kulick, 'Identity Crisis?,' *Language & Communication* 25 (2005): 112.

[62] Ibid.

[63] Sedgwick, 'Axiomatic,' 82.

[64] Larocco, in this volume; Nelems, in this volume.

[65] Donald E. Hall, *Queer Theories* (Hampshire & New York: Palgrave Macmillan, 2002), 67.

[66] Sarah Ahmed, 'Orientations: Toward a Queer Phenomenology,' *GLQ* 12.4 (2006): 543-574.

[67] Note that in this instance there is a difference between 'impartiality', which is about a personal opinion, and objectivity, which is about representing the facts without favouring one or other side

[68] Judith Butler, 'Imitation and Gender Insubordination,' *Cultural Theory and Popular Culture: A Reader*, ed. John Storey (Harlow: University of Georgia Press, 2006.)

[69] Lance and Tanesini, 'Identity Judgments, Queer Politics,' 171-186.

[70] Elizabeth Freeman, 'Introduction,' *GLQ* 1 (2007): 159-176.

[71] Deborah P. Britzman, *Lost Subjects, Contested Objects: Toward a Psychoanalytic Inquiry of Learning* (Albany: State University of New York Press, 1998), 91.

[72] See Nelems, in this volume.

[73] William S. Haver, 'Queer Research,' *The Eight Technologies of Otherness*, ed. Sue Golding (New York, London: Routledge, 1997), 288-291.

[74] Nelems, in this volume.

[75] Weeks, 'Remembering Foucault,' 186-201; David M. Halperin, *Saint Foucault: Towards a Gay Hagiography* (New York and Oxford: Oxford University Press,

1997); Mark Blasius, *Gay and Lesbian Politics: Sexuality and the Emergence of a New Ethic* (Temple University Press, 1994).

[76] Peter Steiner, *Russian Formalism: A Metapoetics* (Ithaca and London: Cornell University Press, 1984).

[77] Peter Steiner and Sergej Davydov, 'The Biological Metaphor in Russian Formalism: The Concept of Morphology,' *SubStance* 6.16 (1977): 149-158.

[78] Ibid.

[79] Victor Erlich, 'Russian Formalism,' *Journal of the History of Ideas* 34.4 (1973): 627-638.

[80] Vincent Quinn and Alan Sinfield, 'Queer Theory,' *The Year's Work in Critical and Cultural Theory* 14.1 (2006):143-151.

[81] Genette, *Narrative Discourse Revisited.*

[82] Donna Penn and Janice Irvine, 'Gay/Lesbian/Queer Studies' *Contemporary Sociology: A Journal of Reviews* 24 (1995): 328.

[83] Steiner and Davydov, 'The Biological Metaphor in Russian Formalism: The Concept of Morphology,' 149-158.

[84] Larocco, in this volume.

[85] Nelems, in this volume.

[86] Judith Butler, *Bodies that Matter* (New York: Routledge, 1993).

[87] Judith Butler, 'Discussion,' *The Identity in Question*, ed. John Rajchman (New York: Routledge, 1995), 129.

Bibliography

Ahmed, Sarah. 'Orientations: Toward a Queer Phenomenology.' *GLQ* 12.4 (2006): 543-574.

Bal, Matthijs P., and Martijn Veltkamp. 'How Does Fiction Reading Influence Empathy? An Experimental Investigation on the Role of Emotional Transportation.' *PloS One* 8.1 (2013): e55341 PloS One 8.1 (2013): e55341- Downloaded on 1 August 2014. http://eds.b.ebscohost.com/eds/pdfviewer/pdfviewer?sid=4dadab4e-ad8b-4a61- 9924-a120dd8394b8%40sessionmgr120&vid=0&hid=112.

Bernstein, Mary. 'Identities and Politics: Toward a Historical Understanding of the Lesbian and Gay Movement.' *Social Science History* 26.3 (2002): 531-581.

Blasius, Mark. *Gay and Lesbian Politics: Sexuality and the Emergence of a New Ethic*. Philadelphia: Temple University Press, 1994.

Britzman, Deborah P. *Lost Subjects, Contested Objects: Toward a Psychoanalytic Inquiry of Learning.* Albany: State University of New York Press, 1998.

Butler, Judith. *Gender Trouble: Feminism and the Subversion of Identity.* New York: Routledge, 1990.

Butler, Judith. *Bodies that Matter.* New York: Routledge, 1993.

Butler, Judith. 'Discussion.' *The Identity in Question,* edited by John Rajchman. New York: Routledge, 1995.

Butler, Judith. 'Imitation and Gender Insubordination.' *Cultural Theory and Popular Culture: A Reader*, edited by John Storey, 255-271. Harlow: University of Georgia Press, 2006.

Cameron, Deborah. 'Gender, Language, and Discourse: A Review Essay.' *Signs* 23.4 (1998): 945-973.

Cameron, Deborah and Don Kulick. 'Identity Crisis?' *Language & Communication* 25 (2005): 107-125.

Cohn, Dorrit. *Transparent Minds: Narrative Modes for Presenting Consciousness in Fiction.* Princeton, New Jersey: Princeton University Press, 1978.

Coplan, Amy. 'Empathic Engagement with Narrative Fictions.' *The Journal of Aesthetics and Art Criticism* 62.2 (2004): 141-152.

Eisenberg, Nancy, and Paul A. Miller. 'Empathy, Sympathy, and Altruism: Empirical and Conceptual Links.' *Empathy and Its Development*, edited by Nancy Eisenberg and Janet Strayer, 292-316. Cambridge: Cambridge University Press, 1990.

Epprecht, Marc. *Hungochani: A History of a Dissident Sexuality in Southern Africa.* Quebec: McGill-Queen's University Press, 2004.

Epprecht, Marc. *Heterosexual Africa.* Ohio: Ohio University Press and Durban: University of Kwa-Zulu Natal Press, 2008.

Epstein, Michele F. 'The Common Ground of Merleau-Ponty's and Wittgenstein's Philosophy of Man.' *Journal of the History of Philosophy* 13.2 (1975): 221-234.

Erlich, Victor. 'Russian Formalism.' *Journal of the History of Ideas* 34.4 (1973): 627-638.

Foucault, Michel. *The History of Sexuality, Volume 1*. Translated by Robert Hurley. New York: Pantheon, 1978.

Freeman, Elizabeth. 'Introduction.' *GLQ* 1.13:2-3 (2007): 159-176.

Stephen Fry: Out There, episode 1. Directed by Stephen Fry, London: BBC, 2013.
Genette, Gérard. *Narrative Discourse: An Essay in Method*. Translated by Jane Lewin. Ithaca: Cornell University Press, 1980.

Genette, Gérard. *Narrative Discourse Revisited*. New York: Cornell University Press, 1988.

Gentzkow, Matthew, Edward L. Glaeser and Claudia Goldin. 'The Rise of the Fourth Estate: How Newspapers became Informative and Why It Mattered.' *Corruption and Reform: Lessons from America's Economic History*. Chicago, University of Chicago Press, 2006.

Goldberg, Jonathan. *Sodometries: Renaissance Texts, Modern Sexualities*. New York: Fordham University Press, 2010.

Hall, Donald E. *Queer Theories*. Hampshire and New York: Palgrave Macmillan, 2002.

Halperin, David M. *Saint Foucault: Towards a Gay Hagiography*. New York and Oxford: Oxford University Press, 1997.

Harry, Joseph C. 'Journalistic Quotation: Reported Speech in Newspapers from a Semiotic-Linguistic Perspective.' *Journalism* 15.8 (2014): 1041-1058.

Haver, William. 'Queer Research.' *The Eight Technologies of Otherness*, edited by Sue Golding, 288-291. New York and London: Routledge, 1997.

Howard, Rhoda E. 'Gay Rights and the Right to a Family: Conflicts between Liberal and Illiberal Belief Systems.' *Human Rights Quarterly* 23 (2001): 73-95.

Lance, Mark Norris, and Alessandra Tanesini. 'Identity Judgments, Queer Politics.' *Queer Theory*, edited by Iain Morland and Annabelle Willox, 171-186. Hampshire and New York: Palgrave MacMillan, 2005.

McLuhan, Marshal. *Understanding Media: The Extensions of Man*. Cambridge, Massachusetts: MIT Press, 1994 [1964].

Merleau-Ponty, Maurice. *Phenomenology of Perception*. Translated by Colin Smith. New York: Humanities Press 1962 [1945].

Nowicki Jr, Stephen, and Marshall P. Duke. 'Individual Differences in the Nonverbal Communication of Affect: The Diagnostic Analysis of Nonverbal Accuracy Scale.' *Journal of Nonverbal Behavior* 18.1 (1994): 9-35.

Patton, Cindy. 'Tremble, Hetero Swine.' *Fear of a Queer Planet: Queer Politics and Social Theory*, edited by Michael Warner, 143-177. Minneapolis: University of Minnesota Press, 1993.

Penn, Donna, and Janice Irvine. 'Gay/Lesbian/Queer Studies.' *Contemporary Sociology: A Journal of Reviews* 24.3 (1995): 328-30.

Quinn, Vincent, and Alan Sinfield. 'Queer Theory.' *The Year's Work in Critical and Cultural Theory* 14.1 (2006):143-151.

Qwelane, Jon. 'Call Me Names, but Gay is NOT OK.' *The Sunday Sun*, South African Edition, 20 July 2008.

Richardson, Brian. 'Recent Concepts of Narrative and the Narratives of Narrative Theory.' *Style* 34.2 (2000): 168-175.

Roberts, Ben and Vasu Reddy. 'Pride and Prejudice: Public Attitudes toward Homosexuality.' *HSRC Review* 6.4 (2008): 9-11.

Scheufele, Dietram A., and David Tewksbury. 'Framing, Agenda Setting, and Priming: The Evolution of Three Media Effects Models.' *Journal of communication* 57.1 (2007): 9-20.

Schultz, Julianne. *Reviving the Fourth Estate: Democracy, Accountability and the Media*. Cambridge: Cambridge University Press, 1998.

Sedgwick, Eve Kosofsky. *Epistemology of the Closet*. Berkeley: University of California Press, 1990.

Sedgwick, Eve Kosofsky. 'Axiomatic.' *Queer Theory*, edited by Iain Morland and Annabelle Willox, 81-95. Hampshire and New York: Palgrave MacMillan, 2005.

Skosana, Ina and Thandeka Moyo. 'Double Stigma Leaves Gay Men with Little Hope.' *Mail and Guardian Online*, 31 July 2014. Viewed on 1 August 2014. http://mg.co.za/article/2014-07-31-double-stigma-leaves-gay-men-with-little-hope.

Sommer, Roy. 'Beyond (Classical) Narratology: New Approaches to Narrative Theory.' *European Journal of English Studies* 8.1 (2004): 3-11.

Steiner, Peter, and Sergej Davydov. 'The Biological Metaphor in Russian Formalism: The Concept of Morphology.' *SubStance* 6.16 (1977): 149-158.

Steiner, Peter. *Russian Formalism: A Metapoetics.* Ithaca and London: Cornell University Press, 1984.

Van Dijk, Teun A. *News as Discourse*. Hillsdale, NJ: Lawrence Erlbaum, 1988.

Weeks, Jeffrey. 'Remembering Foucault.' *Journal of the History of Sexuality* 14.1/2 (2005): 186-201.

Young, Katharine. 'Frame and Boundary in the Phenomenology of Narrative.' *Narrative across Media: The Languages of Storytelling*, edited by Marie-Laure Ryan, 76-107. Lincoln: University of Nebraska Press, 2004.

Zillmann, Dolf, and Silvia Knobloch. 'Emotional Reactions to Narratives about the Fortunes of Personae in the News Theatre.' *Poetics* 29 (2001): 189-206.

LJ (Nic) Theo teaches screenwriting and communication science, and supervises research in visual and mass media, at the Cape Peninsula University of Technology, South Africa. His work is on narrative architectures and communication design in visual and print media.

Art or Science? Formulating Empathy in Vince Gilligan's *Breaking Bad*

Abby Bentham

Abstract

When Vince Gilligan pitched the idea for *Breaking Bad* to studio bosses at the AMC media network, his description of it as 'a story about a man who transforms himself from Mr. Chips into Scarface' proved to be enough of a hook to take the show into production. However, whilst this transformation is indeed breath-taking, perhaps the most fascinating thing about the series has been its attempt to manipulate viewers' emotions. As the show opens, the locus of empathy is Walter White; a terminally ill high school chemistry teacher desperate to provide financially for his disabled, teenaged son and unexpectedly pregnant wife. However, as the narrative arc develops, Walter undergoes a dramatic transformation. His shift from shambling underdog to drug lord poses interesting moral questions which increasingly act as a barrier to empathy and identification with the character. My chapter charts the evolution of Walter White and the characters around him, exploring how their representation in the show affects and manipulates viewer identification through shifts between sympathy, empathy and antipathy. I consider Walter's characterisation in the context of the other male characters in *Breaking Bad* and reflect on why such development is denied to the show's unremittingly negative female characters.

Key Words: Empathy, *Breaking Bad*, Walter White, morality, evil, hero, villain, misogyny, masculinity.

*****

1. The Art of Empathy

In the pilot episode of *Breaking Bad*, Walter White (Bryan Cranston) tells his students: 'Technically, chemistry is the study of matter, but I prefer to see it as the study of change ... It is growth, then decay, then transformation.'[1] The series itself could also be described in these terms, as it charts Walt's evolution from underachieving, downtrodden cancer victim to feared kingpin in a multi-million dollar methamphetamine empire. Whilst that is undoubtedly an audacious premise for a drama series, the most startling thing about the show is not its subject matter, but its skilful manipulation of viewers and their orientation towards the character.

Of course, film and television have a long history of producing charismatic anti-heroes, with characters such as Michael Corleone, Tony Soprano and Dexter Morgan holding privileged places in popular culture. Empathy with such characters is encouraged by a variety of narrative and cinematographic techniques that invite complicity and support identification with the focalising character. Identification, which is distinct from empathy, can be defined as 'a mechanism through which audience members experience reception and interpretation of the text from the inside, as if events were happening to them.'[2] Jonathan Cohen offers a useful overview of identification as a phenomenon that 'requires that we forget ourselves and become the other – that we assume for ourselves the identity of the target of our identification.'[3] He notes that an important extension of this concept was put forward by Bruno Bettelheim, who observed that 'identification does not require actively or wilfully taking on the identity of the other but rather, sharing their perspective and internalizing their view of the world.'[4] Identification is a temporary state elicited by the subject's immersion in a fictional world and whilst it can lead to empathy,[5] transition between the two states is not inevitable. If viewers do experience empathy for fictional characters, the experience can be intense. When an empathetic and identificatory connection is made to a transgressive screen character such as Walter White or Michael Corleone, viewers can find themselves in an uncomfortable moral hinterland where, for the period of entrancement in the fictional world, s/he accepts and endorses actions and behaviours s/he would not countenance in 'real life.'

In his article 'Nobody Here But Us Killers: The Disavowal of Violence in Recent American Films,'[6] Thomas M. Leitch describes a number of techniques used by film-makers on which viewers can base a subjective disavowal, so as to reduce the ambivalence that arises from the passive enjoyment of subversive or troubling material. These techniques typically include the use of music or comedy, or the stylisation of violence. In *Breaking Bad*, for instance, the soundtrack to an early montage of scenes depicting Jesse (Aaron Paul) 'slinging crystal' and smoking meth[7] is the lounge classic 'It Is such a Good Night' by The Charlie Steinmann Orchestra & Singers,[8] whilst the infamous prison killing scene, where Walt orchestrates the strategic murders of ten men in two minutes,[9] is accompanied by the dulcet tones of Nat King Cole singing 'Pick yourself Up.'[10] In both cases, the light-hearted music enables viewers to gloss over the gruesome nature of the material and suspend moral judgement, even though at times the techniques objectively draw attention to the cognitive dissonance which underpins the disavowal process.[11] Such techniques are also at play in *The Godfather* films, *The Sopranos*, *Dexter* and more. Where *Breaking Bad* diverges sharply from its televisual and cinematic forebears, however, is in its shifting locus of empathy. Walt's transformation encourages viewers to move between feelings of sympathy, empathy and revulsion, without providing an alternative figure of easy identification. Rather, every character is flawed and complex and it is this depth and diversity that makes the series so interesting.

The distinction between sympathy and empathy is important here. As Gavin Fairbairn observes,[12] the terms are often confused or used interchangeably. However, they describe distinct states which function in very different ways. Keith Oatley explains: 'In modern usage, sympathy is generally taken as separate from empathy (feeling with), and usually means feeling for someone in their predicament.'[13] Oatley situates sympathy in what he calls 'emotional memories;'[14]

when a particular scene moves a particular viewer to a sympathetic response, the viewer feels not what the focalising character feels, but what s/he her- or himself has felt in a similar situation. By contrast, empathy draws upon a more complex array of emotional and cognitive processes, such as motor mimicry, which Janet Bavelas et al. describe as 'behavior by an observer that is appropriate to the situation of the other person, for example, wincing at the other's injury or ducking when the other does,'[15] and emotional contagion, defined by Steve Larocco as 'an often non-conscious and non-intentional form of emotional transfer or synchronization.'[16] Such processes help the subject feel as the other feels or think as the other thinks during the period of entrancement in the narrative world. Empathy can be induced on screen by screenwriting and cinematography or, in literature, by narrative poetics. In his discussion of emotion in popular fiction, Noël Carroll argues that readers are led to particular emotional states or standpoints by a process he describes as 'criterial prefocussing':

> By that [criterial prefocussing] I mean that the fiction, by means of either visual depiction, enactment, and/or verbal description, organizes or filters the situations or events it presents in such a way that the features the creators select for emphasis are those that are criterially apposite to the emotional states intended to be excited by the work.[17]

For Carroll, 'emotional uptake'[18] is determined by the emphasis the author places on particular elements of the story and this is certainly true of *Breaking Bad*. Much of the show's success rests in its ability to create multiple points of affinity which allow viewers to relate to Walt and his situation.

2. Now for the Science Bit: Formulating Empathy for Walt

Walt is middle-aged and regretful of missed opportunities and unfulfilled potential. His salary is insufficient to meet his outgoings, a fact that probably resonated with audiences when the show first aired during the Global Financial Crisis of 2008. Henpecked at home and under-appreciated at work, Walt's masculinity is in crisis. Resignedly, he accepts his lot, seething with unexpressed resentment and rage. In the first episode, everything about him conveys disappointment and conformity, from his drab, outdated home, to his practical car in an insipid shade of green. A close-up on a dusty certificate reveals that in 1985, Walt's ground-breaking research into photon radiography contributed to a project that was awarded the Nobel Prize in Chemistry. Yet while his former colleagues Elliot and Gretchen Schwarz (Adam Godley and Jessica Hecht) went on to become billionaires, Walt ended up as an overqualified, underpaid high school chemistry teacher forced to work a second job as a cashier at a car wash, simply to make ends meet. Gilligan's careful and strategic criterial prefocussing encourages viewers to sympathise with Walt's frustrations and regrets, as they draw on their emotional memories, recall their own failings and dissatisfaction and feel for Walt in his particular circumstances.

Walt's victim status at the outset of the narrative is also vitally important to the establishment of sympathy for the character. His diagnosis of terminal stage-3 lung cancer spells disaster as his precarious financial position means he is unable to provide his family with long term economic security – an unsettling proposition given that his wife is unexpectedly pregnant, he has a disabled teenage son, and the family has minimal savings. The fact that Walt fears for his family, rather than himself, is presumably intended to endear him to the audience and to establish him diegetically as a good man battling intolerable odds. When he views a news bulletin which shows his DEA agent brother-in-law, Hank (Dean Norris), busting a meth lab from which $700,000 is recovered, Walt decides to start producing meth and the audience is encouraged to accept and endorse not just his dedication to securing his family's future but also his audacity.[19] Although it is likely that very few of the show's viewers would have either the technical skills or the nerve to take such drastic measures themselves, and therefore are not in a position to feel as he does, it is easy to imagine going to extremes to protect and provide for one's family. Such partial recognition is enough to encourage emotional uptake, as Adam Morton observes:

> ...one gets a partial imagination of the motivation of deeds that one would not consider doing oneself (at least in one's current circumstances...) But a partial grasp of motivation is all one ever has: if there is any empathy at all it rests on partial imagination. So... we can empathize with the motives of repugnant characters in part because empathy can be selective in its choice of an imaginative basis...[20]

Morton acknowledges that 'partial imagination' can be sufficient to invoke an empathetic response, although this is not always forthcoming (Morton's use of the word 'if' is instructive here). In *Breaking Bad*, Gilligan's criterial prefocussing encourages viewers initially to sympathise and then, in short order, to empathise with Walt, drawing on their own emotional heritage to imaginatively project themselves into Walt's position and think 'How would I react, in his position?' This kind of cognitive roleplay is the basis of sympathy; it transmutes into empathy when the empath extends their imagining to the point of view of the person with whom they are empathising. As Suzanne Keen explains,

> [e]mpathy in this sense is a more obviously cognitive operation that depends on having a theory of (another's) mind... For narrative theorists exploring the phenomenon of character

identification, this mode of empathy transposes quite neatly to the kind of narrative empathy that follows on artful attention to a fictional character's actions, circumstances, speech, represented thoughts, and reported or inferred motives.'[21]

Identification with Walt is further encouraged by Michael Slovis's immersive cinematography. Slovis makes liberal use of point-of-view camerawork, which is then edited to reflect a subjective viewpoint with which the audience is encouraged to identify. These techniques align viewers with the show's dominant focalising consciousness: Walt. Forced to view situations from Walt's perspective, audiences are pushed towards an emotional (and in this instance sympathetic and then empathetic) response; they see what he sees and feel what he feels. The technique is established in the pilot episode of *Breaking Bad*,[22] during a series of cringe-worthy back-to-back scenes. First, Walt is compelled to clean the tyres on a troublesome student's sports car during a shift at his second job at the car wash. Although the sequence lasts just ten seconds, it is redolent with meaning; its limited length belying the mighty punch it packs in encouraging empathy. Despite being employed as a cashier, Walt has been ordered by his officious employer to help valet the vehicles. A wide establishing shot shows Walt washing a red Corvette, still clad in the same clothes he wore to teach his Chemistry classes earlier in the day whilst his co-workers wear overalls. The difference in attire demonstrates Walt's incongruity; he does not belong in the setting and although he diligently performs his tasks, he looks harried and exhausted. In a close shot, Walt crouches to clean the tyres by hand; the camera cuts away to the opposite side of the vehicle, and, to the sound of approaching footsteps and the words 'Oh my God, Mr. White!', pans around the bonnet to reveal Walt stooped at the wheel arch, hard at work. As Walt peers around the car to see who is speaking, the camera reveals two laughing teenagers, one of whom is the owner of the car and a student of Walt's who had behaved disrespectfully in class earlier in the day. Publicly humiliated, Walt looks mortified as they jeer, photograph him and share news of their discovery with their peers over the telephone. Significantly, although the camera ensures that viewers share the point of view of the teenagers, it actually encourages empathy with Walt rather than his tormentors. By maintaining its focus on Walt, rather than the teenagers, the camera highlights the teacher's discomfort. The low angle accentuates Walt's subservient position and ensures that viewers understand, and to some extent share, his humiliation. Witnessing Walt in such an undignified position is awkward and embarrassing for viewers, and this is arguably the point at which Walt becomes an empathetic character. The implied viewer's emotions mirror Walt's at this stage in the narrative and, although uncomfortable, this emotional proximity subconsciously creates a deeper level of identification with the character, which in turn encourages empathy. Walt's chagrin continues in the subsequent scene when he returns home to find that his wife has thrown a surprise birthday party for him. As he opens the front door to his home, the camera is situated behind the door, so that viewers see it swing open from inside the family home. This creates an almost uncanny sense of unease. Perspectively, viewers, like the camera, are in the sitting room of the home facing out. This should align the audience with the point of view of the excited and expectant party guests, yet instead it invokes Walt's feelings of apprehension and unease. The positioning of the camera gives the impression that there is something unpleasant waiting for Walt – a feeling that is justified when the camera cuts to a shot of the inhabitants of the room rushing forwards to greet him. The slightly canted angle of the camera has a distorting effect which makes the people, and especially his wife Skyler (Anna Gunn), appear bigger and slightly menacing as they loom towards him. Clearly uncomfortable with the attention, Walt looks discomfited, crowded and out of place in his own home. Matters get worse when he is encouraged to hold Hank's gun; when Walt tells Hank that the gun feels 'heavy,' Hank laughingly tells him 'That's why they hire *men*!' Emasculated in front of his peers, Walt squirms with embarrassment; viewers, having been exposed to the extremes of Walt's emotions by the immersive camerawork, are encouraged to feel both with him and for him. Incidents such as these pepper every episode of every season of *Breaking Bad* and they are vital for transforming sympathy into empathy and aligning viewers with Walt's state of mind.

2.1. Walt, Empathy and Politics

Walt embodies the masculine crisis that so dominated the Western cultural and critical landscape in the 1990s and early 2000s. The perceived crisis arose in response to a number of social and cultural spurs, as Jason Landrum observes:

> The state of emergency faced by contemporary men has emerged as a response to the perceived loss of patriarchal prestige. The traditional story of patriarchal decline often focuses on postmodernity's gradual erosion of the power that men, especially fathers, enjoyed in the early-to-mid twentieth century. Privileged cultural practices like heteronormative marriage, the masculine burden of financial responsibility, the fatherly right to disregard day-to-day parental guidance, and workplace superiority, as the story goes, have all been assaulted in so many ways by feminists, liberals, and Hollywood that the resulting post-patriarchy of the twenty-first century has left men adrift and ridiculed.[23]

Walt's characterisation is a direct response to these pressures and his incipient transformation offers a heady fantasy of masculine re-empowerment and fightback. The fact that he plans to achieve his goals by blackmailing former student Jesse

Pinkman into cooperating with the plan can, initially at least, be easily overlooked. Jesse is a habitual drug user and low-level meth cook, with an attitude problem and questionable friends. In the show's early binary positioning of right and wrong, good and bad, Jesse represents a potential source of moral contamination or danger to the straight-laced White family. Yet, as the series progresses, Jesse increasingly provides its moral centre and his empathetic orientation provides a welcome counterpoint to Walt's descent.

Walt's understanding of the criminal underworld is gleaned from popular culture, and his gauche attempts to adopt the hyper-masculine performance of the drug lord or gangster are the source of much amusement both at the level of the diegesis (that is, the narrative progression of the series) and outside of the narrative performance. As noted earlier, comedy plays an important role in helping viewers to disavow their potentially ambivalent response to Walt and Jesse's decision to supply a dangerous drug. Walt's naivety and his unintentional physical comedy are essential to the creation and maintenance of empathy for the character. In the first two seasons, Walt is relatable and funny, and the typical viewer wants him to succeed in his plan to provide for his family, even though by episode three of Season One he has already killed two men. These murders, which are admittedly in self-defence, should be troubling, but identification remains intact and empathy is unthreatened by the juxtaposition of Walt and the 'real' criminals that he comes into contact with. Characters such as meth cooks Krazy-8 (Maximino Arciniega) and Emilio (John Koyama), and psychopathic meth distributor Tuco Salamanca (Raymond Cruz) are ruthless and deadly; when Walt is viewed against them, the audience is reminded that he is a good man doing bad things for good reasons.

Critics of *Breaking Bad* have focused on the show's treatment of race, which they claim is at best unsatisfying and at worst profoundly racist. It has been noted that the show's meth industry is exclusively run and controlled by non-white figures and that Walt's success in the market represents a 'white supremacist fantasy.'[24] Malcolm Harris situates Walt in the well-worn 'Mighty Whitey' trope,[25] whereby a white man enters a non-white world and, by means of his superior intelligence and guile, triumphs over the alien 'other.' In *Breaking Bad* the trope seemingly manifests in Walt's extraordinary success in New Mexico's drug trade, which is run locally by tough Latino gangs, overseen and supplied by a Mexican drug cartel. Krazy-8, Emilio and Tuco may have successful methamphetamine businesses but they are no match for Walt's superior product or his cool rationalism. As Chris Prioleau notes, '[t]hese men supposedly have years of experience in drugs, chemistry, murder, etc., yet the show never hesitates to depict them as buffoons when faced with the great Walter White.'[26] Gus Fring (Giancarlo Esposito) is a formidable adversary, but ultimately he too is beaten by Walt. In relation to complaints about the racial profile of the drug trade in *Breaking Bad*, it should be noted that drug market analysis released by the US Department of Justice reveals that the leading wholesale distributors of methamphetamine in the

New Mexico area are Mexican drug trafficking organisations and criminal groups. Likewise, 'local Mexican traffickers and African-American and Hispanic street gangs' are identified as the primary retail distributors of meth in New Mexico. The research also notes that 'Caucasian criminal groups and independent dealers, prison gangs, and OMGs [Outlaw Motorcycle Gangs] also distribute illicit drugs at the retail level in the region, albeit on a smaller scale.'[27] This research supports the racial profile of the narcotics business in *Breaking Bad*,[28] although of course Walt's positioning as the 'Mighty Whitey' is unchallenged by this. However, it seems that Walt's success is unrelated to race – this is the story of one exceptional man. It's not that non-white people are no match for Walter White – *no one* is a match for Walter White. The white people in *Breaking Bad* are negatively depicted in much the same way as the Latino characters. Although lacking in malice, drug trade colleagues Jesse, Skinny Pete (Charles Baker) and Badger (Matt L. Jones) are 'buffoons' to an even greater degree than their Latino counterparts, and talented chemist Gale Boetticher (David Costabile) is similarly positioned as a figure of ridicule. The more 'serious' players within the network, Mike Ehrmantraut (Jonathan Banks) and Lydia Rodarte-Quayle (Laura Fraser) are also deeply flawed, with Lydia portrayed as particularly invidious.

That said, Walt does seem to enjoy a degree of white privilege in the show. For the anonymous blogger at feministtv.tumblr.com, this privilege ensures that Walt's worst immoral and illegal actions 'are sanitized and masculinized'[29] in a way that makes them acceptable to viewers. The blogger goes on to suggest that by drawing on social and cultural associations of whiteness with purity, Gilligan pushes viewers towards empathetic acceptance of Walt's behaviour – a strategy made clear by the naming of the character:

> Walt's very last name – White – is, I think, the key to delineating who is allowed access to strength and power in this [narrative] universe. Whiteness cloaks Walt's actions in innocence and legitimacy, allowing viewers to privilege his emotional experiences as valid, while rooting for the destruction of the Salamanca Cousins, and later Gus Fring. He is the ultimate performance of white power.[30]

This view is echoed by Prioleau, who notes how the 'moral weight' of death in *Breaking Bad* is also colour-coded:

> ...while brown blood flows, as free and unlamented as tap water, any time a white character is killed it signals a moral turning point in the show, a sign that things may have gone too far. Jane, Gale, Mike, Drew Sharp – these deaths are shown to have moral weight, whereas most every brown life taken is seen as

inevitable. The message here is that while dying in the drug-trade is to minorities basically akin to dying of natural causes, white people shouldn't suffer this way.[31]

This may be true to an extent. However, it is important to remember that *Breaking Bad* is tightly focused on the experience of its focalising character and how this impacts on his closest relationships. The deaths that 'matter' are those that impact on Walt personally; Jane (Krysten Ritter), Gale, Mike and Hank were all closely acquainted with Walt and their deaths directly affect him and those dearest to him in a way that characters like Emilio do not. Drew Sharp (Samuel Webb) stands in relief as a true innocent – his death has more impact than that of the similarly aged Tomás Cantillo (Angelo Martinez) because, unlike Tomás, Drew is neither a murderer nor a drug dealer. The 'moral weight' of the deaths in *Breaking Bad* can therefore be argued to relate to culpability rather than race, and this extends as much to judgements on Walt as it does to the other characters. It is in these judgements that the deaths of Jane, Gale and Mike take on their greatest significance; they demonstrate a turning point in the evolution of Walt's character – and it is on these turning points that the narrative thread of the series hangs.

So, whilst Gilligan's treatment of race is at times troubling, it steers away from politically imperative notions of social (in)justice and operates instead as a means of representing Walt's subjectivity. By positioning Walt in a recognisable world and giving viewers a strong sense of the stratified society in which he lives, it performs an important empathetic function by aligning viewers with Walt's point-of-view. In this regard, the hegemonically wholesome world-view of Walt and his family is juxtaposed against the immorality, cruelty and avarice displayed by the neo-Nazi 'family' of Todd Alquist (Jesse Plemons), which is introduced to viewers via Todd's Uncle Jack (Michael Bowen). As a symbolic counterpart to Walt's role as white patriarch, Uncle Jack's group consists of friends and criminal associates who have come together to create a treacherous and terrifying alternative family. The mutual care and understanding presented at the beginning of the series as the primary motivator for Walt's descent into criminality is replaced by acquisitiveness, hedonism and the pursuit of power. The group functions as a stark warning against the dangers of violating societal and familiar codes of conduct, and performs a crucial role in establishing *Breaking Bad*'s moral framework. Walt's role as provider, when juxtaposed against that of Uncle Jack, therefore serves to establish a criterial prefocussing and psychology which encourages the fostering of emotional uptake and empathy in audiences. By drawing on familiar tropes (both positive and negative) for the construction of Walt, Gilligan encourages viewers to selectively focus on those elements of Walt's behaviour that best suit their theory of his motivations, i.e. his desire to provide financial security for his family before his imminent death. This kind of moral relativity arguably reflects what Larocco has described as the often non-conscious 'culling out'[32] of elements that may threaten empathy; criterial prefocussing on Walt's pro-social motivations provides moral elements that counteract the cognitive dissonance or discomfort to which endorsement of his actions gives rise.

Walt's justification for his crimes – that he is acting altruistically to protect and provide for his family – is crucial to the construction of empathetic acceptance and identification in Season One. It provides a utilitarian moral framework for an immoral act and it aligns Walt with John Stuart Mill's 'Greatest Happiness Principle,' which holds that 'actions are right in proportion as they tend to promote happiness, wrong as they tend to produce the reverse of happiness.'[33] By this rationale, Walt's decision to cook and distribute methamphetamine is acceptable, even desirable, because it will provide an inheritance for his family which will ensure their comfort and wellbeing after his death. Walt is able to override his knowledge of the personal and social problems caused by meth addiction by focusing on his own agenda and the positive outcomes he envisages for Skyler and the children. Walt's pro-family stance also provides a point of identification for the audience, particularly in the United States which culturally, socially and politically places a heavy emphasis on family values which transcend notions of race and class. Carroll contends that

> [m]orality, especially of a fairly widely shared and often nearly
> universal variety, gives the popular fictioneer the interest, or
> project, or loyalty, or touchstone of allegiance upon which
> audiences from similar cultures, and even sometimes dissimilar
> ones, can converge. The protagonists… evince a sense of
> fairness, justice, loyalty, honour, and are altogether pro-social,
> and especially pro-family, at least, where the families in question
> are portrayed as wholesome ones.[34]

This focus on the ordinariness of the previously law-abiding White family not only rationalises Walt's crimes. It absolves viewers of any moral responsibility they might have to castigate and condemn his actions, by juxtaposing them against those of the even more morally abhorrent characters, such as Todd Alquist and his Uncle Jack.[35]

3. Walt's Descent

As the series progresses, Walt's characterisation as beleaguered, moral family man becomes increasingly problematic and this has a serious impact on viewer empathy. His alter-ego, Heisenberg, which he establishes as a means of protecting his identity, becomes progressively central to Walt's identity. The Heisenberg persona is the embodiment of the 'badass' that Walt Jr. jokingly says his father looks like when he is forced to shave his head during chemotherapy.[36] The name derives from Werner Heisenberg, a brilliant, Nobel Prize-winning theoretical physicist who is remembered as a pioneer of the quantum mechanics which govern the physics of the atomic world, as well as for his leadership role in Germany's nuclear fission programme during World War II. Heisenberg therefore symbolises not only intellectual might, but also destructive power and threat. The fact that he was awarded the Nobel Prize reminds viewers of that potential which Walt shares. Significantly, given Heisenberg's link to nuclear fusion, the adoption of this persona converts Walt's thwarted potential into invigorating kinetic energy and imbues him with masculine potency.

Walt first introduces himself as Heisenberg during a tense meeting with Tuco Salamanca, at which Walt uses fulminated mercury to create an explosion, forcing Tuco to agree to his terms.[37] In a chemistry lesson earlier in the episode, Walt used fulminated mercury to demonstrate to his class how rapid chemical reactions can cause otherwise harmless substances to explode, an analogy that aptly describes the evolution of Walt's character. This analogy endorses viewers' empathetic connection with Walt as he can continue to be seen as a 'harmless' man who is increasingly forced to respond in extreme ways to circumstances that are spinning out of control. The notion of control is particularly pertinent to the narrative of masculine crisis, and Heisenberg's 'Uncertainty Principle' has special resonance here. The 'Uncertainty Principle' governs the behaviour of chemical molecules and decrees that 'the more precisely the position [of a moving particle] is determined, the less precisely the momentum is known.' In layman's terms, this means that one can never be sure what will happen in any given situation as there are always unknown variables that cannot be controlled. So, even as viewers are celebrating Walt's success with Tuco, circumstances are established which will ultimately place Walt and Jesse in a far more precarious position.

It is interesting to note that as the Heisenberg persona develops, Walt also takes on a new physical presence by way of the pork pie hat and sunglasses he wears as a disguise. At first glance, the hat simply looks like the misguided choice of a man trying, and failing, to look like a gangster. Hollywood has established a strong visual image of the archetypal gangster and, as Stella Bruzzi notes, '[i]n his armoury, the most consistent of the overdetermined accessories is the essential sharp felt hat.'[38] Freud viewed the hat as a symbol of masculinity,[39] a notion that gained great cultural currency and which is of enormous significance in the context of Walt's self-making and embattled masculinity.[40] The 'sharp felt hat' of the gangster comes most commonly in the form of a fedora or homburg, so Walt's choice is instantly at odds with the traditional image. This demonstrates the performative and initially uncomfortable nature of Walt's 'gangster' masculinity, and points to what Esther Sonnet and Peter Stanfield, in their discussion of the retro gangster movie cycle of the 1990s, describe as 'the dense symbolic exchange around the liminal and provisional status of criminal identity.'[41] However, although the pork pie hat is not the traditional signifier of gangster masculinity, it has important forebears in both history and popular culture which add to its resonance and empathetic power. One of its earliest famous wearers was Buster Keaton, the American actor best known for his physical comedy and stoicism. Other notable wearers include Gene Hackman as Jimmy Doyle in the 1971 film *The French Connection*, and Robert De Niro as Johnny Boy in *Mean Streets* from 1973. The prominence of these characters in popular culture carries a dialogic slew of positive associations which act as cultural shorthand for generating viewer acceptance of the Heisenberg persona. Significantly, the pork pie hat was also favoured by Robert Oppenheimer, the father of the atomic bomb, and this association brings a darker and more menacing context to Heisenberg's destructive potential. Furthermore, the definition between Walt's personae plays an important role in maintaining viewerly empathy with the character. By clearly delineating Walt's 'good' and 'bad' selves, Gilligan encourages viewers to compartmentalise the cognitive dissonance arising from his more transgressive actions whilst remaining accepting and identified with the empathetic catnip of Walt's status as husband, father, teacher and cancer patient.

Walt's evolution from shambling family man to ruthless megalomaniac is played out carefully over the full five seasons of the series, and the psychic difficulties of the changes he undergoes are unflinchingly depicted. As viewers, we are encouraged to empathise with Walt when he weeps as he strangles Krazy-8,[42] and we appreciate the anguish and remorse he feels at his decision to stand and watch – and therefore not save – Jesse's girlfriend, Jane Margolis, as she chokes to death on her own vomit.[43] Walt's involvement in Jane's death places significant strain on viewer empathy for the character, as it is the first time that he is portrayed making a cold and calculated decision to privilege his business over the wellbeing of a fellow human being. However, in so doing he protects Jesse from Jane's malign and corrupting influence. Walt's decision to allow Jane's death, although ethically suspect, therefore represents a further expression of his pro-family stance; Jesse increasingly functions as Walt's alternative family in the narrative, often enjoying a closer, more involved and in some ways more loving relationship with him than his biological son. Although Jane's death is an important stepping stone towards Walt's moral collapse, arguably his true moral turning-point is marked when he mows down two dealers with his car then shoots the surviving one in the head.[44] This too has an arguably ethical justification as the men had just murdered a 12-year old child and in killing them, Walt saves Jesse from also being murdered. By the end of Season Three, however, Walt's corruption is revealed to viewers when he orders the strategic murder of his harmless lab partner, Gale Boetticher.[45] The pursuit of power has become Walt's primary motivating factor and, as hubris takes over, the moral revulsion the audience is encouraged to feel overshadows the empathy they may still be feeling. When a terrified Skyler hears of Gale's murder, she fears for the family's safety and begs Walt to go to the police. His scornful reaction demonstrates the pride and pleasure he takes in his new-found potency: 'I am not in danger, Skyler. I am the danger. A guy opens his door and gets shot and you think that of me? No. I am the one who knocks!'[46] The man who had earlier vowed to do just 11 more cooks to net the $737,000 he estimated would provide for his family for the next 25 years[47] now declares himself to be in the 'empire business.' The extent of Walt's moral deterioration is laid bare when he poisons Brock Cantillo (Ian Posada), the 6-year-old son of Jesse's girlfriend, Andrea (Emily Rios), in order to trick Jesse into believing that Gus Fring, the head of one of the largest methamphetamine production and distribution operations in the US, is responsible for the boy's condition. Walt knows he will be able to manipulate Jesse's rage and guilt and thereby enlist his help in orchestrating Gus's murder.[48] This cynical power grab makes for compelling viewing and whilst the audience may marvel at Walt's cunning and audacity, his moral turpitude is presented as more compelling than the motivations which previously represented him empathetically. Significantly, it is never fully restored as Walt is shown to be thoroughly corrupted. The anodyne family man who struggled to kill in self-defence in Season One is by this point devoid of the relatable characteristics that encouraged viewers to empathise and identify with him. He has been replaced by a scheming, affectless tyrant who will do anything to win; willing even to harm the kind of innocent and harmless figures that he previously held sacrosanct.

As the show's moral complexity develops, the writing and cinematography ensure that empathy and identification become less tenable for viewers and are increasingly replaced with something much more ambivalent. Initially, the vicarious thrill presented to viewers of Walt's violations of social norms provides much of the show's appeal. His extraordinary intelligence and inventiveness allow him to fight back against formidable opponents like Gus Fring and, for the hidden geek amongst viewers, it is exciting to see Walt harness the power of science and intellect to overcome seemingly insurmountable obstacles. To some degree, Walt's defeat of foes like Gus also represents a victory for the ordinary, law-abiding members of society, who in real life are unable to challenge the people they may perceive as destroying their neighbourhoods and luring their children into gang life or drug culture. As the narrative progresses and Walt becomes increasingly motivated by profit and power, his attitude towards his business has the potential to infect viewers via a process of emotional contagion. Although emotional contagion does not require an awareness of the other, its affective resonance works with the more cognitive and deliberate empathetic functions encouraged by *Breaking Bad*. The resultant combination may allow viewers to override their usual beliefs and empathise, somewhat counterintuitively, with Walt's more negative emotions, motivations and actions. This is congruent with Larocco's conception of empathy as 'not simply a disposition to care, but as a multivalent structure of interpersonal orientation.'[49] Viewers of *Breaking Bad* may find that the sympathy they had for the positive valence of Walt's early situation and motivations progressively transmutes into empathy for Walt's growing aggression, belligerence and ruthlessness. This functions in two distinct ways, the first relating to the straightforward synchronization of viewer's emotions with Walt's feelings of arrogance, pique and competitiveness, and the second, with greater complexity, revealing the way that empathy with those feelings impacts upon the audience. As Larocco observes, 'empathy can be a staging post for the narcissistic assimilation of the other's emotions'[50] and the audience's interaction with Walt here takes on a hedonic tone. Empathetic acceptance of, and identification with, Walt's worst behaviours enable viewers to take pleasure in his transgressions.

In his book, *An Introduction to the Principles of Morals and Legislation,* Jeremy Bentham asserts that 'Nature has placed mankind under the governance of two sovereign masters, pain, and pleasure. It is for them alone to point out what we ought to do, as well as to determine what we shall do.'[51] Bentham's claim relates to the determination of action and his study considers how psychological and ethical hedonism impact on behaviour. Explorations of this nature have remained current through the ages, from Plato through to the modern day, and perhaps one of the most notorious theorists in this area is the eighteenth century libertine philosopher and writer, the Marquis de Sade. Sade eschewed social interdictions and moral sanction, arguing that only physical pleasure is of real value and that the individual should be free to perform in whatever way will afford him or her the greatest sensory pleasure. Although this seems an extreme example, it does shed some light on the cognitive processes at play in *Breaking Bad* when viewers temporarily renounce their usual morality and viewpoints in the pursuit of narrative pleasure and emotional satisfaction during the period of entrancement. As Walt is increasingly corrupted by his embroilment in the drugs trade, narrative tension is ratcheted to titillating levels. Viewer may thus be subconsciously motivated to endorse and empathise with Walt as a means of prolonging their psychological hedonism.

However, as Walt's motivations and modus operandi become increasingly ugly and alienating, lower level psychological and emotional phenomena like emotional contagion and psychological hedonism are no longer a sufficient means of maintaining the empathic connection. Instances including the poisoning of Brock Cantillo, Walt's reaction to the murder of innocent bystander Drew Sharp,[52] and his two attempts to contract Jesse's murder result in estranging Walt from the audience. As the atrocities mount, higher level cognitive and emotional functions take over and viewers are enabled to withdraw empathy, renounce identification, and disavow complicity in Walt's schemes. Empathy may be slowly replaced with dread fascination and perhaps a grudging respect, similar to that accorded to Walt's nemesis, Gus Fring. The clinical and efficient disposal of Drew's corpse, which is dissolved in hydrofluoric acid, demonstrates to grim effect how radically Walt has changed since he and Jesse plotted to dissolve the corpses of Krazy-8 and Emilio. Moreover, the fact that Drew and his motorcycle are disposed of in exactly the same way – that a human being is afforded no greater consideration than a commodity – reveals Walt's shift from feeling family man to detached, capitalist megalomaniac.

Yet however heinous and troubling such scenes are (and they *are* heinous and troubling), the affective structure remains rooted in the understanding that all of Walt's actions are explainable in the name of business, survival or expediency. Tellingly, final severance of empathy for Walt is encouraged when he spitefully tells Jesse that he watched Jane die.[53] His revelation is an act of pure cruelty which serves no strategic purpose other than to vent the fury and betrayal he feels at Jesse's decision to inform on him to the DEA. The wantonness of Walt's action, and the devastating impact it has on Jesse, has the potential to change forever the empathetic connection that viewers have with Walt, representing as it does a breach of basic human codes: decent people don't hurt those they love out of spite. Over the course of the series, Walt and Jesse develop a deep bond, more akin to a father/son relationship than one between colleagues. Deliberately wounding Jesse – *wanting* to cause him pain – sees Walt violating the key motivator to viewer empathy for the character: the desire to protect family at any cost. The impact of this cannot be underestimated; *Breaking Bad's* criterial prefocussing and immersive script and camerawork ensure that the alienation of the audience is so complete that even when Walt attempts to make amends to the people he loves,[54] his efforts fail to fully restore viewer empathy for the character.

4. Walt's Counterpoints: Masculinity and Its Discontents

Although the narrative trajectory of *Breaking Bad* is largely determined by Gilligan's focus on Walt's psychological universe, the show's depiction of his moral collapse is also infused with a quasi-moralistic message about the broader risks of über-masculinity. The aggressive, capitalistic pursuit of money and power is portrayed as damaging to the (typically male) pursuer; when this is combined with hubris and violence, the result is often fatal.[55] Conflict-inducing, egoistic versions of masculinity are juxtaposed against alternative performances of manliness, with gentler, family-focused forms marked as particularly deserving of approbation. That the series ends with Walt's exile and death and Skyler's depression and penury is of course significant; it demonstrates how Walt's megalomania has led to the destruction of the only thing that really matters – familial relationships.

As *Breaking Bad* charts the evolution of Walt's character, leading viewers from feelings of sympathy to empathy and ultimately revulsion, his development is shown against a backdrop of overly simplistic female characters. The contrast between the portrayals of the male and female leads in the show is stark: the complexity of emotions induced in viewers by characters like Walt, Jesse and Hank makes the uniformly negative depictions of femininity in *Breaking Bad* all the more apparent. Despite the overall privileging of family in *Breaking Bad*, neither of its leading women enjoy elevated positions that encourage empathy or reflect importance. Rather, both Skyler and Marie (Betsy Brandt) are negatively portrayed, with Skyler a ball-breaking adulteress, and Marie a mentally unstable kleptomaniac. Both are detrimental to the masculine potency of their menfolk. This is a show about masculine crisis, about fathers and family, and invidious womanhood is largely a narrative device used to strengthen the audience's attachment to Walt and Hank. The characterisations do fluctuate – Marie is stoic and supportive of Hank during his rehabilitation, despite his terrible treatment of her, but her mental frailty marks her as undeserving of uncompromised viewerly approbation. Skyler is more complex and in many ways her behaviour mirrors Walt's – she will do whatever it takes to protect her family, whether that is laundering drug money,[56] sending in the heavies to ensure that Ted Beneke (Christopher Cousins) pays the IRS,[57] or suggesting that Walt kill Jesse to prevent him from informing on them to the DEA.[58] When she is engaged in the more audacious – more *manly* – illegal or immoral activity, audience approval[59] of her is higher than it is when she is demonstrating more stereotypically female traits such as hectoring or being fearful of her dangerous husband.

In the earliest episodes of *Breaking Bad*, the audience's antipathy towards Skyler seems to reside in her inability to empathise with Walt. Skyler's behaviour towards her husband is often patronising, dismissive, passive aggressive, controlling and demanding. She belittles him over using the 'wrong' credit card for a transaction, she demands he responds to his cancer diagnosis in a way that privileges *her* feelings and she refuses to offer him any latitude or understanding as he struggles to come to terms with his terminal illness. Skyler rarely shows her husband any true affection[60] or support and, as such, she plays an important role in establishing him as an emasculated man fighting against the odds to regain some control over his life. Skyler's negative portrayal therefore assists viewers' empathetic connection with and acceptance of Walt; as Laura Bennett observes in her op-ed piece for *New Republic*, 'her needling almost helps us to excuse Walt, to validate his quest to reclaim his manhood.'[61]

Yet notwithstanding these fluctuations, which under other circumstances would indicate interestingly complex female characterisations, popular response to Skyler is almost uniformly negative. In her article for *Esquire*, Jen Chaney muses that this is because

> as she's a woman, we *expect* her to be the moral compass… We expect this, perhaps subconsciously, because Skyler is a mom and all of us are conditioned from birth to see our mothers as our ethical barometers… By extension, as a culture, we also tend to be less forgiving of women who do wrong and more understanding of men who cheat… or do a whole host of much worse things. Why? Because men, supposedly, have a harder

time resisting temptation. They deserve some slack and we should all just climb down out of their asses, for God's sake.[62]

Such impulses also suggest a social desire to control women, to police their movements and their bodies, their emotions and their relationships. Society places conflicting demands on women, hailing back to the age-old angel/whore dichotomy and a tendency to depict non-conforming women as mentally unstable.[63] These conflicts complicate and at times confound the affective structures within narrative, hindering the possibility of empathetic connection or identification with female characters.

Popular conceptions of gender stereotypes also inform the construction of *Breaking Bad*'s male leads, particularly Walt, Jesse and Hank. Yet this is not slack writing on Gilligan's part; rather, simplistic constructions of gender drive the diegetic manipulation of the story towards a deeper audience engagement with the male characters. As with Walt, the characters of Jesse and Hank undergo significant change on a notional scale between sympathy, empathy and antipathy, although theirs is an inverse transition to that of Walt. This is made possible by the apposition of the complex viewerly emotions induced by the show's characterisations of masculinity, and the more singular and simplistic treatment of – and responses to – women in the narrative.

4.1 Jesse Pinkman: 'I'm [Not] the Bad Guy'

In his role as the show's deuteragonist, Jesse's stock shifts in inverse correlation to that of his mentor: as Walt's empathetic potential wanes, Jesse's increases. As noted earlier, at the outset of the series Jesse is depicted as a low-level criminal and layabout who stands in stark contrast to the straitlaced and seemingly principled Walt, a portrayal which initially encourages audiences to regard him with antipathy. In the first few episodes of Season 1, Jesse reminds viewers of the thankless nature of Walt's job as a high school chemistry teacher: Jesse was an able pupil who never capitalised on his talents or realised his potential, and who was scornful of his teacher's efforts. In this way, Jesse bolsters the audience's empathetic response to Walt and his plight, and performs an important identificatory function for everyone who has ever been, or has had to deal with, a recalcitrant young person. Jesse's lack of effort at school is mirrored by his incompetence in the meth business, and his mistakes cause Walt significant problems in the early days of their partnership. Despite this, he is a popular character with viewers, due to his humorous portrayal by Aaron Paul, whose comedic delivery of Jesse's 'Bitch!' catchphrase soon gained popular currency. Viewer enjoyment of the character's entertainment value quickly turns into empathy as his 'bad boy' persona is exposed as a ridiculous façade and his essentially gentle, vulnerable and caring nature is revealed.

However, although Jesse is largely a likeable character, identification is strained at times. After Jane's death, Jesse enters rehab where he is counselled that his goal should be self-acceptance rather than personal betterment.[64] Jesse's response is to embrace his 'bad guy' persona and set about making 'some serious cheddar' by selling meth. His attempt to seduce a sweet, innocent gas station cashier into accepting blue meth in lieu of payment[65] is highly disturbing, as it reveals the injurious potential of both drugs and drug dealers – an element of the meth business from which viewers have been shielded until this point in the narrative. Jesse's decisions to push drugs to the members of his Narcotics Anonymous support group and to derail the rehabilitation of his friend Skinny Pete (Charles Baker) are equally alienating to the audience.[66] However, the knowledge that Jesse's grief is at the core of his behaviour ensures that empathy for the character is never fully eradicated and the depth of the pain that Jesse feels at Jane's death serves to bolster viewer empathy.

As the narrative progresses, Jesse's essential goodness is increasingly revealed. It is particularly made manifest in his relationship with children, such as Brock Cantillo[67] and the unnamed youngster (played by both Dylan and Brandon Carr) in the home of Spooge (David Ury) and his 'lady' (Dale Dickey), whom Jesse tries to shield from the effects of methamphetamine use.[68] The parents of both Brock and the unnamed child are meth users and Jesse is determined that the children should not be harmed, compromised or disadvantaged by their parents' drug habits. The depth of Jesse's feelings is revealed when he risks his own life to intervene on behalf of Tomás Cantillo, the twelve-year-old drug dealer who shot and killed Jesse's friend Combo (Rodney Rush) for encroaching on his territory, and who was in turn shot dead by his own gang, when Jesse complained to Gus Fring about the use of children in his distribution network.[69] The sense of moral responsibility that Jesse feels towards the youngsters signifies his inherent decency. His sensitive response to the children is perhaps rooted in emotional memories of his own troubled family life (he has effectively been disowned by his parents who openly favour their gifted younger child over Jesse) and the guilt that he feels over the role he played in Jane's drug relapse, which ultimately led to her death.[70] It seems that, by protecting the children from the effects of exposure to meth, Jesse hopes to prevent them from becoming mired in the addiction that blighted his life and took Jane's. The fact that Jesse's feelings trigger a desire to protect others rather than an instinct for self-care or self-pity is instrumental in endearing him to the audience. Viewers are reminded of the many instances when Jesse has responded thoughtfully and compassionately to the people around him[71] and this helps them to empathise with the character. Jesse's instinct to protect children also has a crucial role in encouraging further emotional uptake, as it aligns him with the hegemonic morality that perceives children as innocent, vulnerable and deserving of protection. Such criterial prefocusing not only encourages viewers to identify with and support Jesse; it also validates their empathetic connection with the character by positioning him as morally sound and therefore an acceptable object of empathy and identification. To a large degree, Jesse also represents the innocence of youth. Although he is 24 years old at the start of the series, he is immature, unsophisticated and technically still a youth.[72] One blogger highlights this by noting how the etymological significance of Jesse's name emphasizes his gentleness and naivety: 'his last name is rooted in color, and pink is usually connotative of femininity/childhood.'[73] Although it is some years since Jesse was Walt's pupil, the dynamic of their relationship remains one of teacher and pupil. The fact that Jesse continues to call Walt 'Mr. White,' rather than enter onto first-name terms with him, signals the power balance in the relationship and indicates that Jesse has not yet attained true adult status. Walt's decision to blackmail Jesse into joining him in the business consequently takes on a far more cynical and sinister cast; it is exploitative and a serious abuse of power. Subconsciously, Jesse's drive to protect the innocent could therefore also indicate a process of his own personal redemption – one that Gilligan seems eager for the audience to share and support.

When Drew Sharp is shot dead by Todd Alquist during the methylamine heist, Jesse feels unable to continue in the business and subsequently suffers a breakdown. The rendering of his emotional and psychological struggles functions as a further identificatory tool for audiences who are encouraged to feel a complex combination of sympathy, empathy and approbation for the character. Jesse's devastation, anger and despair at the killing stand in stark contrast to the sociopathic Todd's apparent lack of affect; when confronted about his actions, Todd merely shrugs and says 'Shit happens.' Jesse's decision to leave the business and his attempts to give away the money he has earned signal his understanding that an ultimate taboo has been broken and, again, the unequivocality of his response aligns him with mainstream morality and therefore with viewers. In his dealings with each of the children, Jesse is confronted with the broad consequences of his actions: that his meth is damaging communities and destroying individual lives. Todd's murder of Drew Sharp brings this into relief for Jesse and for viewers, who cannot fail to observe that Jesse is able to acknowledge his culpability in a way that Walt does not. Although professedly disturbed by Drew's murder, Walt's instinctive response is to protect and expand his empire. When he speaks to Jesse about his regret over Drew's death, his words sound hollow, and what remains is the uncomfortable feeling that Walt is merely paying lip service to the issue in order to manipulate Jesse into remaining in the business. The juxtaposition of Walt's cynical strategising and Jesse's psychologically appropriate response reveals how the binary positioning of good and evil that the two characters originally represented has been transposed and exaggerated, and this in turn encourages in audiences an increasingly reversed empathetic response to the characters.

4.2 Hank: Heroic Counterpoint or the Failure of Alpha Masculinity?

Identification with Hank Schrader, *Breaking Bad*'s heroic lawman, is also challenged at the series' end. Hank undergoes a similar character progression to that of Jesse, with his arc taking viewers from feelings of antipathy to empathy and ultimately to sympathy. This trajectory is framed by the complexity of representations of masculinity in a patriarchal world and juxtaposed against intentionally one-dimensional depictions of femininity.

Hank is a wisecracking, alpha-male DEA agent who represents truth and justice. The heroic police officer is a central feature of standard crime fictions and police procedurals that offers an uncompromised model of hegemonic masculinity. In the first few episodes of the first season his domineering, loud masculinity helps to strengthen viewers' empathetic connection with Walt yet, as the series progresses, Walt comes to contrast increasingly unfavourably with his honourable brother-in-law. Hank's initial representation as crude, bullish, sexist and arrogant encourages viewers to feel antipathy towards his teasing, often unpleasant demeanour and apparently sexist and racist opinions. Yet, as the show progresses, he is revealed to be a warm, humorous, loving and dependable family man. For many, Hank functions as a moral counterpoint to Walt; indeed, Ross Douthat, in his blog for the *New York Times*, goes so far as to claim that Hank is the true hero of the show:

> In the course of the show, as Walt has sunk to ever-lower depths of turpitude, his brother-in-law has been given the classic hero's arc: The repeated testing, physical and moral and physical again; the near-successes in which the prize is plucked away the last moment; the temporary falls from grace; the persistent brushes with despair. And he has followed this arc without either turning into a plaster saint (the flawed, crude, bullying character of Season 1 is still recognizable in the Hank of Season 5) or doing anything bad enough to make him an anti-hero in his own right. (His one huge moral lapse, the beating of Jesse Pinkman in Season 3, took place under extenuating circumstances and was followed by Hank taking full responsibility and accepting his potential dismissal from the D.E.A. without a fight.)[74]

Hank's masculinity is in crisis following several traumatic and life-threatening experiences, and Seasons Two, Three and Four of *Breaking Bad* show him struggling to reconcile his earlier performances of machismo with the panic attacks and depression brought on by his post-traumatic stress disorder. Despite this, he remains a loyal and supportive husband to Marie, a loving and protective Uncle to Walt Jr. (RJ Mitte) and Holly (played variously by Haven Tomlin, Elanor Anne

Wenrich, and Moira Bryg MacDonald), and a faithful friend and brother-in-law to Walt and Skyler – all of which encourages viewer empathy.

Empathy is threatened, however, when Hank realises that Walt is Heisenberg and he is determined to make an arrest, despite the fact that Walt pleads with him to spare Walt Jr. the anguish of finding out the truth about his father.[75] Hank has the option of waiting for Walt to die of cancer, but his masculine pride demands the glory of an arrest and triumph over his nemesis. Hank's failure to prioritise the wellbeing of the family threatens to alienate viewers, and the final vestiges of empathy are eliminated when he attempts to manipulate Skyler into implicating her husband,[76] then risks Jesse's life in pursuit of obtaining taped evidence against Walt.[77] Hank's handling of Skyler and Jesse relies on his ability to empathise with them; having identified their individual drives and weaknesses, Hank is able to tailor his strategy in order to achieve the desired results. In such circumstances, empathy becomes less an instrument of good and more a weapon which can be used against a person. This is not an isolated phenomenon. Fairbairn explores the destructive potential of empathy in his chapter in this volume, when he describes how empathy can be used for ill in a variety of circumstances, including bullying or on the sales floor and even, perhaps, torture.[78]. This same strategy is used by each of the main characters in the series to one degree or another, as they vie for primacy. It is how Gus prevailed over the Juárez Cartel,[79] how his enforcer Mike Ehrmantraut (Jonathan Banks) maintains his crew and provides for his granddaughter, and it is at the heart of many of Walt's machinations. Yet in Hank's case, the technique seems particularly insidious and distasteful. So why is this? Simply, unlike the other characters, Hank is not acting on behalf of others. Gus decimates the Cartel as revenge for the murder of his partner, Maximino Arciniega (James Artinez), by Hector Salamanca (Mark Margolis) in the 1980s.[80] Mike is looking out for his men and providing an inheritance for his granddaughter, Kaylee (Kaija Rose Bales). Walt is trying to provide for his family's long-term future. Each man has been driven to extreme actions by his desire to do (what he considered to be) the right thing for the people close to them, by any means. By contrast, Hank is motivated by personal pride and a desire to restore his professional reputation. Moreover, his manipulation of Skyler and his failure to privilege the emotional wellbeing of Walt Jr. and Holly is distasteful as it represents a betrayal of family – something which Walt would never countenance.

The selfishness of Hank's approach and his concomitant (mis)use of the insight he has into the motivations of others ultimately leads to his representation being couched in sympathetic, rather than empathetic, terms. Viewers are able to understand and sympathise with his motivations whilst maintaining a degree of moral and emotional distance that reflects their affective regard for other characters. Hank's character progression from antipathy to empathy to sympathy works in reverse to that of Walt, perceptions of whom are, as discussed above, encouraged to transmute from sympathy to empathy to antipathy.

5. Conclusions

There is an implicit suggestion that the real danger in *Breaking Bad* is femininity – and this is demonstrated repeatedly via central characters such as Jane Margolis and Lydia Rodarte-Quayle (Laura Fraser), and supporting figures such as Francesca, Saul's PA (Tina Parker), and Ted Beneke's receptionist, Margaret (Catherine Haun). Each of these women is powerful, disdainful and castrating. Somewhat unexpectedly, the exception to this rule is the meth-addicted prostitute Wendy (Julia Minesci). Wendy is a useful ally for Jesse, providing an alibi for him to Hank and standing up to four hours of questioning despite being desperate for a hit of meth. She even agrees, reluctantly, to provide ricin-tainted fast food to the dealers who killed Tomás.[81] Supportive, compliant and sexually available, her unconflicted portrayal suggests that she could just be the perfect woman, particularly when compared to the extremes of Walt's character.

Although *Breaking Bad* appears to valorise masculine ideals and render women as one-dimensional and unpleasant characters, Wendy functions as a subtle, almost satirical reproach to its unabashedly masculinist enterprise. The humour of Wendy's characterisation and the pathos of her situation offers a counterpoint to the excesses of Walt's choices – here is the desperate, depressing reality of methamphetamine addiction, which the audience consumes as entertainment. A montage scene depicting Wendy relentlessly turning tricks at the Crossroads Motel in order to earn the money she needs to fund her addiction[82] is disturbing and grim, yet the jaunty, sunshine pop soundtrack[83] allows viewers to disavow the troubling aspects of the scene and experience it as something jolly and entertaining. Such techniques of disavowal help viewers to reconcile the cognitive dissonance that occurs when they passively enjoy on screen something which they know to be wrong or unacceptable in 'real life.' Methamphetamine destroys individuals and communities and the debasement of desperate, drug-addicted women is never entertaining. Yet *Breaking Bad*'s use of humour and music encourages viewers to overlook these elements of the story and focus instead on character development, psychological hedonism and wish fulfilment. The moralistic framework of the show, skewed as it is, encourages viewers to empathise with the desire to protect and privilege the family above all else. By providing such a universally-accepted point of identification, Gilligan buys the complicity of the audience whilst simultaneously encouraging viewers to ignore what that complicity really entails.

Larocco warns that whilst empathy can 'open us, in sometimes accurate and sometimes distorted ways, to the feeling-life and world orientation of others,' the way that 'we use that possibility remains ethically complex and, at times, troubling.'[84] *Breaking Bad* toys with notions of empathy in ways that productively complicate simple moralities. The thoughtful viewer may admire the icy control and business acumen of characters such as Gus Fring, and cheer as he wreaks his revenge on the murderous Juárez Cartel, yet sanction of the character evaporates when he poses a threat to Walt and Jesse. They are the primary objects of identification in *Breaking Bad* because therein lie the compassion, integrity and humanity that viewers recognise and valorise in themselves and in their communities. This focus on shared humanity encourages viewers to engage in an interactive questioning of their own ethics. *Breaking Bad* juxtaposes complex masculinities with simplistic femininities, whilst playing off the character trajectories of the protagonist and his primary antagonists in ways that encourage audience perceptions to transition from sympathy to empathy to antipathy (for Walt) and vice versa (for Jesse and Hank). These confounding relationships between personalities, (received) morality and circumstances, afford viewers an opportunity to challenge the valorisation of criminal characters in popular culture; they also alert viewers to the role that they themselves play in the transaction, through shifting and contingent empathy. And, perhaps most importantly, it awakens viewers to the founding premise of the show: that heroes and villains are not absolute, and that beauty and horror co-exist in the modern condition despite our best efforts to control it.

Notes

[1] *Breaking Bad*, 'Pilot,' Season 1, Episode 1. Vince Gilligan, AMC, 20 September 2008.

[2] Jonathan Cohen, 'Defining Identification: A Theoretical Look at the Identification of Audiences with Media Characters,' *Mass Communication & Society* 4.3 (2001): 245-264.

[3] Ibid., 247.

[4] Ibid., 247-248.

[5] Keith Oatley, *Such Stuff as Dreams: The Psychology of Fiction* (Malden, MA: Wiley-Blackwell, 2001), 126.

[6] Thomas M. Leitch, 'Nobody Here but Us Killers: The Disavowal of Violence in Recent American Films,' VirginiaTech.edu, Viewed on 21 January 2014 http://www.rc.vt.edu/popculture/violence/files/NobodyHere.pdf.

[7] *Breaking Bad*, 'Crazy Handful of Nothin,' Season 1, Episode 6. Bronwen Hughes, AMC, 2 March 2008.

[8] Written by Paul Rothman. *Like a Breeze: 22 German Groove Classics from the Brilliant-Musik Archives*, Tutzing: Royal Ear Force, 2001.

[9] *Breaking Bad*, 'Gliding Over All,' Season 5, Episode 8. Michelle MacLaren, AMC, 2 September 2012.

[10] Lyrics by Dorothy Fields, composed by Jerome Kern. *Nat King Cole Sings/George Shearing Plays*, Los Angeles: Capitol Records, 1962.

[11] Leitch, 'Nobody Here but Us Killers' 5.

[12] Gavin Fairbairn, 'Reflecting on Empathy', in this volume

[13] Oatley, *Such Stuff as Dreams*, 118.

[14] Ibid., 126.

[15] Janet Beavin Bavelas, Alex Black, Nicole Chovil, Charles R. Lemery and Jennifer Mullett, 'Form and Function in Motor Mimicry Topographic Evidence that the Primary Function Is Communicative,' *Human Communication Research* 14.3 (1988): 275-299.

[16] Steve Larocco, Empathy as Orientation Rather than Feeling: Why Empathy Is Ethically Complex,' in this volume.

[17] Noël Carroll, 'On Some Affective Relations between Audience and the Characters in Popular Fiction,' *Empathy: Philosophical and Psychological Perspectives*, eds. Amy Coplan and Peter Goldie (Oxford: OUP, 2014), 162-184.

[18] Ibid.

[19] *Breaking Bad*, 'Pilot'.

[20] Adam Morton, 'Empathy for the Devil,' *Empathy: Philosophical and Psychological Perspectives*, eds. Amy Coplan and Peter Goldie (Oxford: OUP, 2014), 318-330.

[21] Suzanne Keen, 'Intersectional Narratology in the Study of Narrative Empathy,' *Narrative Theory Unbound: Queer and Feminist Interventions* (Columbus: Ohio State UP, 2015), 131.

[22] *Breaking Bad*, 'Pilot'.

[23] Jason Landrum, 'Say My Name: The Fantasy of Liberated Masculinity,' *The Methods of* Breaking Bad*: Essays on Narrative, Character and Ethics*, eds. Jacob Blevins and Dafydd Wood (Jefferson, North Carolina: McFarland, 2015). Kindle edition.

[24] FeministTV blog, 'White, Pink, Brown, Blue: The Racial Politics of *Breaking Bad*,' *Tubmlr.com.* Viewed on 21 September 2015, http://feministtv.tumblr.com/post/61247485431/white-pink-brown-blue-the-racial-politics-of.

[25] Malcolm Harris, 'Walter White Supremacy.' *The New Inquiry.com*, Viewed on 21 September 2015, http://thenewinquiry.com/essays/walter-white-supremacy/.

[26] Chris Prioleau, 'Walter White and Bleeding Brown: On *Breaking Bad*'s Race Problem,' *The Apogee Journal.org*, Viewed on 21 September 2015, http://www.apogeejournal.org/2013/10/walter-white-bleeding-brown-on-breaking-bads-race-problem/.

[27] See http://www.justice.gov/archive/ndic/pubs40/40393/distro.htm for more information. Viewed on 24 September 2015.

[28] Note that the key distributor of methamphetamine in neighbouring Arizona is a white man name Declan, who is presumably of Irish descent (although actor Louis Ferreira is actually Portuguese).

[29] FeministTV blog, 'White, Pink, Brown, Blue.

[30] Ibid.

31 Prioleau, 'Walter White and Bleeding Brown'.

32 Larocco, in this volume.

33 John Stuart Mill, *Utilitarianism* (London: Longmans, Green and Co., 1879), Kindle edition.

34 Carroll, 'On Some Affective Relations' 174.

35 It should be noted that the wholesomeness of the White family stands in stark contrast to the immorality, cruelty and avarice displayed by the neo-Nazi 'family' of Todd Alquist. Introduced to viewers via Todd's Uncle Jack, the group consists of friends and criminal associates who have grouped together to create a treacherous and terrifying alternative family. Mutual care and understanding have been replaced by acquisitiveness, hedonism and the pursuit of power. The group functions as a stark warning against the dangers of violating societal and familiar codes of conduct, and performs a crucial role in establishing *Breaking Bad*'s moral framework.

36 *Breaking Bad*, 'Crazy Handful of Nothin.'

37 Ibid.

38 Stella Bruzzi, *Undressing Cinema: Clothing and Identity in the Movies* (Abingdon: Routledge, 2004), 76.

39 Sigmund Freud, 'A Hat as a Symbol of a Man (Or of Male Genitals),' *The Interpretation of Dreams* (London: Penguin, 1991), 478-480.

40 The potency of the symbol becomes increasing apparent as the series progresses, with Walt donning the 'Heisenberg' hat at key points in the narrative and with increasing frequency as his megalomania develops. A loose thread on the hat in episode four of Season Five of *Breaking Bad* indicates that Walt's tightly wrought alternative reality is unravelling.

41 Esther Sonnet and Peter Stanfield, '"Good Evening Gentlemen; Can I Check Your Hats, Please?" Masculinity, Dress, and the Retro Gangster Cycles of the 1990s,' *Mob Culture: Hidden Histories of the American Gangster Film*, eds. Lee Grieveson, Esther Sonnet and Peter Stanfield (Oxford: Berg, 2005), 163-184.

42 *Breaking Bad*, '…and the Bag's in the River,' Season 1, Episode 3. Adam Bernstein, AMC, 10 February 2008·

43 *Breaking Bad*, 'Phoenix,' Season 2, Episode 12. Colin Bucksey, AMC, 24 May 2009.

44 *Breaking Bad*, 'Half Measures,' Series 3, Episode 12. Adam Bernstein, AMC, 6 June 2010.

45 *Breaking Bad*, 'Full Measure,' Season 3, Episode 13. Vince Gilligan, AMC, 13 June 2010.

46 *Breaking Bad*, 'Cornered,' Season 4, Episode 6. Michael Slovis, AMC, 21 August 2011.

47 *Breaking Bad*, 'A-No-Rough-Stuff-Type Deal,' Season 1, Episode 7. Tim Hunter, AMC, 9 March 2008.

[48] *Breaking Bad*, 'End Times,' Season 4, Episode 12. Vince Gilligan, AMC, 2 October 2011.

[49] Larocco, in this volume.

[50] Ibid.

[51] Ibid., 1.

[52] *Breaking Bad*, 'Dead Freight,' Season 5, Episode 5. George Mastras, 12 August 2012.

[53] *Breaking Bad*, 'Ozymandias,' Season 5, Episode 14. Rian Johnson, AMC, 15 September 2013.

[54] For example by providing Skyler with information she can trade with the Feds; supplying co-ordinates which will lead the authorities to the bodies of Hank and Steve Gomez (Steven Michael Quesada), and allow Marie the closure that burial will bring; rescuing Jesse from the white supremacists, etc.

[55] Characters such as Tuco, Gus, Uncle Jack and, ultimately, even Walt are testament to this.

[56] *Breaking Bad*, 'Abiquiú,' Season 3, Episode 11. Rian Johnson, AMC, 23 May 2010.

[57] *Breaking Bad*, 'Crawl Space,' Season 4, Episode 11.

[58] *Breaking Bad*, 'Rabid Dog,' Season 5, Episode 12. Sam Catlin, AMC, 1 September 2013.

[59] Audience opinion of Skyler can be measured by the many vitriolic web pages, memes and Facebook groups dedicated to castigating the character. Worryingly, this hatred also spilled over into 'real life' when Anna Gunn, who plays Skyler, became the target of death threats, rape threats and personal abuse. See *New York Times*, 23 August 2003, Viewed on 16 October 2014, http://www.nytimes.com/2013/08/24/opinion/i-have-a-characterissue.html?_r=0.

[60] Skyler's dismissive attitude towards her husband is laid bare in an excruciating two-shot in the pilot episode, when she masturbates him (as a birthday treat) whilst simultaneously conducting on online auction and explaining why he needs to paint the baby's nursery on Saturday, rather than go to a science expo as he had planned. *Breaking Bad*, 'Pilot,' Season 1, Episode 1. Vince Gilligan, AMC, 20 September 2008.

[61] Laura Bennett, 'The True Anti-Hero of "Breaking Bad" Isn't Walter White: Sexual Politics and the Bad Wife,' *New Republic*, 8 August 2013. Viewed on 15 June 2015, http://www.newrepublic.com/article/114245/breaking-bad-review-walter-white-not-antihero.

[62] Jen Chaney, 'Why You Hate Skyler White,' *Esquire*, 5 September 2013. Viewed on 15 June 2015, http://www.esquire.com/entertainment/tv/a24645/why-you-hate-skyler-white/.

[63] See, for example, Sandra M. Gilbert and Susan Gubar, *The Madwoman in the Attic: The Woman Writer and the Nineteenth-Century Literary Imagination* (New Haven, Connecticut: Yale Nota Bene, [1979] 2000).

[64] *Breaking Bad*, 'No Más,' Season 3, Episode 1. Bryan Cranston, AMC, 21 March 2010.

[65] Breaking Bad, 'Green Light,' Season 3, Episode 4. Scott Winant, AMC, 11 April 2010.

[66] *Breaking Bad*, 'Kafkaesque,' Season 3, Episode 9. Michael Slovis, AMC, 16 May 2010.

[67] Jesse speaks out in defence of Brock when Brock's mother, a recovering addict Jesse met at NA, suggests she and Jesse smoke some post-coital meth together in *Breaking Bad*, 'Abiquiú,' Season 3, Episode 11. Rian Johnson, AMC, 23 May 2010.

[68] In *Breaking Bad*, 'Peekaboo,' Season 2, Episode 6 (Peter Medak, AMC, 12 April 2009), Jesse tries to protect the badly neglected child when he attempts to frighten Spooge and his 'lady'(she is never named in the series) into returning money they stole from Skinny Pete.

[69] *Breaking Bad*, 'Half Measures,' Season 3, Episode 12. Adam Bernstein, AMC, 6 June 2010. Walt's attempt to control the situation (by killing the dealers responsible for Tomás's death) leads to events spinning further out of control – proof-perfect of Heisenberg's 'Uncertainty Principle.'

[70] When he met Jane, Jesse was a casual drug user. Upon learning Jane was a recovering addict he attempted to shield her from his own drug use (brought on by a period of depression following the murder of Combo by Tomás, in *Breaking Bad*, 'Mandala,' Season 2, Episode 11 (Adam Bernstein, AMC, 17 May 2009)) so as not to cause her to relapse. Jane opted to join him and quickly escalated their habit, introducing Jesse to heroin and encouraging him to inject it intravenously. So, even here, in such challenging circumstances, criterial prefocussing ensures that Jesse is perceived empathetically by the audience whilst Jane takes on a sinister, corrupting role.

[71] His care for his dying Aunt Ginny, his intuitive understanding of Walt's condition, and his protective relationship with his younger brother are evidence of this.

[72] For statistical consistency between regions, the United Nations considers the term 'youth' to include all people between the ages of 15 and 24 years old. For more information, see the article 'What do We Mean by Youth?' *United Nations Educational, Scientific and Cultural Organization*. Viewed on 21 September 2015, http://www.unesco.org/new/en/social-and-human-sciences/themes/youth/youth-definition/

[73] FeministTV Blog, 'White, Pink, Brown, Blue.

74 Ross Douthat, 'The Hero of 'Breaking Bad,' *New York Times*, 18 September 2013. Viewed on 15 June 2015, http://douthat.blogs.nytimes.com/2013/09/18/the-hero-of-breaking-bad/?_r=0.

75 *Breaking Bad*, 'Blood Money,' Season 5, Episode 9. Bryan Cranston, AMC, 11 August 2013.

76 *Breaking Bad*, 'Buried,' Season 5, Episode 10.

77 *Breaking Bad*, 'Rabid Dog,' Season 5, Episode 12. Sam Catlin, AMC, 1 September 2013.

78 Fairbairn, in this volume.

79 *Breaking Bad*, 'Salud,' Season 4, Episode 10. Michaelle MacLaren, AMC, 18 September 2011.

80 *Breaking Bad*, 'Hermanos,' Season 4, Episode 8. Johan Renck, AMC, 4 September 2011.

81 *Breaking Bad*, 'Half Measures,' Season 3, Episode 12. Adam Bernstein, AMC, 6 June 2010. Jesse encourages Wendy to acquiesce to the plan by empathetically appealing to her maternal instincts and explaining that the men are using children as drug runners. Wendy reluctantly agrees, noting that she would 'do anything' for her own child, but is relieved when the dealers are not in their usual spot when she arrives to make the drop.

82 *Breaking Bad*, 'Half Measures,' Season 3, Episode 12. Adam Bernstein, AMC, 6 June 2010.

83 'Windy' written by Ruthann Friedman and performed by The Association, Burbank: Warner Bros., 1967.

84 Larocco, in this volume.

Bibliography

Bavelas, Janet Beavin, Alex Black, Nicole Chovil, Charles R. Lemery and Jennifer Mullett. 'Form and Function in Motor Mimicry Topographic Evidence that the Primary Function Is Communicative.' *Human Communication Research* 14.3 (1988): 275-299.

Bentham, Jeremy. *An Introduction to the Principles of Morals and Legislation.* Mineola, New York: Dover Philosophical Classics, 2007.

Bennett, Laura. 'The True Anti-Hero of *Breaking Bad* Isn't Walter White: Sexual Politics and the Bad Wife.' *New Republic*, 8 August 2013. Viewed on 15 June 2015,
http://www.newrepublic.com/article/114245/breaking-bad-review-walter-white-not-antihero.

Breaking Bad. Creator Vince Gilligan. New York: AMC, 2008- 2013, Netflix.

Bruzzi, Stella. *Undressing Cinema: Clothing and Identity in the Movies.* Abingdon: Routledge, 2004.

Carroll, Noël. 'On Some Affective Relations between Audience and the Characters in Popular Fiction.' *Empathy: Philosophical and Psychological Perspectives,* edited by Amy Coplan and Peter Goldie, 162-184. Oxford: OUP, 2014.

Chaney, Jen. 'Why You Hate Skyler White.' *Esquire*, 5 September 2013. Viewed on 15 June 2015,
http://www.esquire.com/entertainment/tv/a24645/why-you-hate-skyler-white/.

Cohen, Jonathan. 'Defining Identification: A Theoretical Look at the Identification of Audiences with Media Characters.' *Mass Communication & Society* 4.3 (2001): 245-264.

Douthat, Ross. 'The Hero of *Breaking Bad*.' *New York Times*, 18 September 2013. Viewed on 15 June 2015.
http://douthat.blogs.nytimes.com/2013/09/18/the-hero-of-breaking-bad/?_r=0.

Feminist TV Blog. 'White, Pink, Brown, Blue: The Racial Politics of *Breaking Bad*.' *Tumblr.com*. Viewed on 21 September 2015,
http://feministtv.tumblr.com/post/61247485431/white-pink-brown-blue-the-racial-politics-of.

Freud, Sigmund. *The Interpretation of Dreams*. London: Penguin, 1991.

Gunn, Anna. 'I Have a Character Issue.' *New York Times*, 23 August 2003. Viewed on 16 October 2014.
http://www.nytimes.com/2013/08/24/opinion/i-have-a-characterissue.html?_r=0.

Harris, Malcolm. 'Walter White Supremacy.' *The New Enquiry*, 27 September 2013. Viewed on 21 September 2015.
http://thenewinquiry.com/essays/walter-white-supremacy/.

Keen, Suzanne. 'Intersectional Narratology in the Study of Narrative Empathy.' *Narrative Theory Unbound: Queer and Feminist Interventions*, edited by Robyn Warhol and Susan S. Lanser, 123-146. Columbus: Ohio State UP, 2015.

Landrum, Jason. 'Say My Name: The Fantasy of Liberated Masculinity,' *The Methods of* Breaking Bad*: Essays on Narrative, Character and Ethics*, edited by Jacob Blevins and Dafydd Wood, np. Jefferson, North Carolina: McFarland, 2015. Kindle edition.

Leitch, Thomas M. 'Nobody Here but Us Killers: The Disavowal of Violence in Recent American Films.' VirginiaTech.edu. Viewed on 21 January 2014. http://www.rc.vt.edu/popculture/violence/files/NobodyHere.pdf.

McInnes, Paul. '*Breaking Bad* Creator Vince Gilligan: The Man Who Turned Walter White from Mr Chips into Scarface.' *Guardian*, 19 May 2012. Viewed on 25 February 2014. http://www.theguardian.com/tv-and-radio/2012/may/19/vince-gilligan-breaking-bad.

Mill, John Stuart. *Utilitarianism*. London: Longmans, Green and Co., 1879. Kindle edition.

Morton, Adam. 'Empathy for the Devil.' *Empathy: Philosophical and Psychological Perspectives*, edited by Amy Coplan and Peter Goldie, 318-330. Oxford: OUP, 2014.

Oatley, Keith. *Such Stuff as Dreams: The Psychology of Fiction*. Malden, MA: Wiley-Blackwell, 2001.

Prioleau, Chris. 'Walter White and Bleeding Brown: On *Breaking Bad*'s Race Problem.' *Apogee Journal.org*. 3 October 2013. Viewed on 21 September 2015. http://www.apogeejournal.org/2013/10/walter-white-bleeding-brown-on-breaking-bads-race-problem/

Sonnet, Esther and Peter Stanfield. '"Good Evening Gentlemen; Can I Check Your Hats, Please?" Masculinity, Dress, and the Retro Gangster Cycles of the 1990s.' *Mob Culture: Hidden Histories of the American Gangster Film*, edited by Lee Grieveson, Esther Sonnet, and Peter Stanfield, 163-184. Oxford: Berg, 2005.

US Department of Justice National Drug Intelligence Center. 'New Mexico HIDTA Drug Market Analysis 2010.' *United States Department of Justice Archives*. Viewed on 24 September 2015. http://www.justice.gov/archive/ndic/pubs40/40393/distro.htm

Discography

Charlie Steinmann Orchestra and Singers. 'It is Such a Good Night.' Writer Paul Rothman. *Like a Breeze: 22 German Groove Classics from the Brilliant-Musik Archives* Tutzing: Royal Ear Force, 2001, CD.

Nat King Cole. 'Pick Yourself Up.' Writers Dorothy Fields and Jerome Kern. *Nat King Cole Sings/George Shearing Plays*. Burbank: Capitol Records, 1962, CD.

Filmography

The French Connection. Directed by William Friedkin. New York: D'Antoni, 1971. DVD.

Mean Streets. Directed by Martin Scorsese. Universal City, CA: Universal, 1973. DVD.

Having previously enjoyed a fourteen-year career in the advertising industry, **Abby Bentham** currently teaches undergraduate modules on literature, critical theory and evil at the University of Salford. Her research interests include narrative poetics, transgression, the aesthetics of violence, psychoanalysis, gender, and popular culture. She has published on subjects as diverse as Dickens and *Dexter* and is currently completing a book-length project exploring the literary trajectory of the fictional psychopath.

'Gays Are the New Jews': Homophobic Representations in African Media versus *Twitterverse* Empathy

Charles King

Abstract

In 2006, *The Huffington Post* columnist Danny Miller stated that 'gays are the new Jews', asking if our ability to accept people who are different from ourselves has plummeted to dangerous levels. The world since then has altered substantially, both for better, such as the historic Supreme Court decision to legalise same-sex marriage across the US in 2015, and for worse, with lesbian, gay, bisexual, transgender (LGBT) persons now facing new, unprecedented legal and social challenges in Russia. Similarly, in Uganda, government legislation is anticipated, which will outlaw the 'promotion' of homosexual acts, with possible punishment including the death sentence. Research on the role of empathy in journalism acknowledges that while historically, emotion was considered inferior to reason, increasingly, empathy is seen as critical to the profession, in the belief that empathy is a primary way through which humans emotionally develop and make decisions. In this chapter I explore the relationship and contrast between homophobic representations in African mainstream news media and the unfettered Twitter representations of empathy in direct response to the former. By examining the ways in which African mainstream media and Twitter users relate to empathy, I propose that the *Twitter[uni]verse* has a significant role to play with respect to giving voice to the marginalised, and nurturing emotional development, and in particular, empathy In this way, I argue that Twitter offers a platform for ethical decision-making in response to state-sanctioned homophobia and hatred, thus fulfilling the liberal pluralism media theory that the free exchange of ideas is crucial to a democracy's health. I thus argue that Twitter as a medium has the potential to powerfully counter patriarchal, religious, nationalist and 'traditional' cultural systems of control which are mutually-reinforcing in creating a toxic environment for African queer communities.

Key Words: Empathy, African media, Twitter, homophobia, liberal pluralism, sympathy, gay, emotivism, ethics, compassion, *the other*, African journalism students.

*****

1. Defining Empathy

While attempting to define empathy, I was fascinated to observe that Czech writer, Milan Kundera, who set his best known novel, *The Unbearable Lightness of Being*, in Prague – where the first Global Conference on Empathy took place in

2014 – had succinctly defined empathy's synonym, 'compassion,' in the early pages of his novel:

> All languages that derive from Latin form the word "compassion" by combining the prefix meaning "with" (*com-*) and the root meaning "suffering" (Late Latin, *passio*). In other languages – Czech, Polish, German, and Swedish, for instance – this word is translated by a noun formed of an equivalent prefix combined with the word that means "feeling" [...]. In languages that derive from Latin, "compassion" means: we cannot look on coolly as others suffer; or, we sympathise with those who suffer. Another word with approximately the same meaning, "pity" [...], connotes a certain condescension towards the sufferer. "To take pity on a woman" means that we are better off than she, that we stoop to her level, lower ourselves.[1]

Kundera maintains that the word 'compassion'' generally inspires suspicion because it designates what is considered an inferior, second-rate sentiment which has little to do with love.[2] Thus, to love someone out of compassion means not really to love at all. In languages that create the word 'compassion' from the root 'feeling,' and not from the root 'suffering', the word is used in approximately the same way.[3] However, to contend that it designates a bad or inferior sentiment is challenging. Kundera rightfully argues that the secret strength of its etymology floods the word with another light and gives it a broader meaning.[4] For him, to have compassion (co-feeling) means not only to live with the other's misfortune but also to feel with him/her any emotion – joy, anxiety, and pain.[5] It's this kind of compassion that therefore signifies the maximal capacity of affective imagination, the art of emotional telepathy.[6] For this reason, for Kundera, it is supreme in the hierarchy of sentiments.[7]

Let us now take it a step further, and link 'empathy' with 'ethical decision making,' which will set the tone for what will unfold in this chapter.

2. Ethics and Empathy

Studies on empathy in journalism suggest that in ethical decision making, emotion can be superior to reason, although historically emotion has been generally considered inferior to reason.[8] According to Sandra Davidson Scott in 'Beyond Reason: A Feminist Theory of Ethics for Journalists,' empathy serves as the key principle for emotional development and decision making; she argues that through learning to empathise with other sentient creatures, human beings develop morally.[9] While concurring with the importance of developing empathy, however, I contextualise the notion of morality as the act of expressing or teaching a conception of 'right' behaviour, as opposed to inappropriately conflating empathy with religiously-based moral approval.

In the context of journalism, 'ethical questions can arise' within every aspect of the profession – 'for instance, from investigating news stories, deciding what stories should run, how they should be played, or what kind of pictures should accompany them.'[10] In 'Empathic New(s) Orientations in Narratives about Sexual,' Theo specifically points to the particular ethical decisions involved in reporting on marginalised groups such as lesbian, gay, bisexual, transgender (LGBT) persons who are 'the objects of stories subjected to homophobia':[11]

> Over the past two decades, the Western world has experienced a significant evolution in their understanding and cultural acceptance of lesbian, gay, bisexual, and transgender (LGBT) lives. Consequently, gay and lesbian issues (and increasingly, bisexual and transgender issues) have moved beyond simplistic political dichotomies and toward more fully realized representations, not only of the diversity of the West's communities, but also of our lives, our families, and our fundamental inclusion in the fabric of [Western] society.[12]

This makes their very representation or forms of acknowledgment as the objects of stories an ethical question.[13] This issue of representation is complex, as it is intricately intertwined with what Theo describes as 'communication architectures' because 'the process of mass communication relies on both form and content in concert with one another.'[14] A more complex approach to the issue, he argues, serves to take the exploration deeper than one of (anti-homophobic) content to tease out how communication architectures can confound attempts to change discriminatory paradigms within broader society.[15]

Scott notes the added challenge that tight timelines add to the context of journalism. Reporters and editors working under time pressure are in need of ethical guidance, she maintains, which abstract philosophical theory simply cannot provide.[16] Instead, she proposes a concrete theory of 'emotivism', which she argues:

> ...stresses empathy, and...emphasises the importance of the emotional or emotive content of ethical decisions. Because of its acceptance of emotions, this theory runs counter to most traditional, male philosophy.[17]

Scott maintains that, historically, a failure to appreciate the value of emotions for ethical conduct has accompanied the patriarchal failure to hear women and to appreciate the value of women.[18] It is an unworkable logic that should, by now, be extinct.

> The following "logic'" has held far too much sway: Reason is superior to emotions, Men are rational, women are emotional. Therefore, men are superior to women. Stated in negative terms: Emotion is inferior to reason. Women are emotional, men are rational. Therefore, women are inferior to men.[19]

Not only has this 'perverted logic' harmed women, she maintains, but it has also damaged ethical theory. The value of emotion as an ethical force has been denigrated, because it's seen as too fuzzy a concept, linked to the emotional heart rather than the logical brain. Scott asks whether it is possible that an ethics of using moral imagination to empathise with others - and to progress in moral depth – can also be an ethics through which reasonable people can reach agreement on what constitutes correct conduct?[20] Yes, is her conclusion, and more so than by going through any of the perambulations and rationalisations of reason.[21]

From this perspective, and at long last, emotion is perceived as crucial. And therein lies the embryonic potential for empathy to be incubated: we should not leach our ethical arsenal of the enormous power of emotion; because too much faith in reason is in fact unreasonable.[22] Thus, with this inversion of 'perverted logic', the first in a series of inversions that are highlighted in this chapter is a parallel emergence of the notion of empathy. There is a definite sense that the times they are 'a-changing', for the better; that there is a rise of empathy as a force for good, but also, which I will highlight elsewhere, as the bad, too, is equally emerging.

Further, Scott argues that the historical failure to appreciate the value of emotions has been critical in the construction of women as the *other* in patriarchal societies, and particularly within the mainstream media. This is in addition to the glass ceiling that female journalists and media practitioners encounter in male-dominated newsrooms and organisations, which are 'wired' to filter news for heteropatriarchal societies that continue to subjugate women – and many other *others* for that matter. Heteropatriarchy is

> ...the combination of male – patriarchal – and heterosexual dominance essentially describing the severe sex and gender bias prevalent among the elite ruling classes of nation-states.[23]

Heteropatriarchy thus, in essence, also describes how the white male is the ruling class of post-colonial societies.[24]

In the section that follows I delve further into the concept of the *other* with the aim of exploring not only homophobia, but also why *othering* is contrary to empathy.

3. The Sub-Human, Immoral Other and Moral Imagination

While the first objective of my chapter is to explore the relationship between homophobic representations in African mainstream news media and empathetic *Twitterverse* responses to such homophobia, the second objective is to explore how *the other* is constructed. This is necessary in order to better understand an important aspect of that which upholds and justifies the hatred rained down upon LGBT persons, and other *others*. In this regard, I propose that *othering* is both a process and form of engaging *the other* (with hatred) that works antithetically to empathy. Thus, it is of critical importance to this exploration to better understand the concept of *the other*.

I propose that Twitter – contrasted with the various levels of state-controlled media in 38 African countries (to which I will return later in this chapter) – provides an alternative platform for users to make ethical decisions in response to or retaliation against state-sanctioned homophobia and hatred. In this way, Twitter enables not only empathetic action, but also offers the potential of critically fulfilling the liberal pluralism media theory that the free exchange of ideas is crucial to a democracy's health.[25]

By examining the ways in which African mainstream media and Twitter users act empathetically – that is, compassionately relating with *the other* – or not, I offer insights into the role the *Twitterverse* can play in providing a voice to the marginalised and voiceless (*the other*), while simultaneously offering the potential of nurturing emotional development and empathy.

James Norris writes that '[b]y "othering", we mean any action by which an individual or group becomes mentally classified in somebody's mind as 'not one of us.'[26] He writes:

> Rather than always remembering that every person is a complex bundle of emotions, ideas, motivations, reflexes, priorities, and many other subtle aspects, it's sometimes easier to dismiss them as being in some way less human, and less worthy of respect and dignity, than we are.[27]

This psychological tactic may well have had its uses in our species' distant tribal past when group solidarity was extremely important in the early days of civilisation.[28] Strong demarcation between our allies and our enemies was needed. So as to both survive and thrive, human beings needed to be part of a tight-knit tribe who would look out for us in exchange for knowing that we would help look out for them.[29] Further, those in your tribe, who live in your community, are more likely to have a common culture and dialect and be closely related to you and thus share your genes.[30] I conceive of the *'other'* not primarily as a sociological construction, but rather as a subjective, emotional one, especially in the light of other constructions, such as Edward Said's references to the colonialist 'other,' which is distinctive. For Said, the concept of 'orientalism' was an entrenched structure of thought, a pattern of making certain generalizations about the part of the world known as the 'East'. In other words, generalizations made about *the other.*[31] As Said writes,

> Orientalism was ultimately a political vision of reality whose structure promoted the difference between the familiar (Europe, West, "us") and the strange (the Orient, the East, "them").[32]

*The othe*r is thus perceived of as not belonging, because they are different in some fundamental way, and thus inferior.[33]

> The group sees itself as the norm and judges those who do not meet that norm (that is, who are different in any way) as the Other. Perceived as lacking essential characteristics possessed by the group, the Other is almost always seen as a lesser or inferior being and is treated accordingly. The Other in a society may have few or no legal rights, may be characterized as less intelligent or as immoral, and may even be regarded as sub-human.[34]

While *otherness* takes many forms, the irony is that within the countless and multi-faceted prisms of our world/s, every single one of us is *the other* at all times, every day, everywhere, to varying degrees of course: we are all *others* in the eyes of our *others*: Jews in the eyes of Muslims and Christians, the North versus the South, the West versus the East (as expressed in Said's 'orientalism' above), 'developed' world versus 'third/developing' world, black versus white, female versus male, straight versus gay/LGBT persons, as well the *others* that become silenced by the very framing of this gender binary, such as intersex or transgendered. So the list goes on – not to mention the ways in which these 'us-them' binaries themselves erase other identities, persons or communities who straddle or fit into neither.

Although the list of *others* is an infinite and looping one, somewhere along the line, the cycle of hatred has to be broken. Not only will this serve a better society by seeing it transformed, but it will see individuals empowered. I believe the solution lies in developing, at all costs, an empathetic society, a point that will be elaborated below. Furthermore, in terms of a catalytic infusion of empowerment and transformation, Frantz Fanon insists that 'the thing which has been colonised becomes human during the same process by which it frees itself'. It is this that I believe is fundamental to the parallel approach of both breaking the cycle of hatred while simultaneously building an empathetic society. This is in stark contrast to what Hussein Abdilahi Bulhan calls the 'psychology of oppression'.[35] He insists that Fanon was a pioneer for exactly the fact that he 'combined a commitment to social transformation with the psychological liberation of individuals'.[36]

I refer to Fanon, again, but this time specifically regarding the ivory tower and the role of the academic. At this juncture it is critical to remember that I am not some safe outsider gazing in from a distance; not for a minute must I forget myself, nor detach myself, for that then puts safe-space between me and what then becomes another *other*; I must not for a minute 'speculate' or maintain emotional detachment even in the very writing of this chapter lest I fall prey to exactly what Fanon is so rightfully critical of – i.e. not being fully immersed in the 'social upheaval' of our world. It is one thing to speculate from an academic ivory tower about the upheavals of revolution, to view the gigantic machinery of war from a distance in time and space, to maintain emotional detachment in manipulating lifeless statistics, and reducing the immense travails of anonymous victims into convenient intellectual paradigms.[37] However,

> it is quite another to be totally immersed in the social upheaval, to commit one's life to a cause now looming larger than everything else, to rub shoulders with living persons in the din of battle, and to fully identify with them in victory as well as in defeat.[38]

As Theo discusses in this volume, the 'other' is produced and/or reproduced through communication architectures within media by, among others, the 'pitfalls of the inherent subjectivising discourses of journalistic practices.'[39] This is especially so since in news journalism, news reporting is hawked as exclusively non-fiction, in which 'professional standards of objectivity are pursued as a way to come across as impartial.'[40] Twitter, on the other hand, has enormous potential to disrupt the construction of *the other* embarked upon by traditional media architectures.

Therefore, and in contrast to traditional media, Twitter allows for the possibility of audiences to be 'mobilised', as Theo notes, to 'engage attempts to change discriminatory opinions within broader society by interacting with individuals' as opposed to the sense of 'audiences as a collective.'[41] On Twitter, as opposed to in traditional media (where inflexible communication architectures purposefully concretise discriminatory opinions), communication architectonics can be mobilised (although perhaps unintentionally) by masses of unconnected participants, to engage attempts to change discriminatory opinions within broader society by interacting with individuals.[42]

When such an 'inversion' has taken place (and I use the word 'inversion' purposefully), The Media[43] (hereafter referred to as 'mainstream media,' which comprises both state and private, independent media) fails to fulfil its ideal role within a healthy democracy. In other words, when unreasonable people reach an agreement on what constitutes so-called 'correct conduct' – such as in the case of the recent Ugandan tabloid *The Red Pepper's* front pager exposé of the country's '200 Top Gays'[44] – people were able to step in so-to-speak through the *Twitterverse* to both fill/fulfil that space, completing this inversion.

This stance was further backed by the 2013 Amnesty International report that decried 'the continued criminalization of consensual same-sex conduct in 38 African countries' as a serious cause for concern because these actions 'violate a raft of international and regional human rights norms, and serves to marginalize one group of Africans based on their sexual orientation and gender identity alone'.[45] The report documents the discrimination faced by LGBTI people on the African continent as same-sex conduct ('homosexual acts') in sub-Saharan Africa is increasingly criminalised as more governments seek to impose draconian penalties or expand the breadth of existing laws, including introducing the death penalty.[46] Thus, it is that the 'gay other' has been constructed hand-in-hand with the mainstream media in these countries, such as in the case of Uganda's The Red Pepper newspaper.

The *Twitterverse,* on the other hand – with its myriad of complications and perambulations, especially as this platform is still far from being fully appreciated (looking at the so-called 'Arab Spring' and in 2013, developments in Turkey) or even properly misunderstood – is, instead, an enabler for/medium through which everyday people, i.e. 'reasonable people,' have the opportunity to use moral imagination to empathise with *the other*.[47] Twitter thus fulfils 'the ideal role of the media in a healthy democracy.'[48]

The potential to use a moral imagination to empathise with *others* exists in the *Twitterverse* because it not only offers the opportunity for *the others'* plight to be made known and be heard, but because it also enables *the other* to be the teller of their own story – to be heard in their own voice. Unlike the state-sanctioned news media, Twitter is also a resource for assistance and support, as well as a source of information and knowledge, so that *the other* may retaliate publicly, especially where they are banished from the national media and national agenda except through vilification or unbalanced reporting based on stereotypes and hatred-based coverage where *the other* is not heard in their own voice.

On that note, regarding national or mass hysterias that have historically led to acts such as the public 'burning of witches' at the stake, the concept of 'national empathy', referenced at the First Global Conference on Empathy in Prague, holds particular relevance.[49] In the case of the 38 homophobic African countries addressed in this article, a 'national antipathy' – or hostility, antagonism, animosity, aversion, distaste, hatred, abhorrence, loathing, repugnance, odium, or all of the above – is publicly flaunted through the mainstream media.

Let us also never forget that what is so often sanitised in academic speak (I have Fanon in mind again) in extremely comfortable and safe conference venues, in safe cities, in safe countries, is a matter of life or death for many terrified people in large swathes of the African continent. I am not excited about the fact that in 30 years' time, at another conference in another city, we might be reflecting upon whether our children should or should not be visiting memorials (as has happened relating to Holocaust memorials and museum sites) to the hundreds of thousands of LGBT Africans who had died because of their sexual orientation and gender identity. They would have died because they were marginalised and then permanently muted for being *the other*. A *final solution* so-to-speak.

I therefore argue that Twitter has the potential to become a breeding ground of empathy. That is because it contains all of the ingredients for a progression in 'moral depth' to occur, as all of the seeds are there, which is 'also an ethics through which reasonable people can reach agreement on what constitutes correct conduct,' especially if 38 governments are getting the definition of 'correct conduct' so wrong.[50]

How does one include and incorporate *the other*, so that they are no longer *the other*? In other words how do we begin to transform a society? For one, as Theo in this publication maintains, 'the first step to a more socially transformative paradigm requires a recognition that gender and sexual categories are overly pragmatic and simplistic ways of differentiating between people.'[51] He argues that 'homosexuality' cannot be pinned down in any useful way, and, as with 'heterosexuality,' is not unitary and coherent, nor is it a description of a hidden nature.[52]

Although he also insists that '[a] clearly demarcated journalistic alternative based on a notion of sexuality as *identification* rather than *identity* will always be elusive.' This is in contrast to the mainstream media's simplistic one-dimensional as opposed to multi-dimensional approach (impossibly seeking the notion of balance and objectivity, while discarding any form of emotion, as highlighted earlier by Scott), which flattens out the 'victims'/sources/characters of these narratives. This leaches them of life while simultaneously lessening the possibility of the audience empathising with them. As Theo notes,

> [i]t is one thing to consider disruptions and inconsistencies, and to advise journalists to better reflect the complexity of subjective experience of interviewees, and with that their bodies, sexual acts and sexual objects, all of which mean different things to different people, even within the same sexual identity "category".[53]

But 'how to overcome the pitfalls of the inherent subjectivizing discourses of journalistic practices is quite another.'[54] Especially since in news journalism, 'news reporting is an enterprise touted as exclusively nonfiction, in which professional standards of objectivity are pursued as a way to come across as impartial.'[55] As we know, impartiality is an illusion:

> In linguistic-semiotic terms, journalists use both implicitly and explicitly rhetorical tools to make their stories seem accurate, truthful and verifiable. These tools serve to render the voices of their interviewees by means of largely invisible narrations.[56]

This smoke and mirrors approach hides and obfuscates much, which is why, again, Twitter wins hands down in terms of transparency and realness, unlike the comparatively undemocratic top-down mainstream media:

> As if written as "objective" accounts, their quote-based narratives (inaccurately) imply that [journalists] have no personal interest in the content and ideologies they reflect, and that they are themselves are not emotionally oriented either towards or against the interviewees.[57]

Objectivity remains an illusion; it also tends to muddy the waters further especially because media organisations and many journalists believe that they are functioning from the moral high ground.

> For some, objectivity is the cement of good journalism, the "cornerstone of the professional ideology of journalists in liberal democracies." For others, objectivity is a kind of deception, obscuring cultural, capitalistic or national bias behind talk of a neutral point of view promoting faith in an external truth or ideal, an individualistic viewing position that doesn't exist. Objectivity has been described as a myth and a shibboleth. It can be seen as a lifeblood, a high principle, or just a desire to be accurate.[58]

On Twitter, *the self* as *the other* is able to take their power back, to return themselves to the driving seat, because they are unfiltered by the journalist (whom, despite arguments to the contrary, is incapable of balance and objectivity). Especially because, like Davis, I believe that it is clear that patriarchy, religion, nationalism and notions of 'traditional' African culture can combine into mutually-reinforcing systems of control which are toxic for the likes of African queer communities.[59] Because on Twitter the narrator is *the self, the other*, I maintain that Twitter offers a chance to side-step this lack of objectivity by providing a wide-reaching and almost un-censorable platform for individuals to self-represent.

Thus, there is definite progression in the direction of achieving balance: mainly because those previously deemed 'interviewees,' who were often wronged in the so-called 'reporting process,' are able to tell their own stories. Further, this reclamation can take place on a platform known as a 'breaking news' source, in which journalists' failings can also be communicated to them both directly and publicly. It is not incidental that social media, especially Twitter, has been viewed as a democratizer of news, as a democratising counterbalance to the mainstream media.

Twitter is thus, arguably the link that closes the loop: it allows for the 'interviewee,' *the other* as object, to gain their own voice back as subject, from the journalist or mainstream media, which had taken on the 'responsibility' to speak (hardly ever accurately) on *the others'* behalf. Thus Twitter legitimately acts as a democratiser of news and information.

Referring to the loop, interestingly and in this volume, artist Fiona Larkin in her chapter titled 'Seeing the loop: Examining empathy through art practice,' writes that if the form of an object is always being formed by me, by my inner activity,' then are we merely *meeting ourselves coming back?*[60] Larkin then emphasises:

> It is fitting then to turn to fiction for a response. In her novel *Aliens and Anorexia*, Chris Krauss says; 'Therefore, empathy is not a reaching outward. It is a loop. Because there isn't any separation anymore between what you are and what you see.'[61]

Furthermore, Larkin also quotes Danish philosopher, Dan Zahavi:

> It is not possible simply to insert intersubjectivity somewhere within an already established ontology; rather, the three regions "self," "others" and "world" belong together; they reciprocally illuminate one another, and can only be understood in their interconnection.[62]

She highlights that for Zahavi, objects exist in the 'world' realm 'and while we perceive them as being very different from the bodies of others they have a fundamental connection to our bodies.[63]

Yes, an empathetic approach and/or disposition closes the loop or circle, because of the perspective that we are all one; essentially there is no *other* then: what you are and what you see are one. The distance, the differentiation, the no-man's land between boundaries and borders are thus disappeared.[64]

Irrespective of the above, so early into the twenty-first century we, as an international society consisting of endless prisms of *others*, face constant onslaughts of *other*-upon-*other* violence, such as, for example, perceptions of terrorism, the rise of the 'Islamic State,' and the 2015 xenophobic and Afrophobic violence in South Africa. All of these are hatred-responses to *The Other*. I maintain that 'the Twitterverse is a powerful medium for critiquing any ruling ideology, including the state's discriminatory laws against sexual minorities,' and that, crucially, it performs a crucial role in helping close the loop and shrinking the distance between *them, us,* and *The Others*.

4. Context and Status Quo

Amnesty International maintains that 'the continued criminalization of consensual same-sex conduct in 38 African countries is a serious cause for concern … [and] violates a raft of international and regional human rights norms, and serves to marginalize one group of Africans based on their sexual orientation and gender identity alone'.[65] In Uganda, this includes imposing the death penalty for 'aggravated' homosexuality (yes, you read correctly).[66] Originally, the Ugandan bill, first submitted in April 2009, would have made 'aggravated homosexuality' – which it defines as repeated homosexual acts, gay sex with a minor or someone with disabilities, or when one partner has HIV – a capital offense.[67] However, it provoked international outcry. This is why the Ugandan government subsequently revised the death penalty to life imprisonment so as to allow the 'rehabilitation' of gays.[68] Especially after Ethics and Integrity Minister Nsaba Buturo told Reuters that 'killing them might not be helpful.'[69] The bill also called for gay sex between (consenting) adults to be punishable by a life sentence. As in Russia, the 'promotion' of homosexuality – interpreted to mean any discussion of gay rights – would be a criminal offense. Then, in case that didn't cover all of the loopholes, anyone failing to report a homosexual act could face arrest themselves:

> The last decade has witnessed efforts in some sub-Saharan African countries to further criminalize LGBTI individuals by ostensibly targeting their behaviour, or to impose steeper penalties and broaden the scope of existing laws. Uganda has seen repeated attempts since 2009 to introduce the Anti-Homosexuality Bill – a bill which would seek to impose the death penalty for 'aggravated' homosexuality and which would criminalize anyone in Uganda who does not report violations of the bill's wide-ranging provisions within 24 hours to authorities.[70]

South Sudan and Burundi are not far behind, while in 2011 and 2012, Nigeria and Liberia respectively introduced bills to toughen penalties for same-sex relations and sexual conduct. And Mauritania, northern regions of Nigeria, the southern region of Somalia and Sudan, retain the death penalty for the same.[71]

The role of the mainstream media in these so-called democracies has been inverted such that in these countries, such as Uganda, it fulfils the exact opposite role of what a healthy and vibrant media should play in a healthy democracy: that of the Fourth Estate.[72]

Returning to the word 'inversion,' I return to in fact an entire litany of inversions: The term 'inversion,' 'implying a change in the position, order, or relationship of things so that they are the opposite of what they had been'[73] is derived from Sigmund Freud. Freud 'frequently called homosexuality an 'inversion,' something which in his view was distinct from the necessarily pathological perversions, and suggested that several distinct kinds might exist.'[74] Zimbabwean president Robert Mugabe, notorious for his 'gays and lesbians are worse than pigs and dogs' comment, has repeatedly claimed that Europe is trying to force gay rights on Africa.[75] Ironically, despite his opinion, that 'what is natural is made unnatural. And what is unnatural they want to say it is natural [...] let Europe keep their homosexual nonsense there and not cross over with it here,' it is not the 'homosexuals' that are unnatural, but the so-called 'democracies' of these countries, and their mainstream news media that are. These horrifying class, sexuality and gender inequalities engender state-sanctioned homophobia on the African continent.[76]

By way of a brief overview, below I outline some of the areas that the *Twitterverse* has scored winning goals in the face of the mainstream or 'dominant' media of these African nations' abysmal failings– through which they have scored their own shameful goals and perpetrated toxic fouls. I argue that unlike the mainstream media, Twitter is an incubator for empathy.

The ideal media in a democracy is expected to represent diverse voices and positions in debates, reflective of media theory prior to the emergence of social media and the Internet. Twitter has usurped this role where the media has been corrupted in less than ideal circumstances, such as in the 'democracies' of the 38 African countries under the spotlight in this chapter.

> In any democracy it is arguable that comprehensive coverage of topics in public debate is an important ideal to uphold, as well as to uphold the principle of unlimited public debate, by which I mean that the diverse voices and positions of all strata of society, during debates, should be given unfettered space.[77]

In this context, Twitter as the democratiser provides a counter balance to the fact that mainstream media often represents the voices of the elites and the issues of the elites that are represented.[78] Returning to the soccer analogy, Twitter is undoubtedly shining in contrast to an increasingly outdated and underperforming Dominant Media.

This sees Twitter reflecting varied voices instead of, only, reflecting the agendas of the ruling elite. In other words, it is in the mainstream media, as opposed to Twitter, that one finds the 'unreasonable people' reaching consensus, which is a consensus to be antipathetic.[79]

It is also political opportunism that contravenes human rights, as well as suppresses empathy for 'the other': For example, as journalist Alexis Okeowo has pointed out, '[t]here is little question that former Nigerian president Goodluck Jonathan, who was facing public disapproval over charges of inefficiency, corruption, and a badly fought war against Boko Haram Islamists waging a terror campaign in the north, seized the legislation as a popular, unifying distraction.' Not to mention 'the [significant] influence of American right-wing Christians on the drafting of anti-gay bills on the continent.'[80] As Theo so succinctly notes:

> As most news-aware people probably know, the authorities of Uganda continue to aggressively denounce homosexuals, whom they claim destabilise a purportedly coherent (Christian) national morality. Such simplistic religious rhetoric forms part of the political landscape in many sub-Saharan African countries, where politicians, the right-wing press and other leaders regularly whip up homophobia.[81]

Theo, while referring to South Africa's 'liberal constitution,' writes that, fortunately, it

> promises protection on the basis of sexual orientation, cover which sadly remains wholly imperative in the context of persistent homophobic discrimination and violent sexuality-based hate crimes that serve as evidence of a deeply conservative and homophobic society.[82]

Unfortunately, it is 'liberal constitution[s]' like this one in South Africa, which is exactly what is missing in these countries, in these 'deeply conservative and homophobic societ[ies].'[83]

Furthermore, in a healthy and 'dominant media' there should be 'vigorous debate and dispute over many issues,' as Herman and Chomsky readily acknowledge.[84] They contend, however, that debate within the dominant media is limited to 'responsible' opinions acceptable to some segment of the elite:

> On issues where the elite are in general consensus, the media will always toe the line. No dissent will then be countenanced, let alone acknowledged, except, when necessary for ridicule or derision.[85]

Since there is no toeing the line in the *Twitterverse*, there has, instead, been attempts at pulling, literally, the plug, as happened in March 2014 in Turkey when it restricted access to Twitter hours after its prime minister, Recep Tayyip Erdoğan, threatened to 'root out' the social media network where wiretapped recordings had been leaked, damaging the government's reputation ahead of local elections.[86]

Crucially, it is not that a national mind-set of antipathy will be changed by the vilifying and inverted mainstream media, but rather that the power to change opinion lies in the democratic *Twitterverse*. Thus despite the fact that the *Twitterverse* simultaneously contains homophobic and other instances of hatred, it offers the potential of balance (unlike the one-sided and controlled mainstream state-sanctioned media) with a wide and disparate variety of opinions and pluralist debate.

Further, as Theo importantly suggests, even those 'journalists writing anti-homophobic news articles often do not recognise how their narrative structures might inadvertently fail to encourage an empathic engagement of readers.'[87] Journalists should strive to incorporate narrative frames of (empathic) engagement 'which represent people beyond the identity-based categories of 'the homosexual,' thereby giving them voice as complex individuals,' which is exactly what Twitter allows.[88] This is possible on Twitter because not only does the 'victim'/source of the story have a right to reply, but that right of reply is not via the gatekeeper-journalist nor his media organisation, but directly and unhindered to Twitter's timeline, which is a democratic and open space that can only be limited by Twitter itself, which is rarely the case. The source thus takes her power back and, so to speak, is then again the master of her own destiny. This then immediately also reveals personality and opinion, revealing them to be complex individuals rather than the often one-dimensional and voiceless 'victim'/sources of traditional media stories, where the journalist holds the reins, is in a position of power.

It is particularly important for non-journalists to understand that they have as much and as equal access to a democratic, complex and unlimited international communication platform as any journalist. They have the right to be heard, to tell their own stories, to fill in the blanks, and also to call the journalist out publicly if so required. Furthermore, it is in their power, once they have made the mind shift to move from 'victim'/source in someone else's narrative, to become their own narrator, the potentially powerful narrator of their own story. Therein lies the power of garnering empathy for oneself, and with that the potential to garner assistance, guidance and resources from those who also have empathy for you. It is at that point that Twitter ceases to be a lonely, isolating space.

5. Conclusion

It is no coincidence that the current backlash against LBGT groups comes at a time when advances in rights for gay people – most prominently, the right to marry

– are progressing apace in other parts of the world. To quote Charles Dickens in a different context, it is 'the best of times and the worst of times.'[89]
But what breeds a homophobic climate is not just repressive religious interpretation and conservative politics. Homosexuality goes straight to the heart of gender and heteronormative patriarchy.[90] 'We are dealing with a crisis of heteronormative patriarchy which didn't arrive with colonialism.'[91] Essential to the maintenance of patriarchy is the need to control bodies.[92] It is clear that patriarchy, religion, nationalism and notions of 'traditional' African culture can combine into mutually-reinforcing systems of control which are toxic for African queer communities.[93]

All of these are the antithesis of empathy. So since I am one human being, where can I look to for hope, for light in this dark and long tunnel, and crucially, what can I do?

Despite the fact that empathy might have a reputation as a fuzzy feel-good emotion, I believe that an empathetic approach harbours enormous power and potential. Author Roman Krznaric offers a very different view of the everyday kindness and emotional sensitivity, and being tender and caring towards others, that many people equate it with:

> Empathy is, in fact, an ideal that has the power both to transform our own lives and to bring about fundamental social change. Empathy can create a revolution. Not one of those old-fashioned revolutions based on new laws, institutions or governments, but something much more radical a revolution of human relationships.[94]

More than anything, action is required for such a revolution; so what can I do within my sphere of influence? By looking at my world, at my country and continent through the lens of empathy, there are two things I feel compelled to do: humbly, as an African going forward, I believe that while it is appropriate under the circumstances to express 'my disgust at the rising tide of homophobia sweeping the African continent' on platforms such as these, I also must validate my need to grapple with teaching the concept of empathy to my students, the future African journalists.[95] Because…

> [f]irst they came for the Socialists, and I did not speak out—
> Because I was not a Socialist.
> Then they came for the Trade Unionists, and I did not speak out—
> Because I was not a Trade Unionist.
> Then they came for the Jews, and I did not speak out—
> Because I was not a Jew.

Then they came for me—and there was no one left to speak for me.[96]

The famous, provocative poem, 'First they came ....' written by Pastor Martin Niemöller (1892-1984) was about the cowardice of German intellectuals following the Nazis' rise to power, which then saw the Nazi's subsequent purging of their chosen targets, group after group.[97] The poem deals with themes of persecution, guilt and responsibility.[98]

Thus while I undoubtedly need to teach my journalism students how to use Twitter, I also need to lead them into empathy, to teach them to do something much more than to merely put themselves in the shoes of *the other*. That instead they should strive to be filled with the Kundera'ian compassion, read co-feeling, that he believes 'means not only to live with the other's misfortune but also to feel with him any emotion – joy, anxiety, and pain'.[99] Only then is it possible for them to become potentially infused with an enormous power that then has potential to break the seemingly endless cycle of hatred against *the other*.

In fact, I discovered that I had been teaching empathy without realising it. In all of my classes, I have taught that for a journalist, or for any human being for that matter, to reach a space of compassion (read empathy), especially in the context of journalism, one needs to enter a space of self-consciousness. This is largely about loving yourself before being able to love others, which in turn entails acknowledging and questioning one's own prejudices, in fact interrogating them so as to understand their origins. Only then is it possible to move beyond them and into a liberated space of consciously and constantly striving towards developing, at all costs, an empathetic society, which starts with self.

This entails moving from internal prejudice to a listening and then questioning mode, so that one might competently tell the story of *the other* compassionately, and with empathy, thus, I believe, going about changing the world into a better place one empathetic mind-set at a time.

For Milan Kundera, the secret strength of the word's etymology floods the word with another light and gives it a much broader meaning: 'to have compassion (co-feeling) [read empathy] means not only to live with the other's misfortune but also to feel with him any emotion – joy, anxiety, pain.'[100] As Kundera insists, it is this kind of compassion that therefore signifies the maximal capacity of affective imagination, the art of emotional telepathy.[101] In the hierarchy of sentiments, then, empathy is undoubtedly supreme.[102]

Notes

[1] Milan Kundera, *The Unbearable Lightness of Being* (Croydon, UK: Faber and Faber, 1984), 18-19.
[2] Ibid.

³ Ibid.

⁴ Ibid.

⁵ Ibid.

⁶ Ibid.

⁷ Ibid.

⁸ Sandra Davidson Scott, 'Beyond Reason: A Feminist Theory of Ethics for Journalists,' *Feminist Issues* 13 (1993): 23-24, 24.

⁹ Ibid.

¹⁰ Ibid.

¹¹ LJ (Nic) Theo, 'Empathy in News Reporting: Framing Sexual Minorities in Sub-Saharan Africa,' in *Encountering Empathy: Interrogating the Past, Envisioning the Future*, eds. Veronica Wain and Paulus Pimomo (Oxford: Inter-Disciplinary Press, 2015), 85-97.

¹² 'GLAAD Media Reference Guide, 9th Edition', viewed on 23 September 2015, http://www.glaad.org/reference/.

¹³ Theo, 'Empathy in News Reporting.'

¹⁴ Ibid.

¹⁵ Ibid.

¹⁶ Scott, 'Beyond Reason,' 23.

¹⁷ Ibid., 23.

¹⁸ Ibid., 23-24

¹⁹ Ibid., 23-24.

²⁰ Ibid., 23-24.

²¹ Ibid., 23-24.

²² Ibid., 24.

²³ 'Definition of Heteropatriarchy,' *Collins Dictionary.com*, viewed on 23 September 2015, http://www.collinsdictionary.com/submission/11555/heteropatriarchy.

²⁴ Ibid.

²⁵ Tony Bennett, 'Theories of the Media, Theories of Society,' *Culture, Society and the Media*, ed. Michael Gurevitch (London: Methuen, 1982), 40, viewed 29 May 2015, http://web.mit.edu/211.432/www/readings/Bennett_TheoriesOfMediaAndSociety.pdf.

²⁶ James Norris, 'Othering101: What Is "Othering"?,' *Wordpress.com*, December 28, 2011, viewed on 19 June 2015, https://therearenoothers.wordpress.com/2011/12/28/othering-101-what-is-othering/ Blog.

²⁷ Norris, 'Othering101: What Is "Othering"?'

²⁸ Ibid.

²⁹ Ibid.

[30] Ibid.

[31] Amardeep Singh, 'An Introduction to Edward Said, Orientalism, and Postcolonial Literary Studies,' September 24 2004, viewed on 24 September 2015, http://www.lehigh.edu/~amsp/2004/09/introduction-to-edward-said.html. Blog.

[32] Ibid.

[33] 'The Other,' *CUNY.edu*, viewed on 29 May 2015, http://academic.brooklyn.cuny.edu/english/melani/cs6/other.html.

[34] Ibid.

[35] Hussein Abdilahi Bulhan, *Frantz Fanon and the Psychology of Oppression* (New York and London: Plenum Press, 1985), 150.

[36] Ibid.

[37] Ibid.

[38] Ibid.

[39] LJ (Nic) Theo, 'Empathic New(s) Orientations in Narratives about Sexuality,' in this volume

[40] Ibid.

[41] Ibid.

[42] Ibid.

[43] Here, as in elsewhere in this chapter, I am referring collectively to the mainstream 'media' (a plural verb), which in turn uses various forms of media channels as the means of communication, such as newspapers, television, magazines and radio to reach or sway people extensively.

[44] Associated Press in Kampala, 'Ugandan Tabloid Prints List of "Top 200 Homosexuals" in World News: Uganda,' *theguardian.com*, 25 February 2014, viewed 29 May 2014, http://www.theguardian.com/world/2014/feb/25/ugandan-tabloid-prints-list-top-200-homosexuals.

[45] Amnesty International, *Making Love a Crime: Criminalization of Same-Sex Conduct in Sub-Saharan Africa* (London: Amnesty International, 2013), 7, viewed 2 February 2015. https://www.amnestyusa.org/wp-content/uploads/2017/04/making_love_a_crime_-_africa_lgbti_report_emb_6.24.13_0.pdf

[46] Ibid

[47] Scott, 'Beyond Reason,' 24.

[48] Charles King, 'Between Science, Politics and Human Rights: Media Coverage of the Blood Controversies' (MA diss., University of the Witwatersrand, 2012).

[49] Inter-Disciplinary.Net's 1st Global Conference: Empathy (7-9 November, 2014: Prague, Czech Republic).

[50] Ibid

[51] Theo, in this volume.

[52] Ibid

[53] Ibid.

[54] Ibid.

[55] Ibid.

[56] Ibid.

[57] Ibid.

[58] Steven Maras, *Objectivity in Journalism* (Cambridge, UK: Polity Press, 2013), 1.

[59] Rebecca Davis, 'Queer in Africa: Confronting the Crisis,' *Daily Maverick*, 3 June, 2014, viewed on 18 December 2014, http://www.dailymaverick.co.za/article/2014-06-02-queer-in-africa-confronting-the-crisis/#.VJLXDtKUe-0.

[60] Fiona Larkin, 'Seeing the Loop: Examining Empathy through Art Practice,' in this volume.

[61] Ibid.

[62] Ibid.

[63] Ibid.

[64] Ibid.

[65] Amnesty International, *Making Love a Crime*.

[66] Ibid.

[67] Jessica Phelan, 'Uganda Drops Death Penalty for "Aggravated Homosexuality" from Anti-Gay Bill,' Africa section of *GlobalPost*, November 23, 2012, viewed on 27 September, 2015, http://www.globalpost.com/dispatch/news/regions/africa/121123/uganda-drops-death-penalty-aggravated-homosexuality-anti-gay-bill

[68] Ibid.

[69] Ibid.

[70] Ibid.

[71] Amnesty International, *Making Love a Crime*, 7.

[72] For a discussion of the role of the media, see Theo, in this volume.

[73] 'Definition of Inversion,' *Merriam-Webster Dictionary*, viewed 2 February 2015, http://www.merriam-webster.com/dictionary/inversion.

[74] Michael Peragine, 'Reimagining History: The Turn of the Screw as a Dream, Henry James as the Dreamer, and Freudian Psychoanalytic Criticism as a Means to Uncover Repressed Thoughts,' *Michael Peragine: Academic Essays and Short Fiction*, 30 June, 2014, viewed on 18 December 2014, http://michaelperagine.wordpress.com/2014/06/30/reimagining-history-the-turn-of-the-screw-as-a-dream-henry-james-as-the-dreamer-and-freudian-psychoanalytic-criticism-as-a-means-to-uncover-repressed-thoughts/.

[75] 'Mugabe Slams Europe's "Homosexual Nonsense",' *Mail and Guardian*, 19 April 2014, viewed on 18 December 2014, http://mg.co.za/article/2014-04-19-mugabe-slams-europes-homosexual-nonsense.

[76] Charles King, 'My 1000th Post Is Dedicated to Anti-Totalitarianism: Viva Ann Frank and the Velvet Revolution!' *Beautiful Mind*, 17 November 2014, viewed on 18 December 2014, http://btflmind.blogspot.com/2014/11/my-1000th-post-is-dedicated-to-anti.html. Blog.

77 King, 'Between Science, Politics and Human Rights,' 12.
78 Ibid.
79 Scott, 'Beyond Reason,' 24.
80 Alexis Okeowo, 'Binyavanga Wainaina Comes Out,' *New Yorker*, 29 January 2014, viewed on 18 December 2014,
http://www.newyorker.com/books/page-turner/binyavanga-wainaina-comes-out.
81 Theo, in this volume.
82 Ibid.
83 Ibid.
84 King, 'Between Science, Politics and Human Rights,' 12.
85 Robert W. McChesney, 'The Political Economy of the Mass Media,' *Monthly Review*, January, 1989, viewed on 18 December 2014.
http://www.chomsky.info/onchomsky/198901--.htm.
86 Kevin Rawlinson, 'Turkey Blocks Use of Twitter after Prime Minister Attacks Social Media Site,' *The Guardian*, 21 March 2014, viewed on 18 December 2014, http://www.theguardian.com/world/2014/mar/21/turkey-blocks-twitter-prime-minister.
87 Theo, in this volume.
88 Ibid.
89 Davis, 'Queer in Africa.'
90 Ibid.
91 Ibid.
92 Ibid.
93 Ibid.
94 Roman Krznaric, *Empathy: A Handbook for Revolution* (London: Rider, 2014).
67 Davis, 'Queer in Africa.'
96 'First they came…,' *Wikipedia*, viewed on 29 May 2015,
http://en.wikipedia.org/wiki/First_they_came_....
97 Ibid.
98 Ibid.
99 Milan Kundera, *The Unbearable Lightness of Being* (Croydon, UK: Faber and Faber, 1984), 18-19.
100 Ibid.
101 Ibid.
102 Ibid.

Bibliography

Amnesty International. 'Making Love a Crime: Criminalization of Same-Sex Conduct in Sub-Saharan Africa.' *London: Amnesty International.* 2013. Viewed on 17 December 2014. https://doc.es.amnesty.org/cgi-bin/ai/BRSCGI/AFR0100113-25161?CMD=VEROBJ&MLKOB=32469132929.

Associated Press in Kampala. 'Ugandan Tabloid Prints List of "Top 200 Homosexuals".' World News: Uganda Section, *The Guardian.* 25 February 2014. Viewed on 17 December 2014. http://www.theguardian.com/world/2014/feb/25/ugandan-tabloid-prints-list-top-200-homosexuals.

Bennett, Tony. 'Theories of the Media, Theories of Society.' *Culture, Society and the Media*, edited by Michael Gurevitch. London: Methuen, 1982.

Bulhan, Hussein Abdilahi. *Frantz Fanon and the Psychology of Oppression.* New York and London: Plenum Press, 1985.

Davis, Rebecca. 'Queer in Africa: Confronting the Crisis.' *Daily Maverick.* 3 June, 2014. Viewed on 18 December, 2014. http://www.dailymaverick.co.za/article/2014-06-02-queer-in-africa-confronting-the-crisis/#.VJLXDtKUe-0.

'First they came....' *Wikipedia.* Viewed on 29 May 2015. https://en.wikipedia.org/wiki/First_they_came_...

'GLAAD Media Reference Guide - 9th Edition.' Viewed on 23 September 2015. http://www.glaad.org/reference/

King, Charles. 'Between Science, Politics and Human Rights: Media Coverage of the Blood Controversies.' MA Dissertation, University of the Witwatersrand, 2012.

King, Charles. 'My 1000th Post Is Dedicated to Anti-Totalitarianism: Viva Ann Frank and the Velvet Revolution!' *Beautiful Mind*, 17 November 2014. Viewed on 18 December 2014. http://btflmind.blogspot.com/2014/11/my-1000th-post-is-dedicated-to-anti.html. Blog.

Krznaric, Roman. *Empathy: A Handbook for Revolution.* London: Rider, 2014.

Kundera, Milan. *The Unbearable Lightness of Being*. Croydon, UK: Faber and Faber, 1984.

Maras, Steven. *Objectivity in Journalism*. Cambridge, UK: Polity Press, 2013.

McChesney, Robert W. 'The Political Economy of the Mass Media,' *Monthly Review*, January, 1989. Viewed on 18 December 2014. http://www.chomsky.info/onchomsky/198901--.htm.

Miller, Danny. 'The Blog,' *HuffingtonPost.com*, May 25, 2011. Viewed on 17 December 2014. http://www.huffingtonpost.com/danny-miller/gays-are-the-new-jews_b_18378.html. Blog.

Norris, James. 'Othering101: What Is "Othering"?.' *Wordpress.com*. December 28, 2011. Viewed on 19 June 2015. https://therearenoothers.wordpress.com/2011/12/28/othering-101-what-is-othering/. Blog.

Okeowo, Alexis. 'Binyavanga Wainaina Comes Out.' *New Yorker*, 29 January 2014. Viewed on 18 December 2014. http://www.newyorker.com/books/page-turner/binyavanga-wainaina-comes-out.

Peragine, Michael. 'Reimagining History: The Turn of the Screw as a Dream, Henry James as the Dreamer, and Freudian Psychoanalytic Criticism as a Means to Uncover Repressed Thoughts.' *Michael Peragine: Academic Essays and Short Fiction*, June 30, 2014. Viewed on 18 December 2014. http://michaelperagine.wordpress.com/2014/06/30/reimagining-history-the-turn-of-the-screw-as-a-dream-henry-james-as-the-dreamer-and-freudian-psychoanalytic-criticism-as-a-means-to-uncover-repressed-thoughts/. Blog.

Phelan, Jessica. 'Uganda Drops Death Penalty for "Aggravated Homosexuality" from Anti-Gay Bill,' Africa section of *GlobalPost*, November 23, 2012. Viewed on 27 September, 2015. http://www.globalpost.com/dispatch/news/regions/africa/121123/uganda-drops-death-penalty-aggravated-homosexuality-anti-gay-bill

Rawlinson, Kevin. 'Turkey Blocks Use of Twitter after Prime Minister Attacks Social Media Site.' *The Guardian*, 21 March, 2014. Viewed on 18 December 2014. http://www.theguardian.com/world/2014/mar/21/turkey-blocks-twitter-prime-minister.

SAPA-AFP. 'Mugabe Slams Europe's "Homosexual Nonsense",' *mg.co.za*, 19 April 2014. Viewed on 18 December 2014.
http://mg.co.za/article/2014-04-19-mugabe-slams-europes-homosexual-nonsense.

Scott, Sandra Davidson. 'Beyond Reason: A Feminist Theory of Ethics for Journalists.' *Feminist Issues* 13 (1993): 23-24.

Singh, Amardeep. 'An Introduction to Edward Said, Orientalism, and Postcolonial Literary Studies.' September 24, 2004. Viewed on 23 September 2015.
http://www.lehigh.edu/~amsp/2004/09/introduction-to-edward-said.html. Blog.

Theo, LJ (Nic). 'Empathy in News Reporting: Framing Sexual Minorities in Sub-Saharan Africa.' *Encountering Empathy: Interrogating the Past, Envisioning the Future*, editors Veronica Wain and Paulus Pimomo, 85-97. Oxford: Inter-Disciplinary Press, 2015.

'The Other.' *CUNY.edu*. Viewed on 29 May 2015.
http://academic.brooklyn.cuny.edu/english/melani/cs6/other.html.

Charles King practiced as a freelance journalist for twenty-two years. 2013 saw him make a foray into teaching journalism and media studies. At Cape Town's Cape Peninsula University of Technology, he teaches advanced and specialised reporting, including how to report homophobia and climate change.

Seeing the Loop: Examining Empathy through Art Practice

Fiona Larkin

Abstract

In this chapter I will be using my own artwork, a specific project titled *Backstory,* to explore empathy by reflecting on empathy and art from a phenomenological perspective. This chapter is written from the perspective of the artist/maker and so foregrounds the qualities of specific artworks as a means to consider where empathy and contemporary art might be seen to cross paths. As philosopher Theodore Lipps defined it, empathy is a kind of imaginative projection or *inner imitation* of our own feelings into/onto an object or artwork. In short, Lipps' theory states that the work of art enhances our capacity for empathy as he maintains our sense of beauty results from an ability to identify with the object before us. Empathy as derived from the German *Einfühlung* literally translates as 'feeling into'. In this account, I am not only concerned with exploring our ability to feel empathy, that is, compassion for people directly (though perhaps it is possible with figurative art), but with empathy as a method for activating what Gregory Currie and Ian Ravenscroft refer to as a shift in perspective, particularly with regard to artwork. For both William Worringer and Theodore Lipps, the form of the artwork or object before us is made by the viewers' engagement and their personal insights or inner world. Here, I will be considering my own artwork as a means of exploring orientations, ways of looking, looking as an active process, and how this activity uses imaginative projection to explore empathetic engagement. I highlight four key areas within the practice and consider if and whether empathy and empathic processes are manifest in the artwork. The discussion is presented under the following subheadings: Empathy and Recapture, Empathy and the Substitute, Empathy and Doubt, and Empathy and the Loop.

Key Words: Empathy, art, perspective, orientation, proxy, doubt, loop, translation, phenomenology, Samuel Todes, Edith Stein.

*****

1. Empathy and Recapture

In this section, I am addressing the ideas of 'recapture' and artwork as photographic document. I propose that in artwork, 'recapture' is achieved through a process of engagement on behalf of the viewer. It is the moment the image is experienced and internalised by the viewer. By internalised, I mean made personal through association or reflection. In the work I discuss below, this internalisation is made manifest and becomes a process of expanded collage. We know collage to mean a form of joining one image to the next. Collage suggests a conflation, a contrasting or complimentary connection of one material with another and as such

© KONINKLIJKE BRILL NV, LEIDEN, 2018 | DOI 10.1163/9789004360846_011

is an ideal medium in which to reflect upon empathy's power to connect. I use the term *expanded collage* to mean a layering process that may happen beyond the image itself, for example in the use of layered media as in photos layered with video. Collage also occurs in the method, in that, I often engage others, involving them in the work and therefore develop a dialectical, layered approach.

As part of my art practice, I take snapshot images (which I refer to as *foundational images*) of strangers in the street and then submit these images to a process of opening up or expansion, often through engaging others to respond in some way to the images. These responses, whether written, filmed or drawn, constitute a form of layering, as they add to and expand the original photograph or *foundational image*. In the video and photography project *Yellow De Ne Pouvoir Etre Seul* (Image 1), the chance sighting of a girl in a gallery with an unusual yellow mark on her clothing provided that foundational image, from which began a process of collecting images of everyday yellow things. This activity was carried out as a means of getting closer to or recapturing lost information about the girl in order to explain her yellow mark. However, after a long time collecting images, it becomes clear that these images and this process only serves to delineate a portrait of my everyday life and not that of the stranger with the yellow mark. The video also makes use of a stratified perspective to offer the viewer a more dynamic role. The camera angle places the viewer in my place; my hands become your (viewer's) hands. While this act of orientation may seem subtle, it is not incidental. Certainly the notion of empathy as orientation is relevant and has been explored by many. Amy Coplan discusses the importance of recognizing the difference between 'self-orientated' and 'other-orientated'[1] perspective taking, arguing that the qualities inherent in 'other-orientated' perspective taking make it more faithful to the empathic condition. Steve Larocco sites empathy as a kind of orientation rather than simply a feeling or a state of mind saying: 'it is an orientation of feeling and cognition toward and through the other'.[2] This notion chimes with the process I undertook, where the act of taking the yellow photographs was addressed towards another.

In developing this particular artwork, orientation is also used as a device to engage the viewer, to harness the potential for perspective taking. In the resulting video artwork, the 'other' is considered to be both the viewer of the eventual work *and* the stranger in the original photograph from whom the artwork is derived. Therefore it is my intention in making the work, that the position of the stranger, both the figure in the image and the 'stranger'/viewer of the work, are considered. This requires a certain refocusing of attention and imagination, one that feels like a kind of 'leaning out'. This process of orientating the artwork towards the viewer reflects an attempt to adopt empathic strategies in the working processes.

After completing the work, I realised I had no measure of the viewer's reactions, and wanted to know if my viewer/strangers shared my curiosity and imaginings about the girl with the yellow mark.

Image 1: Installation shot of *Yellow De Ne Pouvoir Etre Seul*, by Fiona Larkin, video, © 2012. Courtesy of the artist.

In his essay 'The Pensive Image', French philosopher Jacques Rancière talks about the image as containing 'unthought thought which cannot be attributed to the intention of the person who produces it'.[3]

So when presented with an image like this:

Image 2: *Backstory,* by Fiona Larkin, c-print, © 2013. Courtesy of the artist.

Where does that *unthought* thought go?

I wondered if the *unthought thought* could be recaptured, through engaging with viewers. Furthermore, I considered whether some kind of investigation of these thoughts could be made a part of the resulting artwork. In *Backstory* (Image 2) I used the above photograph I had taken of a woman quietly sitting at the edge of a lake in a contemplative state to prompt and invite response/interpretation/translation from writers through an open call. I then considered the writers' engagements as emblematic of these recaptured thoughts. The image has the quality of an intimate moment captured and brought into focus through a unique style, however, this image belongs to a common documentary tradition of street photography. Documentary photography has long held an association with notions of truthfulness. Here, the motivation in offering this image to others was, much like my intention in the artwork *Yellow de ne pouvoir etre seul*, to move it beyond the limitations of the documentary – beyond the notion of representation or truth and into the realm of the imaginary. By inviting writers to respond, I drew on their interest in, and ability to shape shift, to empathically engage with the image and create new histories for the figure in the headscarf.

In 'Camera Lucida'[4] Barthes considers the photograph to bear a close relation to death, stating: 'that rather terrible thing which is there in every photograph: the return of the dead'.[5] What is it that causes this return? I propose that the internalising process the spectator experiences on viewing an affective image can cause empathic connection. This connection might be seen to enliven the image; to imaginatively recapture its loss or cause a kind of 'return'. In *Backstory*, the ambiguity in the original photograph acts as a space for imaginative exploration, or fictive reverie. In the photographic document there is always the suggestion that something is missing. While for Barthes, this suggests a sense of death or a passed moment, it is this gap that for me prompts the empathic imagination. In order to imaginatively engage with the image, we must bridge this gap by connecting with the image in an empathetic way. Here, empathy is the nudge that initiates and allows for imaginative unlocking.

My practice of inviting engagement and opening up the artwork to others, as I did for *Backstory*, draws on Umberto Eco's conceptualization in 'The Poetics of the Open Work' in 1962. Eco states: 'The invitation offers the performer the opportunity for an *oriented insertion* into something which always remains the world intended by the author'.[6] In *Backstory*, the viewers/writers allow themselves to be led by the image, but equally by the stranger in the image. In essence, in this way, they follow a stranger. This idea of orientating and following another, echoes phenomenologist Edith Stein's assertion that to experience empathy is akin to being 'led by the foreign experience'.[7]

In the responses from writers, their scripts, prose and short stories clearly conveyed an effort to *re*capture what was missing. Their contributions articulated a wide range of narratives about who the figure behind the scarf was, how she lived, why she sat there and what she might be thinking. Working from visual clues, there was indeed some consensus about age and gender across responses, but the rest diverged sharply in their impressions and constructions.

In *Backstory,* the writer's story telling acts as a form of recovery that recaptures the voice of the silent figure in the image and offers her kaleidoscopic potential. Artist Thomas Hirschhorn says: 'Collages possess the power to implicate the other immediately'.[8] In *Backstory,* I see my method of working as a kind of expanded collage where through invitation the viewer-writers added texture and colour to my foundational image. Their voices add character and tone.

But perhaps collage is an act of substitution rather than a recovery, mixing the silence of this figure and matching it to the voices of various writers. Or perhaps the figure is a mould into which we can cast our own projections. If this is the case, what we call imaginative projections are perhaps simply substitutions, proxies.

2. Empathy and the Substitute

The notion of the proxy is complex as it suggests an act of substitution that may not align with an empathic approach. However it is suggestive of what Gregory Currie calls the simulative approach.[9] In his essay *Empathy for Objects,* Currie turns to cognitive and neural reasoning, reflecting on the recent discovery of mirror neurons.[10.] While the specifics of the cognitive process are beyond the reach of this essay, it supports the idea of empathy being a kind of orientation towards another, reflected in a simulative reaction in the brain's response. Currie notes that the imaginative leap made by people asked to 'describe the handedness of a visual display' can be traced as, he says 'they, seem to answer by 'mentally rotating' their own hands'[11] and this simulative process takes just as long as the real one. This simulation-in-mind process is not unfamiliar to any artist who has experienced the life drawing class. Something between observing and putting pencil to paper allows for a kind of translation. Indeed if you cannot see the object before you but *have* seen it and therefore hold it in your mind's eye, as in blind drawing,[12] you rely on this simulative response or imagined version of the figure to help guide your hand. We might accept then that in turning our attention to the object before us, there is an orientation that occurs not just in sight, but also in mind. This activity occurs certainly in the process of making, but also it seems it occurs, perhaps not to the same degree, in the minds of viewers perceiving the work.

If we are to follow Currie, the simulation or imitative gesture of the artist does not display empathy in itself, but perhaps it offers this point of entry as a nudge to perception. So it seems, as far as Currie is concerned, there is an argument for empathic engagement that arouses imitative responses in the viewer, which in turn aid perception. Edith Stein had a slightly different approach, arguing that empathy is more than a trigger; in her view, it radically alters one's perception altogether: 'The perceived world and the world given empathically are the same world differently seen.'[13] Stein contends that empathic understanding shapes our perception, and therefore inflects our understanding of the things in the world.

There are other key things to consider. Primarily, when considering the art object it is important to note where the object sits in relation to the self. As Lipps maintains, the object is always 'being formed by me'.[14] So the viewer's empathic connection with the perceived object develops or appends the object, even if only for that individual viewer.

In the work, *Backstory*, discussed above, the writers developed imaginative narratives that offered a possible or 'simulated' version of the person they saw in my photograph. Their ability to adopt the perspective of another, often a different age, gender, etc., was notable, as if shape shifting, simulating a version of this figure for the duration of the text. In his paper 'Poetry of Compassionate Empathy', Paulus Pimono offers a thought-provoking argument for how writers engage with their subject He suggests that the process is akin to Buddhist philosophy's conception of the unstable 'I', saying that poets 'don't seem to believe in having a stable 'I' when they do their work.'[15] This mirrors in some way Edith Stein's description of the 'I' as being 'the unity of a stream of consciousness'[16] rather than a fixed and defined thing.

Charles King offers a compelling argument for the use of Twitter as a tool for providing a public platform to the marginalised in society. He also argues that to be a journalist 'one needs to enter a space of self-consciousness'.[17] Thus, it appears that, certainly in the process of making art, the self-conscious act of engaging with another allows for a shift, a kind of immersion in the world of the other. It may be that this immersion provokes instability or allows for a self-conscious questioning of what the self is composed.

It might be said that artists engage with making work in a similar way to writers, tackling a wide variety of subjects, which at times might seem apart from their own life and experience. Regardless, artists are often accused of a complete absorption with the subjects they tackle. This attitude is reflected in J.J. Charlesworth's essay on artist Mark Leckey's artwork. He says it is less about a desire for the object and more about a desire to be the object, a 'flirting with the possibility of becoming other to oneself'.[18] Mark Leckey's own assertion is that he does not want to simply look at things: 'I want to be in them'.[19]This astutely describes a tension and interplay between perceiving and becoming. The sense of immersion that Leckey looks for when making work seems close to the idea of a self-substitute. However, the artist knowingly hints at the impossibility of such - after all, it is only a flirtation. Is Mark Leckey referring to imaginative flights of fancy or something deeper, a kind of becoming the object?

It might be worthwhile at this point returning to the phenomenology of the imagination to help clarify this thought. Indeed Leckey's desire to become the object before him resonates with Stein in her description of empathy: 'when I inquire into its implied tendencies (try to bring another's mood to clear givenness to myself), the content, having pulled me into it is no longer really an object.'[20] So for Stein, our empathic engagement with another removes the objective quality that makes it *other*. Phenomenologist Samuel Todes offers this useful definition of the relationship between perception and imagination:

> What strains my imagination to the breaking point (e.g., imagining a round square) thus seems also to limit what can possibly exist. Perception is self-evidence – in the literal sense that something is itself made evident to us by this way of experiencing it. But imagination is proxy-evidence – in the sense that only a representation of something is made evident to us by this way of experiencing it.[21]

Phenomenologists would argue that empathy is more than a representation of something. However, in our experience of the art object, the empathic connections we make must rely on representation. If we consider empathy as a parallel to a deep imaginative experience,[22] then connections can be drawn where empathy is seen as a form of substitution. We are used to hearing empathy described as an 'in the shoes of' experience, which is a simple metaphor for the act of substitution. To characterise how our perceptual self is interchangeable with our imaginative self, Todes uses the example of seeing someone from behind and construing from this vantage point whether or not they might be an attractive person: 'It is for example by perception rather than imagination that we are aware of the (hidden) far side of a perceived object.'[23] So, for Todes, seeing the back of something helps to explore the phenomenology of the imagination (or limitations thereof). In this instance we have no actual evidence; instead, we have 'proxy-evidence', our perceived version of them from the front. Here we are reminded that empathy too relies on, but is distinct from perception.

We can draw parallels to the example Todes proffers with the art historical tradition of the *Rückenfigur*[24] associated with German Romantic painter Casper David Friedrich. He frequently employed images of a person seen from behind, contemplating a view, to encourage a kind of active viewing from the audience. In *Wanderer above the Sea Fog* (1818), the incomplete nature of the figure encourages curiosity. Indeed, for Friedrich, it was intended to encourage more than that. His intention was that the work would be edifying and indeed transcendental, lifting them out of the gallery and into the landscape. While a bold claim, it suggests that perceiving the work and 'entering' the work are two interrelated though distinctive experiences. Entering the work requires a greater imaginative feat and a kind of connection with the work beyond seeing, although the prompt the work offers to the imagination can be the reason for engaging our empathic 'entry' into the work.

Returning to the context of my own artwork and *expanded collage,* this reflection prompts the question: In offering participants or viewers images to contemplate, am I creating a space to explore 'representations of [the] possible, though not necessarily actual'[25] 'other'? The imaginative 'proxy evidence' that Samuel Todes examines prompts the question: Is imaginative engagement acting as a *substitute* for the limitations of the image in the work? Is it a way to 'flirt with the possibility of becoming other' as Leckey would have it, rather than a truer empathic experience of becoming the other?

Perhaps it is less important to consider which kind of engagement is more accurate after all flirtation holds a notion of intimacy that seems to be a close ally of empathy. Rather, it is more fruitful to explore how these imaginative leaps are made and how they in their own way stimulate empathic connection.

If, through its missing (unseen but imagined) parts, the image acts as a prompt to the imagination, then all of our empathetic reverie is a kind of substitute for what was really there, going beyond the edges of the image. The writers' multiple storylines also made me aware of the possibility of endless versions and revisions - of the possibility for many substitutions. This substitute, authorized and solicited to act on behalf of the gaps, is in some way cut loose, unbridled. It is as if in fracturing and multiplying the possibilities for what happens beyond the image the imagination is in some way set free.

In another film produced as part of the Backstory project, *Scene Three: Where It Is Written,* the camera lens moves as though it were writing over a lake, such that the camera becomes the eyes of the woman sitting and looking. In making this work, I aimed to reflect on the writers' process and to combine the sense of immersion in the image I felt in seeing it anew through the narratives of the writers. Their written reflections had the quality of taking a snapshot, each one a short narrative that reflects some imagined aspect of the life of the person in front of the lens. But beyond this, there was an emotive quality, the sense of an imagined private world being addressed. In doing this, it seems that many of the writers adopt a narrative mode familiar to filmmaking: the point of view. The point of view shot is often referred to as the subjective camera, where the 'subjective' quality achieved chimes with the intimate qualities echoed in the writing. This idea suggests that point of view is an empathic orientation –through adopting as your vantage point the perspective of another. In the video I echoed this idea of the point of view shot orientating the camera toward the lake like the stranger in the image. However, I used the camera to 'write' or to trace text on the surface of the lake.

It seems that speaking on behalf of an unknown other can be liberating. It allows for a kind of becoming that is free of some of the ordinary constraints. The imagined proxy is potentially better, more articulate, and more empathic. So in sharing the work with writers I open up a space for possible, previously unconsidered narratives. The proxy is also a way of thinking about authorship in the work, one that addresses the participants (in this case, writers). They provide the 'proxy evidence', so the resulting agent/image might not be solely of my own making but an amalgam, a collage of ideas.

This provokes a kind of instability regarding authorship, one that Roland Barthes posits in the 'The Death of The Author':[26]

> It will always be possible to know, for the good reason that all writing is itself this special voice, consisting of several indiscernible voices, and that literature is precisely the invention of this voice, to which we cannot assign a specific origin: literature is that neuter, that composite, that oblique into which every subject escapes, the trap where all identity is lost, beginning with the very identity of the body that writes.[27]

Barthes reminds us that engaging with others, even imaginatively, allows access to a variety of voices, thus destabilizing the notion of the artist as auteur. This very method of engaging an other and seeking substitutions and multifarious voices is empathic in intent in so far as it looks to build connections. However, it is unpredictable, as the more versions and substitutions, the more unstable the position of the author, and the more we are made aware of the fissures and gaps. Here we see there are gaps between empathic imaginative engagement and a more exacting phenomenological view of empathy. These gaps, however, are often the point or motivation for empathetic engagement in the first place.

Image 3: *Scene Two: She is Camera,* by Fiona Larkin, still from video, © 2013. Courtesy of the artist.

3. Empathy and Doubt

The substitute is thus necessarily tinged with doubt. In the video *Scene Two: She is Camera* (Image 3), a simple inversion along with the mirroring effect of the lake prompts the viewers to doubt what they see. Doubt becomes an interrupting force, provoking us to consider further what we see in the image before us.

It is by perceiving gaps - the sense that all is not as it seems - in the image that empathy is set in motion. As previously stated, an awareness of difference is key to opening empathic connection. Therefore, it is impossible to engage empathetically with the image without being first aware of the separation between self and other. In the case of artwork, we could say that the awareness of difference is transferred to the object/image. As Lipps undertook, the object is always 'being formed by me'. Danish philosopher Dan Zahavi extends this argument saying: 'It is not possible simply to insert intersubjectivity somewhere within an already established ontology; rather, the three regions 'self', 'others' and 'world' belong together; they reciprocally illuminate one another, and can only be understood in their interconnection.'[28] Thus, for Zahavi, while objects exist in the 'world' realm that we perceive as being very different from the bodies of others, they have a fundamental connection to our bodies. But how can we name this corporeal connection and is the connection empathic?

It would a significant omission to discuss contemporary art and empathy and not mention Jill Bennett's *Empathic Vision: Affect, Trauma and Contemporary Art*.[29] In this work, Bennett contends that our connection to art (particularly art that considers traumatic affect) is not just perceptual but also emotional. The affect she refers to is more than cognitive, it is corporeal. In her opinion, empathic encounters produce the conditions for feeling into rather than seeing into.[30] Bennett defines empathy as a kind of oscillation and, like Nikos Papastergiadis, she sees it as 'a constant tension of going to and fro'.[31] Discussing the work of artist William Kentridge, she notes that 'Spivak has spoken of translation as essential to an encounter with the other, not simply because it renders the experience of the other transparent – it cannot, in fact, achieve this- but because it forces an awareness of difference.'[32] This burgeoning awareness that Bennett refers to might be the unique tool of the affective encounter with art. It might be that artworks allow for open exploration of empathic perception where there is little at stake.

In my project *Backstory*, the act of translation was applied to the foundational image, where writers were invited to respond and communicate what they saw in the figure of the stranger presented. Responses were richly varied and infused with the sense that the writers had 'felt' the character in the image. However, in offering multiple readings, we are made aware of the individual bias of each writer and hence the fracturing quality of translation. It would seem in discussing empathy, it is impossible not to be drawn to an examination on the nature of interpretation and vicariousness, and here enters doubt. At the same time, there is an argument against the limitations of the subjective nature of affect. Bennett demonstrates how art can become a kind of conduit through which subjectivity is negotiated, harnessed even, in order to expose and explore doubt. So the nature of our unique encounter with art, while it may be hard to name, does offer a space to explore our own empathic potential, to see how well we can 'feel into' and not just see other. And so once again, empathic encounters with art lead us back to an examination of self.

Image 4: *Scene One: Her Translation,* by Fiona Larkin, still from video,
© 2013. Courtesy of the artist.

Edith Stein writes: 'Furthermore, this psycho-physical individual only becomes aware of its living body as a physical body like others when it empathically realizes that its own zero point of orientation is a spatial point among many.'[33] Having made the effort to project into the image, to see this other perspective, there is an interruption in our experience of this thing that we see: how might we know it mirrors the other's vantage point? We do not. At best, it is a way of understanding others that doesn't 'bridge the gap' but allows us to be 'led by the foreign experience'[34], implying that empathy is a curious and an uncertain process of *following.*

4. Empathy and the Loop

In his essay Empathy, Expansionism and the Extended Mind, Murray Smith, suggests that engaging with others 'plays an important role in our engagement with fictions'.[35] If his thesis is correct, then the connection between our everyday empathic engagement and our empathic engagement with art, be it narrative or not, are enmeshed. However he states that empathy is 'stretched and refined' through our engagement in narrative arts. Therefore our social empathic connection is fed by our engagement with art and fiction, through a kind of loop. In this instance, art is not simply a safe space to explore our own empathic potential, it is a connected and integral tool to help us articulate and stretch our empathic ability.

From an image I had taken of a woman with her back turned wearing a headscarf, I developed a performance to camera video work, *Scene One: Her Translation.* The video shows a woman caught in the repeated gesture of donning and removing headscarves, here we see an almost mirror image of the woman in the foundational image. However certain elements are accentuated in the video. The act of donning the headscarf is repeated as if caught in an unending loop, putting scarf over scarf over scarf. The video itself, installed, is played on a returning loop, though there is a discernible beginning and end. The strategy of looping video is commonly used by artists as an exhibition method or as a way of temporally displacing the viewer. It dissolves accepted narrative paths and plays with chronology. Birnbaum comments on the effect of loops suggesting they offer the artist a way to control and 'stall' time; 'Loops, circularity, and rotation are modes of visualization, modes of (in)stalling time.'[36] Here it is used mostly as a way of avoiding a *settling down* or fixing of the figure in the headscarf. With each new headscarf, there is a potential doppelganger or mirror figure, but each time this is avoided as the artist/performer continues to place one scarf over the other. Finally, as if in dissatisfaction with the state of mimesis, she removes them all one by one. The gesture is one that echoes something that is temporally beyond the image; in the photo, the woman is wearing the scarf, not performing the act of putting it on. So it might be seen as a way of addressing or extending the temporal restrictions of the photographic object, or as an invocation looking to embody the stranger, or as a connective gesture - a way to feel the scarf on your head as the woman in the image does. In making the work I am developing a way not only to engage with the empathic orientation of the viewer but also to play with how empathy *might* be acted out and made material. However in doing so, am I merely playing with mirror images?

If as art viewers and translators we are following or being *led by* the image, then where are we going? Is the relationship one of influence, translation or appropriation? Following might be misleading and is certainly sticky in terms of questions both of authorising substitutions and of authoring in Barthes' sense. If we return to Worringer and Lipps, understanding that: 'The form of an object is always its being formed by me, by my inner activity'[37], then are we merely *meeting ourselves coming back*?

It is fitting then to turn to fiction for a response. In her novel *Aliens and Anorexia,* Chris Krauss states: 'Therefore, empathy is not a reaching outward. It is a loop. Because there isn't any separation anymore between what you are and what you see.'[38] If indeed the perception of an object is an 'inner activity' and if in empathy 'what you are and what you see' have merged in a loop, then there is room for perspective shifts in the interior life of viewers brought on by artwork. If empathy is a loop then there is room in our perspective shift for an inward turn.

In my practice I am led by a response to a photograph, often an image of a figure, to build something, to construct new images through gesture, text and engagement with others, which are all strongly motivated by intuitive response. This intuition or sense is the inward turn. As Stein suggests, empathy is not just perception or representation 'but a sui generis',[39] a unique experience.

Notes

[1] Amy Coplan and Peter Goldie, *Empathy Philosophical and Psychological Perspectives* (Oxford, NY: Oxford University Press, 2014), 10.
[2] Steve Larocco, 'Empathy as Orientation Rather Than Feeling: Why Empathy Is Ethically Complex,' in this volume.
[3] Jacques Rancière, *The Emancipated Spectator* (London, N.Y.: Verso, 2009), 107.
[4] Roland Barthes, *Camera Lucida: Reflections on Photography* (London: Vintage, 2000).
[5] Ibid., 9.
[6] Umberto Eco, 'The Poetics of the Open Work', *Participation*, ed. Claire Bishop (Massachusetts, London: MIT Press 2006), 36.
[7] Edith Stein, *On the Problem of Empathy*, trans. Waltraut Stein (Washington D.C.: ICS Publications, 1989), xvii.
[8] Thomas Hirschhorn, *ARNDTBerlin.com*, viewed on 10 March 2013, http://www.arndtberlin.com/website/artist_1030.
[9] Gregory Currie, 'Empathy for Objects', *Empathy Philosophical and Psychological Perspectives*, eds. Amy Coplan and Peter Goldie (Oxford: Oxford University Press, 2014), 82.
[10] Mirror Neurons: neurons in the brain that fire in response to observing actions by others. These neurons seem to echo the behaviour they respond to, hence the name.
[11] Gregory Currie, 'Empathy for Objects', 85.
[12] Blind drawing: A process where students are asked to draw the object before them with their eyes shut, this is supposed to sensitize them to the connection between eye and mind.
[13] Edith Stein, *On the Problem of Empathy* (Washington: ICS Publications, 1989), 64.
[14] Theodore Lipps, *Aesthtik* (Leipzig: Leopold Voss Verlag, 1903).
[15] Paulus Pimomo, 'Poetry of Compassionate Empathy,' *Encountering Empathy: Interrogating the Past, Envisioning the Future*, eds. Veronica Wain and Paulus Pimomo (Oxford: Inter-Disciplinary Press, 2015), 35-44.
[16] Edith Stein, *On the Problem of Empathy*, 38.
[17] Charles King, '"Gays are the New Jews": Homophobic Representations in

African Media versus Twitterverse Empathy,' in this volume.
[18] J. J. Charlesworth, *Mark Leckey* Art Review, Summer 2014.
[19] Ibid.
[20] Edith Stein, *On the Problem of Empathy*, 10.
[21] Samuel Todes, *Body and World* (Massachusetts, London: MIT Press, 2001), 130.
[22] Edith Stein's account introduces a closer examination of imagination and its comparative links to empathy.
[23] Todes, *Body and World*, 130.
[24] Rückenfigur, usually considered to be an image of a person seen from behind, often contemplating a view.
[25] Todes, *Body and World*, 132.
[26] Roland Barthes, 'Death of the Author', *Image, Music, Text* (London: Fontana Press, 1993).
[27] Ibid., 2.
[28] Dan Zahavi, 'Beyond Empathy Phenomenological Approaches to Intersubjectivity', *Journal of Consciousness Studies* 8.5-7 (2001): 151.
[29] Jill Bennett, *Empathic Vision: Affect, Trauma and Contemporary Art* (California: Stanford University Press, 2005).
[30] Ibid
[31] Ibid. Here, she is quoting Nikos Papastergiadis from 'Faith without Certitudes: A Conversation with Nikos Papastergiadis' by Mary Zournazi (2002).
[32] Ibid, 121.
[33] Edith Stein, *On the Problem of Empathy*, xxi.
[34] Ibid, xvii.
[35] Murray Smith, 'Empathy, Expansionism and the Extended Mind,' *Empathy Philosophical and Psychological Perspectives*, eds. Amy Coplan and Peter Goldie (Oxford: Oxford University Press, 2014), 111.
[36] Daniel Birnbaum, *Chronology* (N.Y. Sternberg Press), 136.
[37] Ibid., xviii.
[38] Chris Kraus, *Aliens and Anorexia* (Los Angeles, CA: Semiotext, 2013), 150.
[39] Stein, *On the Problem of Empathy*, xviii.

Bibliography

Barthes, Roland. *Image, Music, Text.* London: Fontana Press, 1993.

Bennett, Jill. *Empathic Vision: Affect, Trauma and Contemporary Art.* California: Stanford University Press, 2005.

Birnbaum, Daniel. *Chronology.* N.Y.: Sternberg Press, 2006.

Bishop, Claire. *Participation*. London, Cambridge Mass: MIT Press, 2006.

Coplan, Amy and Peter Goldie. *Empathy Philosophical and Psychological Perspectives*. Oxford, NY: Oxford University Press, 2014.

Currie, G. and I. Ravenscroft. *Recreative Minds: Imagination in Philosophy and Psychology*. London: Oxford University Press, 2003.

Eco, Umberto. 'The Poetics of the Open Work'. *Participation*, edited by Claire Bishop, 20-39. Massachusetts, London: MIT Press, 2006.

Kraus, Chris. *Aliens and Anorexia*. Los Angeles, CA: Semiotext, 2013.

Hirschhorn, Thomas. *Arndtberlin.com*. Viewed on 10 March 2013. http://www.arndtberlin.com/website/artist_1030.

Pimomo, Paulus. 'Poetry of Compassionate Empathy.' *Encountering Empathy: Interrogating the Past, Envisioning the Future*, editors Veronica Wain and Paulus Pimomo, 35-44. Oxford: Inter-Disciplinary Press, 2015.

Rancière, Jacques. *The Emancipated Spectator*. London, N.Y.: Verso, 2009.

Stein, Edith. *On The Problem of Empathy*. Translated by Waltraut Stein. Washington D.C.: ICS Publications, 1989.

Todes, Samuel. *Body and World*. Massachusetts, London: MIT Press, 2001.

Williams, Rhys W. *Oxfordartonline.com*. Viewed on 19 May 2014. http://www.oxfordartonline.com/subscriber/article/grove/art/T092269.

Worringer, William. *Abstraction and Empathy, A Contribution to the Psychology of Style*. London: Routledge, 1963.

Zahavi, Dan. 'Beyond Empathy.' *Journal of Consciousness Studies* 8.5-7 (2001): 151-67.

Fiona Larkin is an artist and researcher currently working toward her PhD at Northumbria University, Newcastle Upon Tyne, U.K.

Printed in the United States
By Bookmasters